FORGOTTEN VILLAGES

RAGGALDS, MOUNTAIN AND WEST SCHOLES

Compiled by
Stan Ledgard

FORGOTTEN VILLAGES
RAGGLADS, MOUNTAIN
And WEST SCHOLES

First Published 2009

ISBN: 978-0-9511013-9-1

Printed and bound by Bakes and Lord, 529 Beacon Road, Bradford

Published by Bobtail Press, 22 Main St, Haworth, West Yorkshire BD22 8DA

This publication is copyright of R. S. Ledgard, 2009.

All rights reserved.
Contents may not be reproduced in any form, except for short extracts for review, without the written consent of the publisher.

Cover photo: West Scholes House, 1980

Introduction

Although a newcomer, in 1975, to the Queensbury area I was immediately fascinated by its 'quaintness'. Born in Manningham, then uprooted to Duckworth Lane area in the 1950's, to me Queensbury seemed very rural, especially as I commuted to Bradford or Leeds or Manchester every day. Eventually I left city life behind, moving to the Mountain and commuting daily to Haworth. I heard stories from the older Mountain and West Scholes residents, saw the last vestiges of local industry, and decided that a record should be made of the hamlets between Thornton, Clayton and Queensbury, since all of these three villages have written histories but which mostly ignore the 'no mans land' between.

I have been fortunate in interviewing many older residents, including the late Phyllis Gledhill, Rennie Briggs and Harry Brooks; in gaining the acquaintance of local historian and author John Patchett; of Graham Hall, archivist and collector of local postcards; Frank Leonard (Thornton) and Steve Wood (Haworth), local historians; and of various other persons who are specialists in their fields. To them all, my thanks.

To all those who 'couldn't be bothered' to tell their stories or dig out their photographs, my regrets as this information may be lost forever.

To all readers of this book, I hope you find it as fascinating to read as I did researching it. I know there are omissions – there will be in any historical work – but perhaps you, the reader, will be inspired to research further.

Photographic credits are given where known but many are from personal collections and of unknown authorship. Modern photos are by the author.

Frequent reference should be made to maps. Sketch maps are included. O.S. maps are useful. A walk around the area is even better.

Stan Ledgard
Haworth 2009

THE ORIGINS OF QUEENSBURY AREA

In modern times the mention of the village of Mountain, the main centre of population in our story, will bring a look of incomprehension from all but those familiar with the locality, since Mountain is now considered a part of Queensbury. And although the full story of Mountain is not to be found in the history books, we do know that it has enjoyed a considerable independence and status, as it still does to those resident in the area who have known the village for most of the 20th century, and whose tales stimulated the compilation of this book.

The focal point of the area now known as Queensbury is the crossing of the A647 main coaching route and turnpike road from Bradford to Halifax and Manchester with the A644 commercial route from Brighouse to Denholme. Along the coaching route were clusters of houses and inns. Near the cross-roads (which around 1700 was known as Causeway End) was the Old Queen's Head Inn named after Queen Anne, and from which the area took the name Queens Head. On the Jeffreys map of 1775, no name is given to this crossroads, the whole area being noted as Clayton Heights. From just north of the crossroads the paved way ended at about Small Page (on the road towards Mountain), but a paved way is shown to Thornton, via Yew Green which the present road probably follows (Thornton Road/Carter Lane), and which may be the same as the Cockam route from Halifax to Bingley of the 1500s.

Handloom weaving became an important cottage industry, together with the development of coal pits and quarries, and eventually real industry came to Queenshead with the founding of Foster's Black Dyke Mill in 1835.

Around 1854 it was felt that a change of name was required – a village named after a pub was perhaps a little unseemly – and a vote was taken in favour of Queensbury, which was used from about 1862, the name being 'Queens' for Queen Victoria and 'bury' from the Saxon 'fortress or stronghold'. For further information on Queensbury see 'A History of Queensbury' (Barrett, 1963).

Three-quarters of a mile up the road to the north, the village of Mountain was suffering no such identity crisis! In the early 1800s textiles brought employment (and people) to the area which developed into a V-shaped village, essentially self-contained and proudly independent (in spirit at least) of Queensbury, although for the purpose of local government, it was administered by Queensbury Local Board (1864), Queensbury Urban District Council (1895), Queensbury and Shelf Urban District Council (1937), which in 1974 was split between Calderdale and Bradford, with Queensbury, Raggalds and Mountain going to Bradford.

FACTS FROM MUSTY SOURCES

If historical details bore you, skip this chapter !

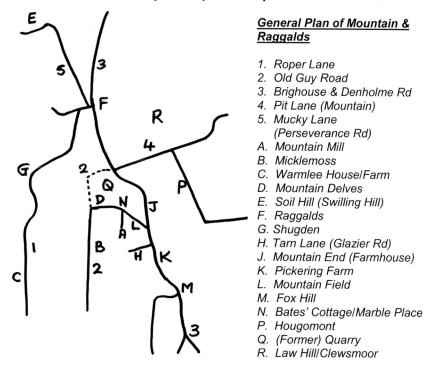

General Plan of Mountain & Raggalds

1. Roper Lane
2. Old Guy Road
3. Brighouse & Denholme Rd
4. Pit Lane (Mountain)
5. Mucky Lane (Perseverance Rd)
A. Mountain Mill
B. Micklemoss
C. Warmlee House/Farm
D. Mountain Delves
E. Soil Hill (Swilling Hill)
F. Raggalds
G. Shugden
H. Tarn Lane (Glazier Rd)
J. Mountain End (Farmhouse)
K. Pickering Farm
L. Mountain Field
M. Fox Hill
N. Bates' Cottage/Marble Place
P. Hougomont
Q. (Former) Quarry
R. Law Hill/Clewsmoor

Information concerning land ownership, council matters and other written comments are continually reappearing, but methodical research is virtually impossible. Items recorded here may, hopefully, add to information gained elsewhere by others.

First, the Enclosures Acts of the late 1700s. These detailed documents relate to Common and Waste Ground being allocated to specific persons, for whatever use they wished, with conditions of mining rights, access to water, and road maintenance being specified. In the Mountain area, for example, waste lands owned by the Duke of Leeds were surveyed, enclosed and apportioned. Mountain has parts in Thornton, Clayton and Northowram areas; Raggalds has parts in Thornton and in Ovenden; West Scholes is part Clayton and part Thornton.

Certain roads extant at the time are mentioned, for which maintenance became the landowner's responsibility:

From Ford across Micklemoss to the Northowram/Clayton Boundary Stone. (This might follow some of the route of the present Fleet Lane.)

From Ambler Thorn, west of Beggarington, over Micklemoss to Roper Delves and Shuckden Head. (This corresponds to Roper Lane.) These were Public Highways.

Private Roads to be maintained for local access included:

From the Turnpike road, north east of Beggarington, over Micklemoss to Mountain Delves at the Northowram/Thornton Boundary. This is Old Guy Road.

When 'waste' land is mentioned, this simply means land not used for cultivation or pasture. Often dwellings were sited there already, the inhabitants of which were allowed to remain.

When enclosed, fields were given names. Some names related to crops grown (Sprout Field, Wheat Field), to minerals extracted (Delph or Pit Field), and some descriptive such as Two Days Work.

Pre-dating the Act, references have been found relating to early habitation in the area, in particular Warmlee Farm in 1315 and Shugden Farm in 1379. Shugden Head appears on record from 1497 (rebuilt 1682), and Micklemoss from 1709. (Queensbury History Society pamphlets.)

Wells Head Farm near Hill Top was already established in 1740, as was James Charnock's farm on Soil Hill (1739).

In 1770 one William Ellis took over a farmhouse and land, being Mountain End. By 1785 two cottages had been added. By 1814 there were 6 cottages, farmhouse and buildings.

Boundary House, built at the highest part of Old Guy Road, was at the meeting point of Thornton, Clayton and Northowram boundaries. It probably dates from the early 1700s when Guy Pearson 'purchased and inclosed' the land. A boundary stone should be built into a wall there, but the land has been raised, so it's probably buried.

Pickering (Hall) Farm dates from around this period, as do many farms and cottages around Raggalds.

Moving forward, in the second half of the 1800s the Speak family, who ran Mountain Mill, were mainly responsible for development in Mountain. Here is a brief overview of lands acquired by them:

The land required for the Mill was purchased in 1818 by Isaac Hirst, a local worsted manufacturer, who proceeded to erect Mountain Mill. By 1821 the Mill was up and running, and in 1831 the Mill was leased to Peter Ambler, then around 1838 to Isaac Stocks. According to deeds (Vint, Hill & Killick files, Bradford Archives), the mill and land were sold to John Clough on 18 July 1844 for £590. With the Mill, listed as 'unoccupied' at the time, came land and three cottages on the site, reservoirs and ancillary buildings.

Clough purchased the adjacent Tarn Field property in 1847. All of Clough's acquisitions were taken over by his nephew Paul Speak in 1854.

The 3 cottages, which had been built around 1811, were at the western end of what is now Fascination Place. They were eventually demolished and Fascination Place and Montrose Place were erected in 1873/4. Most domestic development took place in the late 1850s to 1880.

On 30/5/1861, James Jowett 'and others' sold part of Mountain Delves land and dwellings to Paul Speak. In October 1871, Hannah Fawthrop sold another part of Mountain Delves land (undeveloped) and 3 cottages (Marble Place) to Speak's. These same properties are again mentioned in January 1881 as being purchased by Paul Speak – presumably they'd been mortgaged and now repaid.

Cornelius Drake Cottages

The land was taken from Micklemoss in 1829. Two cottages had been 'recently erected' there (probably about 1819), with an access 'road' leading directly to Tarn Lane behind North View. These cottages had been built by Cornelius Drake. They and the land were purchased by a Mr Fawthrop in 1829 and Glazier Row (8 cottages) was erected by the early 1840s.

The land south of the mill, bounded by Tarn Lane, and containing Glazier Row and Cornelius Drake's cottages, was bought by Speak's in 1871, but not redeveloped.

Bates/Lees Cottages

The two back-to-back low-decker cottages, in one of which lived John Bates, were built at the edge of a quarried area. The cottages were acquired by Speak's some time after 1873, but not redeveloped. They are sometimes shown as Mountain Cottages.

The quarry area by Bates' cottage, which later included the area of the cricket field, was also acquired by Speak's. Opposite Bates' Cottage, was Spring Cottage, demolished in the early 1850's for construction of Speak's Time Office and the new approach road to the Mill.

Mountain Delves

Documents of the 1730s mention one Joseph Booth building a cottage on wasteland at Micklemoss Delves, probably near Percy Street.

Three rows of cottages had been built at Mountain Delves by the 1830s. In 1851 the land and housing was purchased by Jonas Robertshaw, mortgaged to Speak's. As a result of default, the property was auctioned in 1873 and was acquired by Paul Speak, being redeveloped as Jester/Luddenden Place.

Mountain End Farm

Of the six cottages listed in 1814, some were probably in the area opposite, across the main road, part of which was later rebuilt as 'The Eagle' in the 1860s. The area behind 'The Eagle' became Wareham's (or Wainhouse) Fold. Mountain End land was acquired by Speak's by 1861 (except the Eagle to Snug Cottage triangle), and some roadside land to the north, (e.g. the area around Hougomont which was acquired in 1880 but excluding Hougomont itself).

Pickering Farm   (From the Speak Institute Deeds)

Owned by Ellen Perkinton (Widow of Joshua) and John and Ellen Bentley, the deeds refer to the area bounded by the main road, the 'Catsteps', Blind Lane and Low Lane (called Back Lane), being 5 fields and the farm buildings. The area was situated at 'Corken Edge'. In 1817, it was sold to Thomas Perkinton for five shillings.

Thomas Perkinton died on 18/12/1859, and the farm was sold for £140. In the title deeds 27/1/1913 reference is made to the documents of 16/11/1886 of the sale to Samuel and Catherine Webster, together with Bohun Henry Chandler Fox – whoever he was ! On Samuel's, then Catherine's, death it passed to their daughters Emily Fabling and Edith Webster. On 6/5/1911 it was sold by the Webster sisters to John Speak, for £240.

John Speak had the Institute built adjacent to the farm, and on 27/2/1913 transferred Pickering Park Farm, and the Institute with its furniture, to the Trustees of the Speak Institute. The Speaks involved were John, of the Grange, Kirton near Boston, and Paul II and Paul III both of Laurel Bank. It was noted that some land adjacent to the main road had already passed to Queensbury Council for road widening in 1905.

★ ★ ★ ★ ★

Properties in Mountain not acquired by Speak's include:

Mountain Field

This included the area of Derwent Place, Mountain Place and South View. In 1847 it was bequeathed to Isaac Patchett. It had 10 cottages, a shop (Mountain Place) and a pub (Fleece). In 1858-61 more buildings were added behind Mountain Place ('Patchetts' on the 1861 census). The properties were sold in 1864.

Jonas Bairstow Houses

In 1834 John Bairstow built 6 cottages on the site which is now adjacent to No. 19 Mountain. These passed to his son Jonas in 1844 who also acquired other land and dwellings nearby, including Abel St, and North View and East View. The name Able or Abel Street was retained until the late 1800s, and probably refers to the track running from the Fleece to Glazier, and named after Abel Ackroyd, resident in Stocks' Houses opposite the lane top.

Reservoir Place

In the late 1700s, parts of the Fleet estate were sold. Sam Tooker and Richard Holden held the area south of Tarn Lane down to Fleet Lane, and sold to T and W Bradley 18/11/1802. Bradleys sold to Isaac Brear 21/11/1804, the area being known as Brear Farm, and which included the Tarn Field, Betty Field and Micklemoss. Isaac died in 1829. Benjamin Waugh bought parts and sold the Tarn Field to Speaks, a small part of Betty Field to Michael Smith and, later, the rest of Betty Field to Queensbury Council.

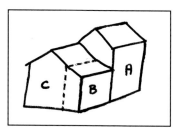

A - originally two back-to-back
B - extension, probably about 1900
C - original through-by-light

In 1838 three cottages were erected by Michael and Martha Smith. Two were back-to-back (nearest Micklemoss), the other being a through-by-light. In the rear wall of the back-to-back is a date stone: S M M 1838.

The main residence of the three was then occupied by Abraham Smith, the other two being rented out. On the 1881 census it is listed as Smiths Buildings. Abraham's son Benjamin took ownership by 1891 and, together with Abraham's son-in-law Squire Bentley of Hill Top Farm, sold the properties to George Wallace, Mill Manager, of 6 Montrose Place.

Wallace had the back-to-backs made into one, and (probably) had the front extension made to the other house. He occupied one himself and either rented or sold the other.

Stocks

Opposite the top of Abel Street were two blocks – Stocks' Houses and Stocks' Buildings, totalling some 5 or 6 cottages. One block was parallel to Glazier Road, and one at a 45° angle. Built around 1800, they were demolished in the late 1800s.

Fox Hill

Before the building of Fox Hill School, a couple of cottages stood at the top of Harp Lane (now part of the school yard). A track led from here to Fox Hill Farm just beyond the northern tip of the school yard boundary. On the

Queensbury side of Harp Lane was the stone quarry of David Knowles, active from 1823 until the mid 1800s.

Active into the 1890s was Mountain End Coal Pit. This extended from Blind Lane top to the Mountain side to the present school boundary.

Across the road was Pineberry Moor. The main features were the large quarry, active into the 20th century; the Pineberry beer house; and a few yards up Fleet Lane, on the right, on the first bend where the road seems excessively wide, were four cottages whose gardens occupied part of this now wide road. The cottages were demolished about 1900.

Micklemoss Farm

Documents of 1801 relate in rather detailed terms to the previous ownership of the area (taken from the wastes in the main), being 'the Most Noble George William Frederick, Duke of Leeds .... and George Cherry, executor of the Will of Charles Brett who was the surviving trustee of the Rt. Hon. Mary Countess Dowager Gower, also William Mawe of Kirton, West Yorkshire, and the Rt. Hon. James Godolphin Osborne (Lord Francis Godolphin Osborne), and the Most Reverend Father in God by Divine Providence Lord Archibishop of Canterbury Robert Lord Stobart Charles abbot.' Hopefully known to his friends as Charlie !

The land referred to is shown in the following diagram, marked M and comprising about 35 acres, plus 2 acres by Chapel Lane, north of 'Israel Robinson's Field' (which had been owned by him since 1779 and known as Red Delph). Another part was at Priestley Hill. The whole was eventually bought by Isaac Brear with the farm being known as Brear Farm. In 1837 the estate was split (right hand diagram). From 1853 to 1885 areas (1) were owned by a Mr Scott, then by a Colonel Stanhope and/or Captain Rhodes.

In December 1904 Captain Rhodes sold to Prince (first name, not royalty!) Rushworth, with Sam Fielding providing the mortgage. In October 1939 it was sold to George Irish who rented it to George Feather. In July 1953 Mr Irish sold to Thomas Marsden and Charles Allan Scott, of Tobills Haulage, Tyne and Wear. Thomas died in 1966, Charles in 1985, and most of the land was bought by Mr T W Bradley (not related to the Bradleys of 1802) who farmed and ran a haulage business.

The area between the farmhouse and Mill Lane had been sold separately to Speaks, and eventually used for housing development (4 and 5) in the late 1900s.

To digress briefly, the Red Delf field probably contained a pond (possibly a small former stone quarry). At the end of the 1800's, it was owned by Israel's grandson Ellis Robinson. An interviewee born in 1902 recalls "the lads used to go swimming in Ellis o' Israel's pond", which probably lasted until 1922 when Ellis became bankrupt and the field was sold.

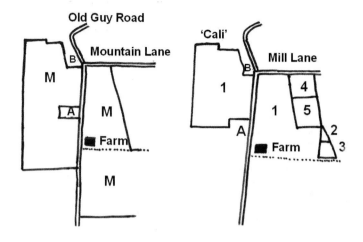

1. Bought by Mrs Lancashire and Mrs Brooks.
2. Bought by Benjamin Waugh
3. Bought by David Ackroyd, then to John Foster (1871)
4. Purchased by Paul Speak (1873)
5. Purchased by Paul Speak (1865)

A = Percy Street   B = Moorside Place

★ ★ ★ ★ ★

SPEAKS ASCEND THE MOUNTAIN

In 1818 Isaac Hirst, bought land at Mountain and had Mountain Mill built. It was in production by 1821, run by Thomas Hirst, and beating Black Dyke in Queensbury by 14 years or so. Terraces of cottages were built for the workers, seeming to push up against the low crofters cottages already there. In 1831 the Mill was leased to Peter Ambler who went bankrupt, then to Isaac Stocks (of a family of entrepreneurs scattered around the Queensbury area) in 1838.

Meanwhile in Keighley, Robert and John Clough ran Grove Mills at Ingrow. Their business flourished, and while Robert continued with the original mill, John first leased Ingrow Mill, then moved further afield. In 1844 John bought Mountain Mill and, with his nephew Paul Speak, set about redevelopment. There were problems at first due to lack of staff – many had left the area because of low employment.

However, in the 1851 Census, Paul is shown as employer, living at Mill House, and employing 109 men, 12 boys, 132 women and 46 girls, more than half of the population of Mountain.

In May 1854 Paul bought the mill from Clough, and it was immediately mortgaged to a Miss M Marshall in order to provide capital, until November 1858 when he was able to repay it. He began a period of upgrading and expansion. He bought land and properties, in particular Mountain Delves, and others adjacent to his land. By 1873, the mill gates and time office and most mill improvements were complete.

Mr Paul Speak
1816-1878

The two names outstanding in the Speak family are Paul and John. However, several individuals bore these names, so let us adopt the American terminology of Paul I, II, III and so on, and plot the main characters in the family:

Paul I (11/10/1816 to 24/12/1878) son of John I, a Keighley farmer of Royd House, Keighley and Alice Speak (née Clough). In Mountain, Paul was referred to as a shepherd (which he wasn't). He learned textiles at his uncle's mill (Clough's) in Keighley. He married Nancy Drake, a domestic of Skipton, and they moved to the area around 1844. Paul worked with his uncle and took over the business in 1854. After his programme of expansions, Mountain Mill became known as Speak's, producing fine worsteds (serge). When Paul I retired, he handed the business to Paul II.

One story quoted about Paul I is that during the strikes of the 1850s he rode his horse among the strikers, cracking his whip and reminding them that the local employers were also local magistrates ! Deportation was still an option and one could be deported for such minor offences as stealing handkerchiefs or a fish from someone's pond. More serious crimes, such as assault, could result in hanging.

Mrs Nancy Speak
1815-1884

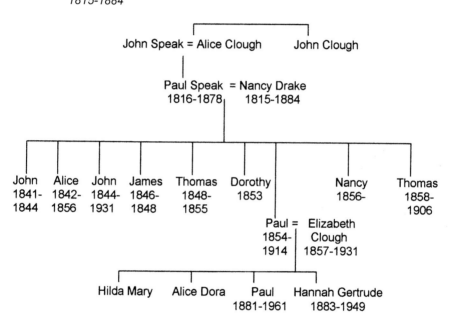

Now Paul II (b. 1854), apart from his associations with Mountain, was a member of Queensbury Council. He laid the foundation stone for the Council Offices in 1895 when he was presented with 'an ebony mallet with the Speak crest' on it – the nature of the crest has not been determined and it seems more probable that it was the Council logo He married Elizabeth Clough (1857-1931) of Steeton, and for a while they lived in the Mill House until he bought Laurel Bank, in the valley near Holmfield.

They had three daughters – Hannah Gertrude, Hilda Mary, and Alice Dora, and one son – Paul III (b. 1881) - who took over the business and Laurel Bank when his father died in 1914, remaining there until 1937.

Due to a severe and prolonged illness, Paul III retired in 1937 and the Mill was sold to the Parkland Group though Paul retained other land and properties which he gradually sold off. Paul never married, hence this lineage ended with his death in 1961. Paul III is remembered as being 'bowler hatted, slightly bent over, swinging his arms, and a regular attender at chapel'. He was actively engaged in local affairs, and benefactor of places of worship. Even so, he is remembered by some as interested in "nowt bar brass" (nothing but money).

Paul Speak
1881-1961

Let us trace one of the other members of the family, being John II (1844-1931). His interest in Mountain was considerable but his interest in the family business was minimal. He was a wanderer, and was so right up to his death, visiting off-beat places throughout the world and collecting souvenirs wherever he went. As with the last Paul, he never married thus ending this Speak line. He was a supporter of the chapel in Mountain, and erected the Speak Institute during 1912, in memory of his father and mother, and being for the benefit of all the villagers. John died at the family estate (purchased by Paul I) Kirton Hall in Lincolnshire where he had gone to live in 1914 having rented Warmleigh Hall, Roper Lane, previously. He is remembered for his civic work in Queensbury, and for presenting the clock and 3 faces to Queensbury church in 1885. (Subsequently the tower was relocated and a fourth clock face added in 1907.) His funeral was at Queensbury Parish Church on 17 January 1931. His collection of cultural souvenirs was distributed to museums in West Yorkshire and Manchester when the Institute closed.

John Speak
1844-1931

When Paul I died much of his estate was willed jointly to John II, Paul II and Thomas. In 1880 the lads got together to sort things out for individuals. For example Paul II took Black Carr Farm (Boggard Houses) with its 'pumps and the engine' for an agreed sum of £933. The pump and engine provided water.

It was also agreed that whoever controlled the Mill, their mother Nancy could live at Mill House, rent free and for as long as she wanted, and with an allowance of £140 per annum to keep her cows and horses.

Paul I had shares in many companies, especially to do with transport, such as the Great Western Railway, the Glasgow and South Western Railway, the Grand Trunk Railway of Canada, and the Finsbury Tramways. The company also owned a warehouse at Charles Street in Bradford, which was rented out.

Paul I left all the household effects (excluding cash) to "my dear wife Nancy", plus £500.

Daughter Dorothy was granted the Whaplode Saint Catherine Farm in Lincolnshire; daughter Nancy got 'another' estate; John II gained Kirton Hall, and Thomas gained Swineshead and Donnington estates.

Paul II died in 1914, leaving 60% of his estate to Paul III and 20% each to daughters Gertrude and Hannah. His wife Elizabeth received £1000 per annum. Daughter Alice was excluded – she had married Samuel Watkinson, the son of a Halifax wool merchant, and for some reason had angered Paul. Alice and Samuel had a son John (oh no, not another one!!) possibly out of wedlock. By codicil, Paul II later bequeathed £10,000 to John Speak-Watkinson when he attained age 21, provided by reducing the cash legacies to Paul III, Gertrude and Hannah.

Elizabeth Speak died in 1931. Daughter Hilda had married William Ellis Sugden. She, and Hannah Gertrude, received all the household effects. Paul III and Hannah shared '2 pianos and the motor car'. Legacies were provided for the Sugden offspring, and for any children of Paul III and of Hannah (they achieved zero). Elizabeth left an annuity to her brother Sir Robert Clough; and to Harry Elwis who had married Elizabeth's mother Nancy after Paul I's death.

In 1949 Hannah died at Laurel Bank 'spinster without parent'.

✦✦✦✦✦✦✦✦✦

SPEAKS AT THE MILL

Plan of Mountain Mill c 1930 – Also known as Ambler's or Speak's

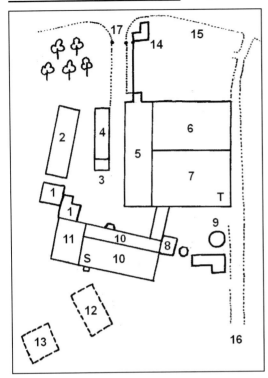

1. Mill House and Tarn House.
2. Stables
3. Office (2 storeys)
4. Stores
5. Smiths/Engineers on ground floor, front. Burling and mending on first and second floors.
6. 'New' weaving shed c.1866. Originally with skylights.
7. Weaving shed c.1861, with skylights. The raised toilets situated at T.
8. Boiler House
9. Gasometer
10. Spinning (2 storeys). The other toilet at S.
11. Drawing (2 storeys plus 'attic')
12. Hot Reservoir
13. Cold Reservoir
14. Time Office. Lodge / roller covering. On the other side of the driveway was 'the Plantation'.
15. Mountain Lane, later becoming Mill Lane
16. This road provided access to the boiler house for coal deliveries and the exit route for the soil cart !
17. Mill Gates

In 1854, Paul Speak purchased the Mill and Mill House residence for £3650. The original Mill, for both spinning and weaving, was the two/three-storey block [10 and 11 on the plan]. Paul's first expansion was the new weaving shed [7], and the gas works. From 1860 to 1873 he added [2] which had formerly been a barn; blocks [3, 4 and 5]; weaving shed [6]; also, the time office [14] at the top of the new approach road. In 1873, an ornamental garden is shown behind [11], facing Micklemoss. There were two 'reservoirs' for the Mill, a cold one fed by a spring on the Tarn Field and one (sometimes shown as two) hot, adjacent to the back of the Mill. The boiler house and gas facility were approached down a narrow paved road at the side of the new weaving shed. This had been the way into the mill until Speak came along. Several cartloads of coal per week were obtained from local pits, latterly from Stocks' at Ford. About 1 ton a day was required. For gas production the cheaper 'smalls' was used. At the top of the yard was the 'plantation', an area with trees; and the Mill was almost surrounded by open grassland prior to 1860.

Mountain Mill, looking North. Beyond the Mill, L to R, is Bates cottage (white), a shed (white roof) beyond which is the back of Wareham's Fold and The Eagle. Next right is the Sunday School and Chapel, with Harmony Place and West Royd beyond. A space at the side of the Chapel is where St George's Buildings, or Greenwoods, block stood. Next is Changegate block of shops and houses, a sort of T-shape with Snug Cottage nestling at the foot. Beyond is Evelyn Place, and in front is Derwent Place and Stone Street. The space to the right of the Mill chimney was the site of Speak's gas works. (Photo courtesy: Mr Les Chippendale, Mountain Mill)

The original mill house, occupied by a Mr Whitaker, was attached to the mill [1] with a bay window facing Micklemoss Farm. When Speak bought the Mill, he had a larger, rather plain, property added, forming a zigzag plan. The new house was called Mill House; the original occupied by Mr Whitaker became Tarn House. By 1871 the whole block became Mill House. The Mill House was occupied by Speaks, latterly by Nancy after her husband's death in 1878. After Nancy, Mill House was again divided into two – one was occupied by Mr Wallace Cockcroft, a Manager who moved from Marble Place. The other was occupied by Mrs Amelia Davoren – unusually of Catholic persuasion, (most on the Mountain were Methodist) and whom some describe as a 'fine lady'. She had a daughter, Amy, who wrote poetry (as a serious pastime). Some remember her huge tab rug which she'd get the mill lads to shake out for her each week. Paul III would ride on horseback to the Mill from Laurel Bank, taking the shortest route and jumping walls, and he'd take lunch with Mrs Davoren. Perhaps in return for this (though others have suggested more than just lunch !) she lived there rent-free. There was no canteen at the Mill so a large gas boiler was installed at Mill House where the workers could make 'mashings' – in the 1920s, only 6d a week, milk provided, but bring your own tea and a pot.

As well as Amy Davoren, another intellectual at the Mill was burler and mender Florence Cockroft, who frequently regaled her workmates with extracts from Dickens. Her sister Lucretia married Clifford Robinson [See Shopkeepers].

The Mill didn't have flush toilets. Some toilets 'just ran into the fields' [S on the plan] but the main block [T] in the weaving shed was reached up a few steps. The 'waste matter' went down a chute into a waiting cart, to be taken for fertilizer. Waste from the wool processing had also been a problem – Queensbury Council often complained of the "intolerable nuisance of suds from Paul Speak's mill blowing down Blind Lane and Laneside." (Council Minutes, June 1887). So it must have been pretty messy in Mountain itself !

Speak's cricket team pose proudly. The year is 1923 and Mountain Mill CC have won the Bulmer Cup and the Wallis Charity Cup in the Bradford and district league. Those present are: L-R, back row: J. Parkinson (patron), W Priestley, A F Farrar, F Firth, J W Berry, H Balmforth (Treasurer), E Cook (Secretary).
Middle row: G Bleazard, J Firth, Paul Speak (President), F Read, R Parkinson, R Whitelock. Front: A Rushworth, H Grange.
In the background, left to right, is the corner of the Time Office; the 'new' weaving sheds; the former weaving shed, now Burling and Mending, and Engineers; the Stores (first low gable); the Stables block as built but later reduced to single storey (gable with windows). (Photo courtesy: Yews Green Cricket Club)

The Queensbury Council Medical Officer also tried to lay blame on Speak's for contamination of several pumps (wells) used for domestic water supply in Mountain. (Paul Speak was Council Chairman !)

The Council Nuisance Officer had cause to complain in 1905. He noted the filthy state of ashpits and privies at Glazier Row (Speak's properties). It was required that they be thoroughly cleaned; have two coats of good quality lime-wash; and have lockable doors fitted so that the resident keyholders could be held responsible for any future mess.

May 15th 1897 was declared Diamond Jubilee for Speak's Mill. To celebrate, a 'treat for the old folk' was organised, and the workers and local children were invited to Laurel Bank (quite a walk !) for refreshments and entertainment. In the evening 'a bonfire was provided on the Mountain'.

To be trained for mill work, an agreement or indenture had to be drawn up. This example is for a Warp Dresser and Twister:

Extracts from the Indenture of Tom Brooks to Paul Speak

Dated 11 June 1888.
Paul Speak, spinner and manufacturer, T/A Paul Speak & Sons.
Between Benjamin and Sarah Bartle, and son Tom Bartle Brooks.
Indenture for five and a part years to 30 August 1893.

During which time "his said Master well and faithfully shall serve, all his Secrets shall keep, his lawful Commands shall do, Fornication or Adultery shall not commit, Hurt or damage to his said Master shall not do .... At Dice, Cards, Tables, Bowls or any other unlawful games he shall not play ... Matrimony within the said Term shall not contract, nor from his Masters Service at any time absent himself ...."

For the term of the apprenticeship, his mother and father (or their heirs or executors) had to agree to provide the said Apprentice (Tom) "sufficient and suitable meal and drink, lodging and washing and all necessary wearing apparel, medicine and medical attendance during the term ...."

The wage was 7/- per week for the first year, rising a shilling per week per year. No sick pay. There was the little clause of "and shall assist in any other work required by his said Master" – the "any other duties" clause of which one must still be wary today !

Queensbury and Mountain areas were among those suffering unemployment in the first half of the 19th century, so regular work in the second half was welcome. However, there were occasional rebellions as in October and November of 1892 when there was a strike in protest at management wanting each weaver to mind (operate) two looms instead of just one. And at the same time, a general reduction in pay was to be made ! This provoked riots. Like his father in the 1850s, Paul II now rode his horse amongst the rioters – and was pelted with eggs! Several rioters were hauled into Court later.

There were occasional protests from the Headmaster at Raggalds school about Speak employing under-age labour full-time (and children under 10 years old were sometimes working there part-time), but he was generally ignored. On census returns, children as young as eight are listed as having a mill or mining job.

Until 1871, the Mill closed at 2pm on Saturdays but then, following Foster's example, work stopped at 1pm. Diplomatically the workers were told of this idea, and approved it – as if they had any choice !

At Mountain, in 1914, Rennie Briggs (who was then 12) recalls the wages for his age group were: Full-time 4/6d, part-time 2/6d per week. For attending every day for a fortnight there was a 1/- bonus, 6d for part-timers. If you were late for a shift you'd find the gates closed (there was a big double gateway for wagons and a small pedestrian gate). Then you had to go into the time office corner door. You were fined by the Penny Man one penny (off your wage at the end of the week) and entered the mill yard through the adjacent corner door, thus bypassing the closed gate.

The Time Office
'Penny hole' and pedestrian gate 1990

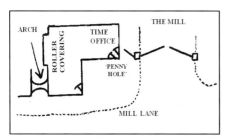

The Time Office, Penny Hole, Gates and Arch

At the time, work was from 0600-0800; breakfast; work 0830-1200; lunch; work 1230-1710 (the extra ten minutes is well remembered, but not the reason why). Contributor Fred Jagger was (briefly) a doffer at Speak's in 1930. His pay was 21/- a week. In 1931 it was reduced to 19/6 (economy measures?) so he left ! In 1932 another ex-employee reckons it was down to 17/6, with an 0630 start.

By 1937 (another ex-employee remembers) the wage was 27/- a week for adults, and the hours reduced to 0700-0830, 0930-1200, 1300-1700. In 1938, Irene Holdsworth, then 14, started work as a bobbin pegger at Speak's, for 19/- a week. At the time she lived with her folks who'd moved from Denholme to Hougomont, "where there was a well in the cellar" (house marked B on the Hougomont plan). Irene remembers visits to the Mill by Paul III in the late 1930s "about once a fortnight", even though he'd sold to Parklands in 1937.

Working conditions were on a par with those in other mills of the time. Much of the housing was owned by Speak's and rented to workers. Some were supplied with gas from the Mill until the late 1920s when supply was taken over by Halifax until 1969, and thereafter by NEGB, with conversion to natural gas in June/July 1972.

Thursday was Paul's day at Bradford Wool Exchange, to get orders for the quality blue and black serge cloth which the Mill produced (30 warp 60 weft). Often he seems to have overestimated the mill's capacity and found himself having to haggle over discounts with the buyers when production was late. Speak's had an office at 208 Swan Arcade in Bradford for a while.

Friday was wage day. Granville Rushworth, (the Treasurer) and Jack Binns (the Penny Man), would go to the bank in Queensbury for the cash.

The Mill was sold in 1937 to the Parkland Group. The company still traded as Paul Speak & Sons (Queensbury) Ltd, but, by 1948, was registered at Clyde Street, Bingley – another of Parkland's businesses. In 1949, the registered office became Albion Mills, Greengates (yes, Parkland's!) and Mountain Mill was then sold by the group, becoming Mountain Mills Co Ltd, a mortgage being raised with Lloyds Bank, covering the Mill property, the Lodge, Montrose Place, Fascination Place and 'other properties'. All other domestic properties were sold off by Paul III to individuals in the 1940s and 1950s. For example four lots were sold in February 1944 being Hillside Cottages nos. 34, 36, 38 (these were the first block of 3 beyond the Eagle), and nos 1-19 and 2-22 (Jester/Luddenden) and three cottages being Marble Place. The Time Office became domestic property. Last to be sold was the Institute in 1952.

After cloth production ceased, the Mill was divided into units and included a bakery and a double glazing company. In the late 1980s the last of the mill property was demolished. Some stone was used to rebuild the roadside wall along the main road between Glazier Road and Pineberry. The Mill site (except for Mill House) was left void for some years until planning was granted for housing. The cold reservoir proved difficult to fill adequately – the older locals fully expect the houses built there to sink !

The Mill after Parklands (Photo courtesy of Mr Les Chippendale, Mountain Mill)

A Mill House (white)
B Original Mill
C Weaving Sheds
D Site of Gas Works
E Time Office
F Bates/Lees
G Sunday School
H Warehams Fold
J Luddenden Place
K Marble Place (site)
L Jester House
M Reservoir Place
N 'Norman Keep'
P Glazier Road
Q Cornelius Drakes (site)
R Site of Quarry

The paved track to the Mill boiler house, between Derwent Place (left) and Fascination Place. New houses beyond occupy the site of the weaving sheds.

Warmlee/ Warm Lea/ Warmleigh Hall

Situated on Roper Lane, this was occupied by John Speak from the late 1870s until his removal to the family estate (Kirton Hall) in Lincolnshire in 1914. At present the property is private housing adjacent to a caravan site.

Laurel Bank

Situated at Holmfield close to Holdsworth House, it was a relatively plain property when purchased by Speaks. It consisted of a 2-storey structure, with a single-storey service block at the rear, forming an L-shape. Adjacent to that was the stables and barn building to the left. To the right rear was the vegetable garden; to the right front, a tennis court (slightly sunken)

Laurel Bank frontage and conservatory

was constructed; to the left front and built on to the house was a large conservatory; an S-shaped tree-lined drive led from the main road to the house; a separate driveway crossed the adjacent field direct to the barn. The property was bought by Paul Speak II in 1879 and subsequently occupied by Paul III until 1937. Laurel Bank is currently a nursing home.

Laurel Bank. (Photo courtesy Laurel Bank nursing home)

The Mill site. Everything has been demolished except Mill House in the centre. (L to R behind) Far left is Jester House (white), Jester Place, modern terrace on 'The Plantation', Bates cottage (white), the Time Office, and the end of Montrose Place.

Mill House from the Time Office side. Beyond is Micklemoss Farm.

THE SPEAK INSTITUTE 1913-1952

In the village of Queensbury the mill owner John Foster constructed a considerable production facility known as Black Dyke Mill, and a grand hall, known as Victoria Hall. This building, situated close to the main crossroads and almost opposite Foster's original home Prospect House, was for the recreation and education of the villagers of Queensbury in general and his workforce in particular.

By the end of the 19th century additional recreational and social facilities were deemed desirable on the Mountain. There were, of course, several pubs, and from 1898 there were events organised by the chapel. Otherwise you had to travel to Queensbury, or further. Perhaps inspired by the construction of Victoria Hall, John Speak (the adventurer) paid for the erection of a similar but smaller structure for his workers at Mountain. This, costing £3000, was called The Speak Institute (known locally as t'Tute) and dedicated to the memory of his parents, Nancy and Paul.

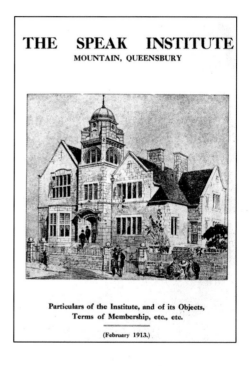

The opening ceremony was performed, using a gold key, by John Speak on a warm, sunny but breezy Saturday, 25 January 1913. On that day and continuing on Monday 27th, an estimated 900 persons attended for 'tea and entertainment'. On the Tuesday it was a day for the children, with games, a conjuror and a ventriloquist. (The Institute was, as always, closed on the Sabbath.)

Invitation tickets, printed in gold on bright coloured card, were issued, the colour relating to which day you should attend, in order to partake of 'Tea at 5 o'clock. Concert at 7.30.' A billiard match against Saltaire Cycle Club was arranged for the Wednesday.

The Institute was built adjacent to the Queensbury-Denholme main road. A local 'legend' relates that the road peaks around this point (by Snug Cottage) because spare earth from the footings was dumped there during construction. Certainly Snug Cottage is below road level but that was brought about with road reconstruction, either in 1905, or more likely when it became a turnpike in 1821.

The building is complete with tower (of no useful purpose except to hold a water tank) and cupola. Designed by Herbert Hodgson of Bradford, it stands proud and compact overlooking the main road and was within sight and easy reach of Speak's Mill. It is a notable structure seen on the skyline from many parts of West Yorkshire, perhaps not so easy to spot as Lister's Mill chimney or even that of Black Dyke, but to the inhabitants of Mountain it was as familiar as Blackpool Tower is to holidaymakers !

The structure is of Yorkshire stone, which is naturally a cream/brown colour. The roof was tiled in red, with several elegant chimney stacks, which carried tall chimney pots. The windows were metal framed with small panes. A short flight of steps led to the main entrance, which was separated from the main road by a dressed stone wall with iron fencing, heavy stone gateposts, and a plain strip of lawn.

The exterior of the Institute was incorrectly drawn on the cover of the commemorative brochure, including the inscription over the door which proclaims it to be 'The Mountain Club'! A photograph of the opening ceremony (published by O. Cockcroft of High Street, Queensbury) shows:

On the right of Cockcroft's photograph (taken from the road at the Queensbury side) is a mobile hut belonging to 'Thompson & Co, Joiners and Builders. Tel 179 Bfd' – presumably the contractors who were still working there. The side steps to the caretaker's house have a metal rail; and there are chimney pots.

Cockcroft's postcard of the opening ceremony. See text. (Graham Hall Collection)

Also on the Cockcroft photograph: A flagpole, with unidentified flag (it was a breezy day !), is fixed to the front Queensbury-side corner of the tower (brackets still existing); two lines of bunting run from the gateposts to below the front semicircular tower window; a flag is being flown from a horizontal pole above the Co-op; there is a pavement of setts or flags only across the Institute front for the length of the 'fancy' wall, (which is topped with iron railings). There is a gas lamp on this pavement.

There are two means of access to the grounds: Opposite the main door for pedestrians, and a wider one for vehicles nearer Pickering Farm. Both have the same style of gatepost and double wrought iron gates. The main road is 'dross'. There is a group of perhaps 100 persons all in their 'best outfits', watching the ceremony taking place outside the front door.

The front of the structure faces a little west of true south. All three storeys of the rear NE corner of the building were for the family of the resident caretaker (originally Mr Maud then Mr Dobson, and finally Mr Stead). Grassy banking fell away to the rear, overlooking fields. There was a double door rear entrance on the lower ground floor for easy access to the dining room, and a single door from the rear into the caretaker's basement. To the west was the grass Tennis Court, about 3m below road level, while to the east was Pickering Farm house across the front garden of which was a gently upward sloping path leading to the crown bowling green beyond. No provision was made for vehicular access to the Institute grounds, except for coke deliveries, with chutes to the boilerhouse to the right of the main steps.

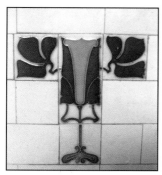

Decorative tiles in the hall and staircase. Dark green with yellow centre on plain white background. A line of small, rectangular, light blue and green tiles ran above, topped by dark green 'moulding', and with dark green tiles as a skirting.

Let us make an inspection of the Institute in pre-WWII days. Entering the double doors at the front, passing immediately through a second pair we are in the entrance hall, the floor of which is terrazzo with a simple green and black pattern around the edges. The walls are covered to 120cm high with green and white tiles, the higher wall being plastered and painted a buff colour. To the right, a heavy wood-panelled door (all room doors are of this type) leads to the Ladies' Meeting Room (referred to as Reading Room on the original plans) which is heated by a coal fire, and intended for pursuits such as sewing and gossip. This room is not particularly well used as 'ladies only', but is also used for Whist Drives, and so on, when men are allowed in.

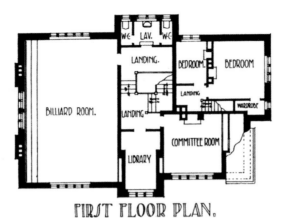

FIRST FLOOR PLAN.

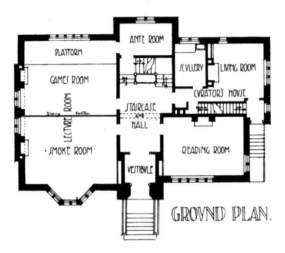

GROUND PLAN.

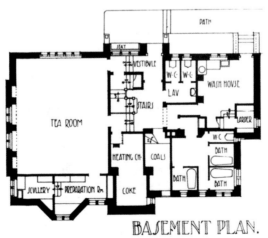

BASEMENT PLAN.

Two doors on the left of the hall (the further one at the bottom of the stairs, being extra wide and in two parts with one part door edge-hinged, the other, larger part being of a folding type) lead to the main room, which has a small stage at the back with an access door at stage level to an ante-room used by performers. The main room is used for dances, lectures and concerts. A wooden partition can be drawn across, thereby dividing the room into two, the front part of which becomes the Men's Smoking Room, the rear the Games Room. A piano is in the Games Room. Spittoons are provided in the front for those who like to 'crack baccy'. There is a coal fire in each half, and central heating throughout the public part of the building. Fireplaces have a dark green tile surround with brown tile backing and an arch over the grate.

At the far end of the hallway a broad arch (which is echoed on the floor above and the floor below) leads us to the staircase, which has stone stairs and a banister of wrought iron surmounted by a wooden handrail, and wooden corner posts. The walls are decorated the same as in the hall. We note a door to the right which leads to the caretaker's apartment. Up the first flight of 3 steps, ahead is a door leading to the ante-room. Turning clockwise, up 3 more short flights brings us to the arch on our left, leading left to the Committee Room, used once a month, functionally furnished without being pretentious, and with the usual tiled fireplace and hearth. It could also be used as a reading room etc, if no other room was available.

Another door leads to the County Library room (situated immediately over the hall). Continue to the very top landing, where the door ahead is to the gents toilet, and the door left is to the Billiard Room, which has two tables illuminated by gas lamps; chairs, card tables, and a clock obvious on the wall, and with the usual wall decorations for the main rooms – bottle green lower, pale green band and buff upper paintwork. The main roof timbers dominate overhead, with two arches. There is a central roof ventilator, operated with wires. Apart from billiards, card games are popular. Gambling for money is forbidden, but the Institute issues ½ and 1 tokens like brass coins, which are often used for bets. These were purchased at 12 to the shilling and exchanged at 13 to the shilling !

Return to the staircase, the walls of which exhibit souvenirs, such as spears, boomerangs, shields and bows and arrows from Mr John's world-wide wanderings. On summer mornings we see the whole of the upper staircase is illuminated in brilliant colours by sunlight shining through five stained glass windows, which depict (left to right) a symbolic figure (unknown), Paul Speak 1816-1878, John Speak, Nancy Speak 1815-1884, and a symbolic figure of Justice, all situated above the Gents on the top landing. The left hand symbolic figure is not known – it was removed after the Institute closed and no-one seems to remember what it was !

The Speak Institute.

*Left:
Entrance Hall, staircase and door to ante-room. The door on the left is the folding part of the Concert Room door. John Speak's souvenirs adorn the walls. The original gas light hangs in the hall. The windows down the descending staircase provide illumination from the rear vestibule.*

*Below:
The Billard Room, looking to the front.*

The Men's Smoking Room with bay window

The Dining Room (labelled Tea Room on the plan), looking towards the rear

The centre pane shows John Speak looking to the right, and carries the wording: John Speak who built and endowed this Institute in memory of his parents Paul and Nancy Speak AD 1913.

Returning down the staircase, four short flights below the hall take us to the lower ground floor – ground level at the rear of the building. Facing the bottom of the stairs is the Ladies toilet; to the left the rear door and glazed vestibule, wherein and to the left, three steps and a short passage lead to a single door into the dining room. Ahead from the main stairs and bearing slightly right is a short wide passage tiled up to 120cm in plain brown. A left hand door goes to the caretakers cellar kitchen, labelled 'Wash House' on the plan. A right hand door to the slipper baths. This room contains a toilet and three cast iron baths, partitioned from one another with stone slab walls. The bath cubicles are about 2m sq. There are hooks on the wall for clothes, and the lower outer walls are faced with white glazed bricks up to a height of about 2 metres and white painted above. One bathroom is complete with low ceiling, and is known as 'the sweater'.

Leaving the baths and proceeding straight ahead past a door leading to a store which partly overlaps the boiler, and with the main staircase on our right, we descend three steps, and observe the boiler house and coke store behind a wall to the left. The boiler and ancillary equipment was installed by W Nicholson & Co of Bridlington. The heating engineers were Richardsons of Darlington.

Double doors lead in to the dining room, which has trestle tables and chairs for up to 72 guests. Preparation and wash-up rooms with windows are partitioned off on the left (the front of the building). Again it is functionally furnished with the usual décor. The Institute has its own crockery, white with black motif 'The Speak Institute, Mountain'. On the underside is: 'Royal Vitreous. John Maddock & Sons Ltd, England'. The dining room is available for Mountain Mill employees 'and others' for refreshment, and for private hire. There are windows to the rear, and two windows on the west wall.

The Institute motif

Back upstairs to the entrance hall, the caretaker's quarters can be entered from the main landing, though the outside door is the usual means of access. Inside is a short corridor, with a door left to the scullery with double windows; and a door right to the cellar.

Ahead opens into the living room with a fireplace on the left, a small single window to the rear and a triple to the east, where we turn right through a door into a small lobby. Ahead is the door to the outside stairs, or turn right to go up a dark staircase to the two bedrooms, one fitted with a large closet.

Both bedrooms have fireplaces. The décor here is the usual green and brown. There is no bathroom.

Going down a dark stone staircase from the caretaker's hall brings us to the cellar kitchen with the door to the slipper baths corridor and public area. The walls here are in red brick, whitewashed. There is a large York range in place, backing on to the lower toilets room.

Activities, Rules and Regulations

The Institute was opened 25 January 1913, 'to further the social, moral and intellectual interests' of Speak's employees and the villagers of Mountain.

It was controlled by John Speak as president through a committee consisting of Messrs:

Lumb Wadsworth	Treasurer (he was the Mountain Mill Cashier)
Martin Robinson	(ex schoolmaster)
Sydney Mann	(Chapel committee member and overlooker at Black Dyke Mill)
Sam Gledhill	(overlooker at Mountain Mill and a bell ringer at Queensbury Parish Church)
Wallace Cockcroft	(a manager at Mountain Mill)
Herbert Hodgson	(the architect who designed the Institute)
A Bairstow	(Councillor)

Paul Speak II and III were Trustees and Vice Presidents.

From October 1913, the committee was elected annually by the members.

'No Gambling, No Alcohol, No Politics' were the members' rules, though rooms could be rented for political meetings. On a day-to-day basis (Monday-Saturday, closed Sundays) the 'front room' (Ladies Room) was not intensively used. The menfolk adjourned to their 'front room' or to the billiard room for card- or board-games, or dominoes. A few, both male and female, might use the library (which had its own stock of books plus West Riding County Council books to borrow).

Events held included lectures – 'Lady Fisher-Smith gave a talk with lantern slides about Oberammergau' – which were free. Concerts were held, which were quite well supported: Later there were more 'popular' concerts (even jazz !), and dances were held (Saturdays or Wednesdays) which latterly cost 9d or 1/-, and featured a trio or quartet on the stage.

Some of the dancing was not approved of by parents. One of our correspondents recalls her father dragging her out of the Institute – she'd been dancing 'The Lancers', and the lights had been dimmed. Scandalous !!

The slipper baths initially cost 1d to members (3d non-members) for soap, two towels and a bath; women all day Wednesday and Thursday, men all day Friday and Saturday. The 'sweater' bath is remembered as 'very hot'. The Curator (or his wife on women's days) ran the bath for you. The taps had a key, so you couldn't run in more water !

Billiards cost 2d per game of 20 minutes if light was used, or for 30 minutes if gas was not used.

Institute membership was 2d a week or 2/- per quarter (lady members half price). Library membership (if not an Institute member) 2/- per year. Institute membership was for over 18's only initially, except for the Library and the Slipper Baths.

Here are some comments, provided by Mary Hargrave, whose father was the final curator (caretaker) at the Institute (1938-1952).

"My father became curator in 1938. We'd lived in Mountain since 1925. My father had been unemployed for a long time during the depression. Previously he had been caretaker of the chapel.

Living at the 'Tute made us feel like Royalty. And what a view ! It was a pleasure washing up at our kitchen sink.

The 'Tute was open Monday-Saturday 0800 to 2200. Anyone could come. Consumption of alcohol was prohibited. The building was gas-lit until after the War. We had quite a lot of dances before the War, music being provided by piano and drums. Admission 1/-.

Most people who came during the War were older men, retired. They liked to argue with one another, and were scandal-mongers. They liked to crack baccy, and spittoons were provided, being cleaned and refilled with sawdust each day.

During the War, blackouts were fitted. The preparation room (off the Dining Room) was fortified with thick timbers, and taken over by the ARP, 24 hours a day. The Home Guard came here as well.

My father was paid £1.10s.0d a week plus free rent, coal and gas. This was considered good pay then, and there could be 'overtime' in running the canteen from our cellar. When the war ended, so did the overtime. Soon after the War, my father asked for a rise, but Paul Speak and the Committee decided rather to close the Institute, so we had to look for a house."

On 21/12/1951, Paul Speak sold Pickering Hall Farm (as it was then called) and 4 closes (ie minus the Institute land) to John William Sutcliffe, alias Pig Willy. The Institute was sold 21/4/1952 to Greenwood and Shackleton.

THE INSTITUTE AFTER SPEAKS

Although the mill was sold to Parkland Group in 1937, the Institute remained owned by Speaks and controlled by Paul and the committee. After the War, conditions in the area did not return to 'as before', and on 21 April 1952 the Institute and Tennis Court were sold for £800 to Messrs Tom Greenwood and James Shackleton of Queensbury, property developers. The Bowling Green went to Pickering Farm.

The rear of The Speak Institute in its original form except that the topmost row of windows of the Billard Room have been blocked up. When converted to flats, it was known as Mountain Villas.

Mr Shackleton, who was born in 1910, seems to have been the one most familiar with the Institute. He remembers firing and maintaining the coke central heating boiler, later converted to gas. The property, which was said to be 'in good condition' when purchased, was in part converted ('on the cheap') to inexpensive rented flats, and called Mountain Villas. The accommodation areas became: 2 in the Billiard Room, (a new doorway and 3 steps being made from outside the library), 2 in the concert room, and one being in the caretakers apartment. It seems likely that the Ladies Room was let also. Individual toilet facilities were not provided – residents had to visit the nearest communal toilets ! The flats were let at 30/- per week to 'poor families'. Mr Shackleton recalls this venture was one of the worst they undertook! Better was the construction of 3 'bungalows' on the former tennis court, which they sold freehold in 1966, with number 43 going to Albert Mitchell, 45 to Francis Spencer, and 47 to Ida Bray.

On 30 December 1966 Greenwood & Shackleton sold the Institute to Arthur Dobson for £1000. The property alternated between him and Leslie Dobson, changing hands on 10/12/1969, 3/5/1974 and again 2/7/1980, each time for £1000 ! Around this time a survey was done. The Institute land, with a frontage of 112 feet, a depth of 90 feet, and an area of 1120 square yards, was considered to be worth £5000 as building land for 4 houses, if the

Institute was demolished. Arthur was the one who lived and had his printing business there. The Billiard Room flats – cheap partition walls with a low false ceiling – became darkroom, staff room and ancillary rooms, and the original door to it from the top landing by the Gents was blocked up. The Committee Room was the office. The Concert Room was the Press Room, where the printing was actually done; the Dining Room was stripped out to house cutting and finishing machines. Outside all the gate posts and part of the front garden wall were removed. At least one gate column was built into the retaining wall adjacent to Pickering Farm, with only two gate post tops remaining at the front. Arthur also had the rear and side yards levelled, partly concreted, and a ramp built at the back for servicing motorcars.

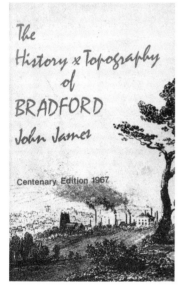

Example of a Mountain Press reprint, from 1967

The business and building were known as Mountain Press, doing jobbing printing, reprints of previous-century books (eg 'History of Bradford' by James) and a minor sideline in literary erotica – well-known to the locals and the local constabulary who said that when lights were on at night in certain rooms, Arthur was printing his 'mucky books'! Examples of some – extremely tame by today's standards – were found in the underdrawing in the former Committee Room during renovations.

An exceptional reprint was one called 'My Secret Life' by 'Walter', written c. 1850 to 1870. When Arthur reprinted this in the 1960's he found himself in court. Various experts testified against him, agreeing that the book was pornographic and of no literary merit (one 'expert' was an authority on Dickens – unlikely to give Walter, an anonymous author, any credit). The judge described it as 'filth'. Arthur was given a 2 year jail sentence. Ironically, 40 years later, 'My Secret Life' is readily available in book stores and is regarded as of socio-historical importance, commenting as it does on the bits of Victorian Life that other (mainstream) authors left out !

Entertaining, cut-price flamboyance and appalling taste in decorations seem to have been some of Arthur's qualities. Maintenance of the fabric of the building seems to have been of no interest. Rather than repair a leaking roof, even though spare tiles were to hand, a plastic sheet was fixed inside to divert the drips. One unusual but presumably essential repair was to a main roof timber which was reinforced with a concrete beam! Water permeated the whole building. The heating was shut off. Dry rot and interesting fungi wrecked timber and loosened plaster from walls. Huge rolls of paper rotted in the basement.

Arthur, now a loner, and perhaps becoming a little paranoid, had every single door in his domestic area fitted with intruder alarms, even that between his clothes closet and bedroom! The former Ladies Room was converted into a dining/entertaining room, a new access from the living area being created by breaking through the wall just inside the caretaker's apartment door from the main Hall. (This was actually through the flue from the main boiler – hence the end of central heating !) This room then received a bright red carpet, red flock-patterned wallpaper, lap panelled ceiling with Roman-style cornice (very badly fitted), a huge imitation stone fire surround and hearth with an electric heater, and two equally out-of-proportion plaster ceiling mouldings from which hung large chandeliers. Small gas convector heaters were fitted in various rooms.

Arthur, however, became seriously ill, and died in 1987. 'The Family' descended on the building which was immediately put up for sale. An auction was arranged for commercial items – what wasn't sold was just abandoned. The domestic part was stripped – even light fittings and wall-mounted gas heaters. The estate agent handling the sale was DeRome in Bradford.

MOUNTAIN HALL HOTEL 1988-2003

[The former Mountain Press/Institute was purchased by Shirley and Stan Ledgard. They resided on the premises, and this chapter was provided by them during this period.]

As soon as the sale board appeared on the Mountain Press building, we contacted the estate agents and put in an offer but were out-bid. Despite several potential buyers expressing interest, nothing was signed over. After about a year, the Estate Agent, Mr DeRome, contacted us to see if we were still interested. "Make an offer – it's in poor condition", he warned us. So we did - £6000 less than we'd offered a year ago (and £10,000 less than The Family had wanted !), and the sale was agreed in 1988.

Shirley, Stan and Nina the lurcher pose in front of Mountain Hall

The domestic accommodation was habitable, after the installation of central heating. Plans were drawn up and passed for the conversion we wanted, and work began with the roof being completely re-tiled, and the asphalting of the three flat-roof areas. In the tower, the supporting timbers for the cupola looked to be deteriorating so steel reinforcements were added. Alterations then continued slowly down the building, with 72 new window frames (the original ones being metal and well rotten), an intermediate floor in the Billiard Room and two new staircases there, handmade to fit. This became two floors of bedrooms, the library another one, the committee room was two, and the gents toilet extended out onto the stairs top landing was another, totalling 13. The original billiard room doorway was re-opened to provide an 'emergency exit'. The concert room became lounge-bar to the front and restaurant with a spacious galley kitchen to the rear. The former dining room became two lecture rooms. The anteroom became ladies' toilets. Unfortunately, the open areas from the main staircase to the three levels had to be screened off to comply with the fire requirements. The original tiling in the hall and staircase was covered since much was damaged and not repairable. And various ceilings were lowered in the interests of heating efficiency and to hide the new plumbing. Outside, the building was re-pointed, drains re-laid across the yard, and levelling done. A grassed banking was prepared at the rear of the property, but the adjacent landowner then petulantly demanded that a drystone wall be constructed 'to keep the sheep in' (neither we nor he had any sheep !). So more digging and a reinforced concrete wall partly stone-faced was installed – which actually gave us a more useful rear yard. This was the 'Great Wall'.

<u>Above:</u>
The completed Mountain Hall Hotel. The dome was painted by Master Decorator Bert, together with an assistant. They edged round, holding on with one hand – Bert with the paintbrush, his assistant with the paint, and fuelled by lager, judging by the cans we found afterwards! Health and Safety? Pickering Farm cottage is on the right.

<u>Left:</u>
Girders for the new upper floor are slotted in through the window.

Left:
Master joiner Dennis Prescott, in what was the Men's Smoking Room, manufacturing new stairs for the upper bedroom area.

Below:
The upper bedroom floor before the creation of the rooms.

To the rear of Mountain Hall was car parking, a ridge of lawn, and a terrace bounded by the Great Wall. Here resident lurcher Nina relaxes on the lawn. On the terrace, Shirley sits at the tea-table. Above Nina's head can be seen the old pumping station with Clough House beyond. In the middle distance above Shirley's head is Laneside disappearing into the trees. The nearer long building is a joinery.

During re-roofing, resident terrier Trudy tests out the hoist.

The 'fancy wall' by the side steps was a Dobson addition.

Why did we buy the building? For years it had looked an ideal size and location for our idea of a residential adult education centre. When we first viewed it in 1988, even in its dilapidated state it felt 'right' – good vibes, man! We weren't the only ones to feel that. Part way through the renovations, Harry Thompson the Holistic Healer of Queensbury – a friend and colleague – called. He stood on a pile of brick rubble filling the hallway and also pronounced that "it felt right"! Visitors who allowed themselves 'feelings' all agreed. Others viewed the project as a lot of work and considered us quite mad. In fact, the projected cost of the work proved quite accurate except for the plumber who charged some 40% over estimate due to failing to keep to agreements (moral: always get it in writing). Around 1990, some resident (or transient) spook in the building scared the excreta out of the plumber on occasion by causing old plumbing (which he'd isolated) to suddenly sound as if activated. Being a God-fearing soul, he refused to be in the building alone after that, the other tradesmen told us.

Another (or the same) spook would call the name of our joiner: "Dennis!" who would respond by calling: "Hello" and make a tour of the building to see who wanted him ! More time wasted !!

To digress in a ghostly manner, one of the few apparitions seen is an indistinct form on the staircase. Probably a woman, but nothing is known about her although several people have seen her.

To 'help' with the ghost hunting, the local radio station brought the medium James Byrne to visit (prior to a show he was to do in the area), to communicate with any spirits which were present. And it was to be a live broadcast. Now James is a nice enough guy, and likely a good medium when allowed to do it naturally. But he was in the throes of becoming a stage medium – a showman, entertainer – and he became very conscious of his radio audience and especially of his manager of that time – whom some might rate as an obnoxious plonker – and who was present. On air, James began well, picking up on a colleague of ours who, in spirit, seems to be a frequent visitor. But then we had to have the shock/horror garbage – "There's spirit at the top of the stairs, connected with a murder, probably of a child. In the 1800s. Do you know of this?" "No". "Well it was. And I'm told the body was taken from here out into the field ………" etc, etc. Even when I pointed out that the building was only erected in 1912, being a field prior to that, the manager wouldn't accept it ! If he'd done any preparation, he'd have noticed the commemorative date stone over the entrance.

Another spook has been spotted in what used to be the billiards room – a gent walking round seemingly lighting the gas lamps there. Other presences, some with names, have been detected but unfortunately have not checked out. They don't seem to want to do anything except go about their own business. The vibes still feel good. It's a very peaceful building. However some of the living guests can be a big scary …..!!

Returning to physical reality, in years to come excavations in the rear yard might reveal an irregular lump of concrete weighing several tons, buried just below the surface. This is 'Steve's Folly'. When putting in footings for the 'Great Wall' at the rear, Steve, the manager of the job, found he couldn't get concrete shovelled in fast enough (I think part of the banking collapsed into the trench) so much of that readymix delivery solidified in the yard. Difficult to break up, the next time an excavator was on site, we had a hole dug, and the concrete mass dropped in it. R.I.P. Concrete !

With the advent of Mountain Hall – a fairly obvious name, chosen for the most imposing building on the Mountain, and complementary to Mountain House (formerly Mill House) and Mountain Lodge (alias Law Hill Farm) – little was changed externally apart from the provision of fire escapes and the removal of unsafe chimney pots. The caretaker's quarters remained, but the former cellar kitchen and slipper baths were partitioned off from the rest of the guest accommodation. Thirteen bedrooms were created and the whole concept was geared to a residential capacity of 24 persons.

Until 2003, various unusual adult courses were offered – continuing Speak's original concept but lowering the minimum age to 16 – as well as hiring the facilities to groups and educational institutions.

Residential courses run by Mountain Hall were mostly to do with Complementary Therapies or with the Paranormal. All meals were provided, with a 3-course dinner menu chosen according to the weather and the peculiarities of the students. These menus usually had a Yorkshire/Lancashire theme, or Greek (for some reason !).

The chefs who provided for guests were mostly two characters Ken and Stan. They, together with the head waiter/barman Allan, were usually well 'lubricated' from the bar before service began, and dinner was often an hilarious event both within the kitchen and in the restaurant.

In sober mode, both Allan and Stan were also tutors at Mountain Hall as well as for Bradford/Calderdale Education Boards. Ken was Executive Chef at a local hospital, and missed slaving in a kitchen !

A note on the menus stated: "All wines served at Mountain Hall have been tested to oblivion by the proprietors" - which was perfectly true !

****

In 2003 Mountain Hall was sold to a Dr Hussain for a private residence. Many alterations were begun but mostly not completed. In August 2007, the building was abandoned.

The original Men's Smoking Room became the lounge-bar

The former Games Room became the Restaurant and Kitchen.

The two chefs, Ken above, Stan below and an example of a Greek-style menu with rather dubious spelling!

Kolokithakia
(Courgette with Cheese & Tomato. Grilled.)
Kremydosoupa
(Greek Onion & Yoghurt Soup)
'Manos'
(Marinated Feta, grilled & served on Asparagus)

Stifado
(Beef cooked with Tomatoes and Onions)
Kabak Moussaka
(Courgette, Mushrooms, Red Onions, Aubergine)
Kotopulo 'Zygos'
(Chicken cooked with black Peppercorns and Leeks)

Mila Psita
(Baked Apple with Fruit, Walnuts and Brandy)
Cretan Pancake
(Pancake filled with Cottage Cheese and Honey)
Coffee

MOUNTAIN - THE CENTRAL AREA

Development within this area was completed and static from around 1870 until 1930, after which time changes began and continue. Some of the main developments are mentioned here and on the following diagrams.

In 1858-1864 the Fleece pub was revamped. The 'fill-in' shop (butcher's) was built, joining the pub to the Mountain Place block. Snug Cottage which was two low-deckers had, in the early 1800s, three cottages behind it. Between 1851 and 1861 these were demolished and a block of 4 dwellings (including shops) was built in the area behind Snug and bounded by Mill Lane and the main road. A few years later two more were added at the Raggalds side. Originally known as Gate End, they became known as Changegate, then Commercial Buildings (1901), and Providence Buildings (or Changegate) in 1961. A ginnel was between them and the next block which was built along Mill Lane about the same time (to replace 3 cottages known as Royd Gate). This block became known as St George's Buildings, or Greenwood's. It had two properties on Mill Lane, back-to-back with 3 others. The Mill Lane pair had a common cellar with access via steps from the ginnel, the cellar being used for habitation pre WW II.

Continuing up Mill Lane next was the Sunday School; Lee's (where John Bates lived) and Bairstow's (Marble Place). Along the main road was the Chapel then Wainhouse (or Wareham's) Fold. From around 1860, this consisted of two cottages, and a barn with a cottage at a right angle, joining on to the newly-built 'Eagle' beerhouse, which replaced an earlier domestic property.

On the opposite side of the main road was Harmony Place (opposite the Eagle), West Royd, built during WW I (opposite the Chapel); next a space (formerly part of Mountain End Farm) on which a house was built in the late 1900s and Evelyn Place opposite the central shops. The back of Evelyn Place had three levels. Those at ground level were 'cellar dwellings'. Above was a steel-and-stone walkway giving access to houses back-to-back with Evelyn Place. These were called Grand View, but colloquially known as t'Landin (the Landing or Balcony). Next towards Queensbury was the Co-op block of three, and the snicket to Low Lane; the Institute Tennis Court (later bungalows), and the Institute itself.

Apart from the addition of porches, Harmony Place is much as it was, with small gardens to the front and plain flat-topped walls. The larger gardens at West Royd had wrought iron fencing atop the walls. Evelyn Terrace had only paving, now stepped up above the more recent pavement.

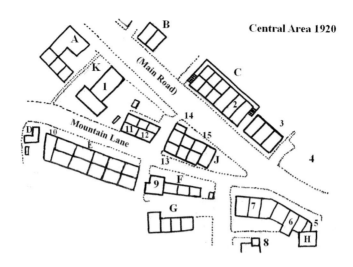

1. Chapel/Sunday School
2. Post Office
3. Co-op
4. Tennis Court
5. Robinson, Butcher }
6. Original Co-op } Mountain
7. Cloggers } Place
8. Fleece brewery

9. Binns, Hardware became Post Office/Off Licence
10. Jackson, Grocer
11. Cloggers
12. Greenwood, Grocer
13. Ingham, Fish Shop } Change-
14. Barn/Dobson Grocer} gate
15. Bairstow, Grocer }

A. Mountain Eagle
B. West Royd
C. Grand View/Evelyn Place
J. Snug Cottage

F. Derwent Place
G. Stone Street
H. Fleece/Fin Inn
K. Jackson Ginnel

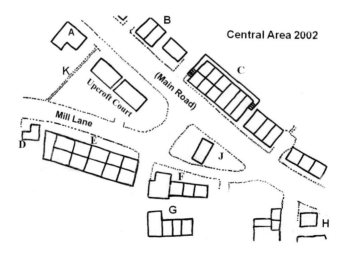

Bates' cottage, actually two cottages back-to-back and also known as Lee's. The slightly lower building on the right is a post-Bates extension.

The low deckers behind The Fleece. The track through the trees provides access to South View. The low building on the right was the Fleece brewhouse.

Speak Institute in the 1950s, featuring the frontage wall, (the vehicular access gate has been blocked up), the lamp, Snug Cottage (painted white) and Changegate, and the Chapel in the distance. (Graham Hall Collection)

Snug Cottage hides away at the junction of the main road and Mill Lane in 1989. The last shop in Mountain still trades behind on the far left.

View from Low Lane. (L to R) The Institute, bungalows on the former tennis court, Co-op building, Grand View, new house, West Royd.

View from Low Lane: West Royd on the left and Harmony Place..

View from Catsteps snicket of The Landing (the rear of Evelyn Terrace), the new house and West Royd.

Close-up of The Landing, looking towards The Institute

SHOPKEEPERS AND TRADESMEN

Mobile Traders, 1900-1960s

Probably the most well known (or, at least, most often quoted) was Paraffin Irvin (Rev. Irvin Scott), a resident of Myrtle Farm, Roper Lane. He travelled the area with a donkey and cart, selling paraffin which he dispensed from old milk churns. Of small build, he was known for rarely washing his hands and always smelled of paraffin ! He was also a local Methodist preacher. A man with a dry sense of humour, he is quoted as saying upon the death of his first wife: "My light has gone out". However, on remarrying he claimed he'd "struck another match". At the time, paraffin was essential for lighting – either that or candles ! Gas was supplied (by the Mill) to a few places – the Institute being one – though in houses gas was usually only downstairs. In general, electricity didn't arrive until the 1930s, but some places were on paraffin until after the second War.

'Salt Jim', a trader with a notable proboscis, came from Wibsey with rock salt and donkey stone. Donkey stone is made from the softer sandstone of 'mares' (faults) in a mine vein. This is ground into sand, mixed with crushed lime ('cement') and formed into blocks. Originally used from Victorian times to scour wood or stone, colour additives were used to enable stone steps to be decorated as well as cleaned. 'Yellow-stone', for example, was coloured with iron oxide. It is possible that the 'Salt Jim' remembered here was, in fact, Tommy Jones. The 'real' Salt Jim (James Ashley) was a well-known beggar who didn't <u>sell</u> salt but carried a lump with him so he could claim to be a legal hawker not an illegal beggar. He died in 1911. Tommy succeeded him – as a genuine hawker!

Also remembered was a trader with only one-arm. He brought a sack of oranges which he sold at 14 for 1/-, but he seems nameless.

Cyril Trufit was a greengrocer with horse and cart, whose visits were frequent since he was 'bothering' with the landlady at the Foresters, it was believed. He had a shop at 38 Sandbeds, Queensbury.

Willy Dobson, a travelling greengrocer, lived at Evelyn Terrace. He kept his horse in a stable at the back of the Eagle yard. He had a house-shop also, being the Raggalds end of Evelyn Terrace, which his wife Ada ran. Later he took a shop property opposite Evelyn Terrace. He was Curator at the Institute until 1938.

Newspapers were delivered by handcart from Queensbury, though Sunday papers were distributed from a house in Harmony Place.

Later in this period, and operating from Queensbury, was Herman Whiteley a coalman who habitually wore a dickey bow and bowler – a gentleman coalman !

Bottom of the league for transport, perhaps, was Amos Harrison who sold linens, carried in a parcel on his head and a sack on his back. He had a shop in Halifax. He called on a Friday (= pay day at the Mill), and sold all manner of clothes and cloth which could be bought 'on tick'. He's remembered for asking his customer: "Av ah ta laise dahn?" (Have I to open the pack?)

Mobile, though not strictly a tradesman, was Sam Spencer, a gentle giant of a man. He had a huge barrow, brush and shovel and cleaned pavements from Queensbury to Mountain. Like others in his family, he suffered a cleft palate and called himself 'Tam'. He lived with his family at 4/6 Stone Street, then moved to 3 Luddenden Place. His father John had been a bread baker, but did watch and clock repairs after the move. Sam also trained as a bread baker before taking up roadsweeping. Bread making seemed a family occupation since when in Luddenden Place, mother Betty and Sam and his sister Alice still made bread to sell from the house.

Mobile traders of pre-1900 days have not been recalled. By their nature, they were either local producers, or transients. Of the latter were hawkers: In the 1861 census, there is mention of two hawkers living in the area. Hawkers might specialise in the sale of particular goods, and would move from area to area, staying only as long as necessary for business. They travelled the streets with horse and cart, handcart or simply selling what they could carry. The two mentioned are both from Kendal and "recently arrived here" with their families. One Joseph Wilson, Licensed Pott (sic) Hawker, has with him his wife and with children born respectively in Fouregg, Adenfield, Weely Lane and Colne (all in Lancashire) and Whitehaven. His neighbour, Enoch Vase, hawker, has his wife with children born in Kendal, Clitheroe, Burton (Lancs) and Blackburn. This gives an idea of the wanderings of these mobile traders.

Asa Nicholson

Asa was a farmer and quarryman (employee) from Keelham. In the bad winter of 1897/8 he looked for additional work, and began training with T H Binns in Halifax, making oatcakes. Rather than take the train from Thornton, he'd walk to Holmfield then take the train. Similarly on his return but en route via Bradshaw or Mountain, he'd stop off to sell his oatcakes. He lived at a small farm next to Stocks House, at Bottomley Holes, and turned one of the outbuildings into his 'bakery' – it housed his horse and trap also – from around 1900. Notwithstanding this activity, he is still listed as 'Farmer' in 1909. He began regular deliveries round the area. From the 1920s he became mechanically mobile, with a second-hand Ford T flat truck. Having had no driving experience, the vendor gave him a 10 minutes 'lesson' and left him to it ! By the 1930s there were 6 vans operating from the extended bakery at the farm, now known as Oats Royd. The present bakery, next to Keelham school, opened in 1948, and is still owned by Asa's family.

Asa Nicholson's kindly provide the following information about Havercake (also known as Oatcake, and locally as Haverbread). It is thought to be of Norse origin and is made from oatmeal, wholemeal flour, water and a raising agent. The mix is stored overnight in an earthenware or wooden tub which had contained the previous day's mix without being washed out. This dough has the consistency of thick cream. A small amount is poured on to a scored wooden board covered with dry meal. This is transferred to a cloth on a second board. "With a highly specialised action", the mixture is flung from the cloth onto the hot bakestone (originally clay, then stone, slate or metal). When freshly baked it is soft, like a limp washleather, but can be hung to dry out on the kitchen creel and can be kept for a week or more. Producing Havercakes is skilled, labour-intensive, and slow (at best about 3 per minute). Asa Nicholson's still produce them weekly.

If you want to make some yourself you may use this recipe:

One teacup oatmeal, one heaped teaspoon baking powder, one-third teaspoon salt, one teacup water. Mix all ingredients and leave to stand overnight. Pour a small amount into a hot (dry) cast iron frying pan. Turn over once. Ready in seconds!

The Co-Op Cometh

 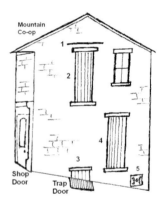

The photograph shows the Mountain Co-op block as originally built with the corner shop door and single display window. The diagram emphasizes the end features.
(1) hoist support, (2) upper stockroom door, (3) cellar store door,
(4) ground floor stockroom door (added 1913), (5) coalgrate.

In 1856 the Queensbury Co-operative Society opened in Chapel Street, Queensbury, selling staple food items cheaply. Branches were subsequently opened at Thornton, Shelf, Denholme, Bradshaw, Sandbeds, West End and Ambler Thorn, but one of the earliest branches was on the Mountain. In 1858 premises at Mountain Place were rented, the line-up being Fleece, butcher's lock-up, house, Co-op rented shop, another house and three low decker cottages. In 1870, two cottages opposite the rented shop were purchased (part of Mountain End estate), were demolished and a new shop and storage built with 2 attached cottages. This opened in September 1871. A newspaper article reports: 9 Sept. "A teaparty was held at the new building of the Mountain Co-op. Tea for 200 people was provided in the shops and there was a public meeting in the chapel. The new shops are commodious and are being fitted with the most recent improvements for carrying on a large drapery and grocery business".

'Shops' is slightly puzzling. Obviously the rented shop in Mountain Place opposite was still functioning but was not being refitted. In the new building, all of the ground floor of the shop was presumably sales space, with drapery to the rear. When the shop front was remodelled in 1913, drapery was abandoned, the rear of the shop being partitioned off as stockroom and a new door added as shown in the diagram. The shop door was moved from the corner to the shop front and replaced with a window. 'Union is strength' and the date '1913' were inscribed above the windows.

This branch closed in the 1960s, shortly after Roy Murgatroyd the manager was convicted of fraud. He'd noticed that stock at the shop didn't tally with the books. He panicked and 'adjusted' the paperwork which was soon detected.

One local recalls that for a while there was a 'tin shed' situated in the garden of Snug Cottage. This was used by the Co-op "at odd times in the week", to sell fresh meat, which was brought ready-prepared from the butchery department in Queensbury.

As with many Co-op stores at the time (pre-1945), you could take your radio accumulator there for re-charging. The bigger Co-ops (such as Queensbury) did shoe or clog repairs 'while-you-wait'.

Down the main road just beyond Harp Lane at Hill Top, was the Gala Field. In 1906 Queensbury Co-op applied to the Council for approval for a piggery at Hill Top. It was approved and six fields were purchased in 1907 from (the wife of) Greenwood Robinson. Two parts were within the harp-shaped area of David Knowles: The half parallel to the road with his filled-in quarry, and the more sloping lower part. The road side became the bakery in 1924, and part of it (at the Fox Hill end where the quarry had been) became the Gala field, with fine trees along the roadside. The bakery was of red brick. In the highest gable facing the road was carved in relief:

QUEENSBURY IND SOC LTD
19 BAKERY 24

As at many bakeries, the public could take their own bread there to be "oven'd". The bakery closed just after WWII and was bought by Grimston's (pre-fab garages) in 1951. They purchased the Gala Field also in 1960. The property was later occupied by a car wreckers, who had the brick-built offices (of Grimstons) completely encased in reclaimed stone for use as a house, which they called Foxhill Lodge.

'Foxhill Lodge', formerly the brick-built offices of Grimstons, now clad in stone. In August 2005 it and the Bakery were demolished, and the site levelled, by Lynskey on behalf of housing developer Asquith. The site remained void for several years.

The former Co-op Bakery, which was the two gable-ended buildings. The lean-to was added by Grimston.

Mountain Shops

Several shops were established in the central area. In the late 1850s these included those of Jonas Bairstow, Jonas Chatburn, George Normanton, Jonas Robertshaw, Martha Smith and Thomas Smith. All are listed as 'Grocers'. There were cloggers also, being Joseph Firth, Joshua Benn, and Joshua Robertshaw, and 'clog sole cutter' Joseph Dean who had moved from Clog Street Raggalds to Mountain.

Please refer to the Central Area diagrams in the previous chapter. Going back to the first half of the 1900s, based on personal memories of older inhabitants, the village traders are recalled thus:

In the 1920s the middle property in Marble Place (opposite Luddenden Place) was a lock-up shop (sweets and general) owned by Harold Walker. Several locals maintain that he ran it previously as a fish shop, but none have personal knowledge of it.

Next to the Mill Time Office, the first use as a shop seems to be around 1890 when John Benn opened a grocers shop there. This became Samuel Saunders from 1908 to 1927, then 'Gertie Bootie' Jackson's. The bad-tempered geese she kept by Glazier Road are well remembered!

At the other end of Fascination Place lived Joshua Benn, a clogger. In 1900 he is listed as a 'dealer in antiquities', his stock being stored in one of the low deckers in Mountain Place.

In a block of five properties opposite Fascination Place was Joshua Benn's shop [11], and Greenwood's (grocer, and who also sold coal) [12], both facing on to Mountain Lane, with three houses behind. Mr Greenwood's sales pitch for his coal was "These coals burn like burning silver". In their cellar lived (for a while) a character known as 'Sam-at-our-Mikes'. This was the only true cellar dwelling known to be on the Mountain, where the whole apartment was below ground.

At the upper end of Derwent Place was Binns Hardware [9]. Mr Binns was timekeeper at the Mill. Mrs Binns ran the shop. In the main block opposite was the fish (and chip) shop of Emily Ingham [13], facing on to Chip 'Oil Ginnel, the throughway between this block and Greenwood's. Later taken by Arthur Kirkbright, he had his fish delivered, once a week, to Queensbury station, when he or a 'contractor' transported it to Mountain. Mrs Kirkbright prepared the fish, and would sell wet fish from the shop. Arthur would take a basket of fish to sell to householders down on Laneside, at West Scholes and Yews Green. During the 1930s, Kirkbrights sold pies supplied by Susannah and Lavinia Barratt who baked at their house on the Cali.

On the main road side of the main block was greengrocer Willy Dobson who had the corner building [14]. Next a house, and then another grocers, Rhoda Bairstow, whose family ran a shop from the 1850s [15]. This became Gray's, in the late 1920s. In Evelyn Terrace opposite was the Post Office [2], opened in 1900 and run by Wright Sutcliffe, who was also a boot and shoe seller. Previously he'd been at Travis Cottages. In 1927 the Post Office passed to his wife Olive. In its own block was the Co-op [3]. Over the main road, next to the Fleece, was the lock-up butchers shop of Clifford Robinson [5]. He had a small slaughterhouse near Stone Street. He'd bring a cow up for slaughter on a Sunday morning – which fascinated some of the local kids! In the block (which at this time consisted of: Robinson's lock-up shop, three houses, three low-deckers) the middle low-decker was a cloggers [7], and the third house was Herbert Cawthra gents hairdresser open Thursday and Friday nights – Herbert had a 'salon' in Queensbury also.

From the Fleece up the track (Abel Street) towards Glazier Row, were two cottages, remembered as the joinery and funeral parlour of Mr Bairstow (later becoming Knowles' joiners, then Farnell's). Edgar Farnell bought the buildings and over 1000 square yards of land (up to Glazier Road) from Paul III in 1939 for £93. 9s. In Glazier Row itself was the spice shop (sweet shop) of Ike Crump, essentially sales from a house. Up beyond and behind Glazier Row were Cornelius Drake's cottages, used by a builder/plasterer.

View along the main road, with the Co-op shop frontage on the right, and now filled in. It has been converted into two flats.

Over the years, shops began to close earlier – say 7 or 8pm instead of 11pm which had been the norm in the area from the mid-1850s. And closed on Sundays, of course.

View down Mill Lane from Bates cottage, showing the Arch, (giving access to domestic privies), the former shop (white door) of John Benn and Fascination Place, with Derwent Place beyond.

Further down Mill Lane is Derwent Place. The first building with the extended frontage was Binns shop, latterly the last Post Office and shop in Mountain. The former Fleece pub is in the distance.

The former butcher's shop of Cornelius Robinson in the yard of the Bradshaw Tavern. Grandson Clifford's shop next to the Fleece on the Mountain was somewhat smaller!

By the early 1930s some of the shops (and characters associated with them) had disappeared. But Mountain was still well provided. Around the time of WW II the shopping area included:

Next to the Fleece was Clifford Robinson butcher (later becoming Kenneth Wrightson's). Clifford made deliveries – certain days to certain houses – carrying meat in a large handbasket. Since most folk had regular requirements, he knew what to take even if not specifically ordered. His grandfather Cornelius had a butcher's shop at Bradshaw (at the side of the Bradshaw Tavern). Clifford and his wife Lucretia lived at No. 21 West Royd, a property built by Cornelius' uncle William. When built, during World War I, the two West Royd properties were the only houses in the village with bathrooms. 'Cretia (as she was known) sold groceries from the back of No. 21, these being supplied by MacDonald's of Queensbury, who also toured with a sales van, selling fruit, vegetables and fish. At No. 23 West Royd was Edgar Farnell, a joiner, who used the barn (which had been Willy Dobson's greengrocers) opposite Evelyn Terrace as a joiner's shop, before taking over Knowles'.

After Robinson and Farnell left West Royd, the houses were occupied by two milkmen, Ernest Corkwell in one, and Len Mawson in the other - he was unfortunately killed by a vehicle when crossing the road after a session in the Eagle. Adjoining Farnell's barn, along the main road towards Queensbury, was next a house, then Emanuel Gray general grocer and provenders of excellent home-made apple pasties! This later became Miss Brown's bought-in sweets and confectionery. She is remembered as being distinctly odd, and had the habit of counting by tapping a finger against her cheek.

Still in business on the ginnel side of the block was Arthur Kirkbright's fish shop, with two houses between it and Snug Cottage. The fish shop had originally been run by Emily Ingham in the 1920s. She 'trained' Ada Kirkbright and sold the business to her. Later, when Kirkbrights wanted to leave, Ada Ingham (Emily's daughter) bought it back and ran it until its closure around 1970. Although of two storeys, Kirkbrights used it as a lock-up shop – they lived at Pickering Farm then at East View.

On the main road, the Co-op was in fine form, and the Post Office, run by Ivy, daughter of Olive Sutcliffe, at the second house in Evelyn Place, did a good line in shoes, slippers and things from the Grattan catalogue, where Ivy's sister worked. Home-made ice cream was sold, for a time, from a house in Harmony Place.

John Benn's former shop became Mrs Jackson's, groceries, chickens, eggs, and off-licence. Next it was run by Mrs Elliot and later by Mrs Bentley from 1960.

Binns hardware shop (equivalent of a DIY, or make-do-and-mend store) was still on the end of Derwent Place – paraffin, gas mantles, coal, nails, cotton, pans, and lots of other useful or essential items. And particularly for clog irons. This then became a general store and, in 1968, the Post Office. Latterly it was owned by George Page for about 12 years, and finally closed in 1990, the last shop on the Mountain.

A mobile trader in greengrocery and firewood was Bethel Cockroft who had a smallholding next to Travis Cottages at Raggalds until 1945.

Postal Services

A wall-type post box, listed in 1893, is thought to have been at or near Marble Place. It was moved to Evelyn Place when the Post Office opened there around 1900. When this Post Office latterly moved to Derwent Place, a wall-box was fitted there. When it closed, a post-mounted box was placed adjacent to Snug Cottage, on the main road.

One time postman was Rufus Hird. His son Hubert was also a postman. Hubert and his mother had a house-shop at 16 Perseverance Road. (Another 'house-shop' is remembered at number 11.) Hubert's round covered Raggalds, Mountain and surrounding farms – on foot, of course ! Later a post woman Gladys Balmforth took over – she was a general gossip, and many suspected she opened envelopes before delivery. The roundsman had to collect the post from Queensbury Post Office. Until 1949, trams conveyed the mail to and from Bradford. Rennie Briggs was a tram driver at the time and is remembered for stopping outside the Office, clanging his bell until someone came out – other tram crews would call in at the office.

Going back to 1822, we read that it cost 3d to send a letter from Queensbury to Bradford, or 11d to London. So there wouldn't be many letters going from Mountain.

In 1871 complaints were noted in the Halifax Courier about postal deliveries in the Queensbury area. It was claimed that deliveries were now only once a day (previously 3 times), and that some outlying areas didn't receive that until noon!

Miss Dorothy Kitchin, counter assistant at Queensbury Post Office during the snows in 1947, remembers having to deliver a telegram to Perseverance Road. It was to tell a Navy lad not to report for duty the next day. She duly struggled through the snow and delivered it. "I wasn't going to travel back in this weather anyway", he said. On the way back she took a wrong turn, and ended up being lifted over snowdrifts which Italian PoWs were trying to clear. She arrived back, soaking wet, and was sent home for the rest of the day.

Serving all the farms around Soil Hill involved a lot of footwork. One postman who delivered here also did sewing – alterations and so on. He'd take garments one day and return them the next, with the mail !

Hird's former shop on Perseverance Road. It was run by Hubert Hird and his mother for several years and known locally as 'The Co-op'.

MOUNTAIN CHAPEL

The general area of Queensbury was said to be 'an old and formidable area of Dissent', and abounded with preachers, it seems ! On the Mountain the only group of note were the Methodists (Weslyan Reform) who originally (1863) rented a room over one of the shops next to the Chapel site.

The chapel (single storey) was planned as being 49 feet x 37 feet. The foundation stone was laid by James Drummond of Bradford on Saturday 10 November 1866. Work continued through the winter until 4 March 1867 when the whole of the Chapel front wall fell in ! (A strong north-east wind was blamed.)

Mountain Chapel with the 'new' Sunday School towering behind.

Though unfinished internally, the building was used for the 4th anniversary services on 2 June that year. Later a tea party for some 170 people was held in the new extended weaving shed at Speak's Mill, and in the evening a public meeting attended by some 300 people was held there when various monies were pledged towards the construction (Paul Speak gave £20, being one of the most generous) On the next day, two services (for 'large congregations') were held in the shed. One report (1867) claimed the Chapel had seating for 600 people – something of an overestimate, or very cramped seating ! Other sources give it as a more realistic 200.

The land for the Chapel was purchased from John Leedham of Mountain End Farm – or from Timothy Ambler of the same, depending on your source.

In 1874 there seems to have been a 'rival faction' for the religious needs of the inhabitants of Mountain. The vicar of Queensbury (C of E), Mr Hyatt, had collected £150 towards the construction of a new church at Mountain. This money was handed to Paul Speak I who invested it in his own name to gain interest. Nothing further happened – and Paul died in 1878. It was said that it was a whim of Paul's, as there was no evidence of popular support, and it is thought probable that the only, or main, investors were Paul and Foster's (Black Dyke). In 1924 Paul III wound up the fund, stating that of a population of around 400, only 8 families in Mountain professed to be C of E (most were Wesleyan); that the population was unlikely to increase; and that most families lived in 2-room cottages and were mill-workers or labourers (presumably not considered C of E material !) The investment, now £787. 7s. 6d, was withdrawn and the Charity Commissioners informed.

Built on to the back of the Chapel, a Sunday School building was erected in 1877. This had two classrooms on the lower floor and one larger one above. In 1897/8 the Sunday School was rebuilt as a larger two-storey building, attached to the chapel to form a T-shape. It was partly funded by Speaks, Paul and John giving £100 each, with further gifts of £450. The new Sunday School was built outside of the existing one, which was pulled down when the new walls were up. The building was designed by Hubert (or Herbert?) Hodgson of Bradford, probably the same person who later designed the Speak Institute. The Chapel was square to the main road. The Sunday School block completed a 'T', resulting in a triangular yard at the Mill Lane side. Substantial boundary walls were built front and rear only, with heavy stone gateposts, wide concave wall tops and wrought iron gates and railings. The side walls were simple with triangular section copings.

Entering the Chapel (main road entrance), there was a centre block, four pews flanked by aisles, and outer blocks of two pews. Unusually, there was no gallery. The communion rail at the far end ran across the 'stage', to the left hand end of which were stairs descending to the vestry under the stage. The choir was arranged facing the congregation either side of the (pipe) organ, all of which, together with the lectern (pulpit) were raised on a stepped stage. Steps on the right gave access only to the stage and choir. Steps on the left extended up to a door passing on to a landing. From this point, which was in the Sunday School building, one could go up to the one main room and the main door on Mountain Lane; or down to the other rooms. In this lower part, the largest room was referred to as the 'supper room', and there were two smaller rooms and a kitchen. The Sunday School had its own crockery, with a light blue motif, and a narrow gold and a blue band round the rim.

Sunday School Crockery
*Printed on the underside was:
'Supplied direct from the Crown Pottery, Stoke-on-Trent, by the Ceramic Art Co Ltd'*

The upper school room had a stage at the end nearest the Eagle. Toilets were outside "across the yard" (at the Mill Lane side, Queensbury corner).

In 1930, the electricity supply was being laid from Queensbury, along the main road. The company Electrical Distribution of Yorkshire Ltd was contracting to supply anyone who wanted electricity. At the Chapel this happened in 1933. On 28/1/1934, to raise funds, there was a sponsored switching-on – 43 of the congregation paid 5/- each to be first to switch on one of the lights.

Paul Speak and his sister, Hannah, were frequent attenders at the Chapel. There were two pews, the first as you entered on the left side of the central block, which would be reserved for them if they were likely to attend. It was said to be 'well-used' by Speaks. One worshipper remembers young men being required to occupy these pews until Speaks arrived. Others reckon upturned chairs were used.

One especially attentive worshipper got the name of Sidney Boxarse because of the time he spent sitting on the wooden pews.

Apart from Sunday School (twice a day) the school building hosted concerts, and wedding receptions. Seating was on long wooden benches. Also remembered for 'Pie Neets' – a concert followed by a meat pie - and there were sometimes family concerts on Fridays or Saturdays with supper after. And it was right next door to the Mountain Eagle for 'extra refreshments'! Some locals make no distinction between 'pie neets' and 'at 'ome neets' (at home nights). In the 1930s the 'at 'ome neet' was actually three nights in February, (Saturday, Monday and Tuesday). Each night would be a different play, each performed by a different Methodist Amateur group. The food after was often supplemented with fishcakes from Kirkbright's fish shop.

A performance in May 1936 of the operetta 'May Day and Well-a-Day' by the Mountain Wesleyan Reform Sunday School, on the Sunday School stage. (Marion Bentley collection. She is 4th from the left.)

Another attraction in winter was the Magic Lantern Lecture – "lime leet picters". The projector actually used a gas mantle as the light source.

Several locals remember tall chimney stacks on houses being whitewashed for Whitsuntide, and some associated this with the Chapel Anniversary, or in connection with the Mill Anniversary which was claimed to be in mid-May. On the last Sunday in June two services were held (2.30 and 6.00 pm), and extra choir singers were brought in from other chapels. Such was the attendance that extra chairs had to be placed in the aisles. Paul Speak attended, arriving in an open carriage. It was 'forbidden' to hang out washing on this day ! And it was tradition that you could call at any house and be made welcome with a pot of tea.

Also at or around this date was the Whit Walk from the Chapel. The Chapel group would visit the Mill to sing for Paul (when he lived there), then walk around the whole of Mountain and Raggalds to sing for any residents too ill or infirm to attend the Chapel. The men carried a harmonium which was about 4' x 1½' x 3' high with handles at each end. The group then returned to the Cricket Field opposite the Mill gates for tea and buns, and "competitive games with prizes of 1d, 2d, 3d."

The Chapel Anniversary is remembered as being celebrated into the 1960s, on the last Sunday in June.

A local concert group of the type of which Jonas Rushworth would have been a member (Geoffrey Hainsworth Collection)

One of the founders of the Chapel was Jonas Rushworth, who was then in his 60's. He played string bass in a concert group, but his eyesight was failing a little. If a fly settled on his music, he'd swat it with his bow – next time he played that music he'd play the squashed fly as a note, it was said.

Other individuals remembered in connection with the Chapel include: Moses Wallace of Reservoir Place, organist in the 1920s; Granville Rushworth, of 18 California Row (1930s), choirmaster and active Reccabite; Mrs Harrison of Low Well Cottage in Pit Lane, a long-time preacher.

One circuit preacher was known as Black Jooa. His prayer was mainly: "It's glorious! It's glorious!" repeated over and over. Another was 'Jacop'

(Jacob), a Hell-fire preacher, and very strict. There is mention of him with Tom Bartle Brooks in the 'Personages' section.

A certain dutiful chapel-goer wouldn't swear - he'd say "Jam it an' butter it!" And Ada Ingham, local fish shop owner and devout chapel-goer, had cause to go to the pharmacist in Queensbury for arsenic (readily obtainable over the counter at this time, used for rat poison). She didn't like to say this name so alluded to it as "bumnick"!

Sidney Mann, of 1 Fascination Place was a mainstay of the Chapel. Up to World War II he ran a 'branch' of the Yorkshire Penny Bank on Friday nights in the Sunday School. He is probably the Sidney Boxarse mentioned previously.

Some terms associated with Chapel activities include:

To book a wedding/put the banns in was to "put t'spurrins in".To aspire to the choir was to 'get in t' singing seat'. It often went to their head – "Shoo's getten all ikey sin shoo gate i't' singing' seeat" (She's become conceited since she joined the choir).

On the Sunday School Anniversary was the 'sittin'-up', which was singing from a stepped platform erected outside. 'Sittings up' is a general term for a festival of religious music or songs.

On special occasions at the Chapel, everyone dressed up, of course. The women wore 'falls' (veils) and the men wore 'sparra-lap' coats (frock coats). For funerals, the poorer folk often had to borrow 'decent' clothes from neighbours.

Dinah Charnick (Charnock) assisted by 'liggin 'em aht' (laying out) when anyone died.

In the late 1960s the condition of the Chapel was giving cause for concern. Inspection found rampant dry rot. The services, now with a much diminished congregation, were held in the Sunday School.

After the closure of the Chapel and School in 1973, it was bought by a property developer based in Keighley. It soon fell into disrepair. In the 1980s the roof was stolen, by a gang cleverly disguised as workmen, and who went so far as to advertise on a board 'Materials for Sale'. It just happened that the owner drove past and called the police. In 1992 it was demolished.

The date-stone from the re-built Sunday School was removed to the rear yard of the Institute.

1995. The scant remains of the Sunday School walls, with the Time Office on the left and Bates cottage on the right. This cottage was sometimes called Lees after Sam Lee, blacksmith, who lived back-to-back with Bates in the 1850s. When excavations were being done for Upcroft Court car park (the land in the foreground), the cellar dwelling of Greenwood's block was revealed.

View from the former Co-op, 2001. Snug Cottage is on the left, Upcroft Court is being erected on the Chapel site, and Mad Ma Jones (former Eagle) is beyond.

TEMPERANCE PLACE and surroundings (from Speak's deeds)

In the corner of Mill Lane and Old Guy Road, where a semi now stands, was Temperance Place, a block of 8 back-to-back houses. They were unusual in that each had a small coal-keeping cellar under it which had a lockable door from a large wash cellar for use by all tenants. There were no yards. Privies were at the mill end of the block. By 1880, blocks [2, 3, 7] had been demolished. In place of [3] was a row of back-to-backs, being Jester Place facing [B] and Luddenden Place facing [A]. The Temperance Place houses facing [A] were numbers 21-27 (odds), which followed on from Luddenden Place (1-19 odds). The other side of the block was known as Parkinson Street, in fact a very narrow alleyway with a row of 4 cottages opposite, the numbers of Parkinson Street being 1-15 (odds), which included both sides of the alleyway. The four cottages were demolished about 1903. Temperance Place survived until about 1970. Jester Place has even numbers 2-20 from the mill end. Roughly opposite numbers 14 and 16, a row of 4 cottages were at almost a right angle, with even numbers 22-28 and known as Rushworth Street, plus Rushworth House [5].

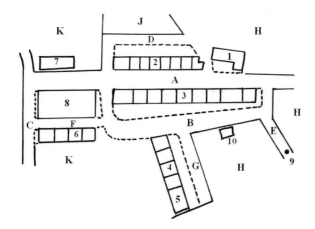

Plan of 1873, prior to Speak's re-building (from Speak's deeds)

1. Marble Place (3 houses)
2. 8 one-storey cottages
3. 9 one-storey cottages, the original Jester Place Nos 1-9
4. 4 single-storey cottages
5. Two-storey house. Became Jester House after (4) demolished.
6. Four cottages
7. 3 Cottages. Mountain Delves.
8. Temperance Pl. – 8 back-to-back houses
9. Public well
10. Block of 'conveniences'.

A Mountain Road or Lane
B Old Road
C Old Guy Road
D John Street. 15 feet wide.
E Intended road. 15 feet wide.
F Parkinson St (both sides of the alley which was about 8 ft wide)
G Rushworth St. 15 feet wide.
H Speak's land
J Jonas Bairstow's land
K Colonel Stanhope's land

Blocks 1, 2, 3 and 4 had yards, middens and various house designs.

ON THE CALI

California Row, shown as a hotch-potch terrace of houses, was situated on the most exposed spot on the Mountain. If you walk from Moorside Place up the dirt road (Old Guy Road), you will notice a kerb on your right, a rubble-base to the road and a manhole for the drains. Where the kerb ends, look about 75° to the left. In the field is a flat strip, where the foundations of California Row can be found. The land was owned by Mrs Lancashire and Mrs Brooke, and was sold off in plots in 1853. The access road was marked out, then the houses built in blocks by the plot owners – first 4-10, then 24-30, then filled in with 16-22 (even numbers only). Numbers 12 and 14 were occupied in 1853 – the year the land was purchased – which indicates either a quick building job, or that the houses already existed. Number 2 (nearest Old Guy Road) was a low-decker, all the others being two-storey through-by-light, except 26, 28, 30 also low-deckers. All had a small garden to the south. From 1976 to 1978 all were purchased by the Council, and demolished.

The Cali is remembered as being 'nice houses' during the first half of the 20th century, and housed many members of families long associated with Mountain – Rushworth, Sutcliffe, Drake. The whole block 16-30 was owned between the Rushworth family from 1875, selling off units as the family members died. The last Rushworth was Ida at No. 22 from 1937 to 1972. She was a well-respected teacher at Foxhill School.

Number 2 is remembered as being a very small one-room dwelling. There was a well in the yard protected by a cupboard-like structure. The last occupant, in the 1930s, was Miriam Ambler, who was regarded as an eccentric or a witch – much the same to many locals !

At this time, Susannah and Lavinia Barratt took over tenancy of Number 6, on the death of their father Solomon. The ladies baked and sold excellent pastries at their house, and also supplied Kirkbright's fish shop with pies.

The field in front of the Cali, known as The Moor, was owned (in the 1853/85 period) by Mr Scott of Micklemoss Farm. Originally Cali residents paid 1/- a year to him for the right to hang out washing on his land.

At the edge the field beyond the back of the Cali – the back being the Raggalds side - was a well "dug by John Willie Sutcliffe, on his own". In the field is a pile rather like spoil from a pit. It is, in fact, mostly horse dung piled over the remains of a stone crusher which was used in the mid-1900s to make sand from stone waste. The area had been a stone quarry in the early/mid 1800s.

HILLSIDE PLACE AND MOUNT PLEASANT

First beyond the Eagle was Hillside Place, actually two blocks. All houses were through-by-light. Access to the first block of 3 houses was up steps adjacent to the farthest house into a communal yard. One, two or all of this block are remembered as having been a sort of Working Mens Club prior to the opening of the Institute. Privies were at the Mountain end. Next a block of 5, each having its own garden, with individual access from the pavement. The walls had triangular section copings, and there were wrought-iron gates.

After a gap of about 30 m was Mount Pleasant, again as two blocks. The first block was of 5 houses, then a space, then a block of 6. Each house had its own yard with steps up to the house and with privies between the two blocks. Opposite Mount Pleasant was a 'Tardis' type police box in the mid 1900's. Hillside and Mount Pleasant were sold by Speak in 1944.

All the properties were deemed 'unsanitary' and compulsorily purchased by the Council in the 1960s and demolished. Locals reckon the 'unsanitary' description was the opinion of Queensbury Doctor Sullivan who reported to the Council on these properties, California Row and others. During the smallpox epidemic of 1962, the Health Inspector had found no such problems, indeed rather that the householders took a pride in their houses.

In 2001 the cricket field was sold. The new owner fenced off the sites of Hillside and Mount Pleasant as his own, even though it was Council property. Guy Nick boundary 'disappeared' also.

The stone foundations of Hillside Place were dug up to build the Weavers Court boundary wall.

The two terraces of Mount Pleasant. Beyond is the end of Hillside Place. On the left is Pit Lane, and the 'Tardis' police box. (Harry Brooks Collection)

MOUNTAIN RESERVOIR

The original reservoir (on the site the present one) was authorised in 1887 and opened on 7 December 1889. There were many delays, first in organising the finance; then in finding a site. In March 1888, Mr Edwin Waugh offered to sell a field of about 2 acres – known as 'the Betty Field' – for £250. It is shown on deeds as Betty Field (part) – the other part was already taken with Smith's Buildings. It was December 1888 before the council authorised the purchase. By May 1889, tenders for the works were being considered, finally being awarded to E & E Balmforth of Halifax. Somehow, the job was done in just 6 months, notwithstanding changes decided by the council during construction.

Queensbury Council considered the placing of a commemorative stone at the reservoir, but nothing was decided. The council's engineer, Mr John Drake, saw the project through, together with on-going problems and roads in poor repair. The Reservoir featured in the 1890 council meetings, with frequent references to the alleged non-payment of monies due to Balmforth's – Queensbury seemed typically Yorkshire in driving a bargain, which often ended with disputes about quality. The whole works cost £3132, plus land.

Bradford supplied the water and there were frequent demands made for more water to be pumped – "The reservoirs can hold enough for two months supply but there is rarely more than for fourteen days". Bradford tended to ignore these pleas. One unusual excuse was that the supply was restricted because water was being used for tramway extensions !

The reservoir was uncovered, and occupied an area of about 58 yards square, and about 11 feet deep, with a capacity of around 2 million gallons. A high, single-storey square stone tower situated on the right just inside the gates, supported a header tank – the structure was known locally as the Norman Keep.

Initially, supply from Mountain was to Queensbury. It took another 9 years before supplies were organised for Mountain. By October 1898 a water main had been laid to Stone Street. The Sunday School, at the opposite side of the road, asked for a water supply, but, being in Thornton District, was told it would have to apply to Thornton. Application from Mountain Co-op in 1902 brought the same response, for the same reason. Local distribution and maintenance was the responsibility of Queensbury Council.

The reservoir became known as Rodney Dock, a Rodney being an idle or useless person in late 1800s parlance. Hence the dock where no ships ever came.

The entrance to Mountain Reservoir.
QUEENSBURY LOCAL BOARD is inscribed on the left top stone.
On the right top stone: WATERWORKS 1889.

The pump house on Low Lane at the bottom of Blind Lane stands out like a true blot on the landscape. The Institute is at the top of the field behind.

In 1958/59 covered storage tanks, reducing the capacity to 700,000 gallons, were constructed in the old reservoir at a cost of £30,000. The work was protracted. The contractors were threatened with penalties, it is claimed, and eventually completed the project in 1960. All water supplies were taken over by Bradford Council in 1962. A pump house (to feed water from elsewhere to Mountain) was erected on Low Lane at the bottom of the field behind the Institute. There was a standby generator for times of power failure or other problems. When the water ceased to flow at the Institute, the arrival of the Water Board man at the pump house was watched for – he'd start up the generator which, being outside the building, was clearly audible, and water would flow, since Mountain is higher than the water level in the reservoir.

In 1997/98 a new storage reservoir was constructed at Soil Hill. A new pump house was built in the Pit Lane/Headley Lane area, with a subsidiary control building opposite Old Foresters, Raggalds, and the Low Lane pump house was closed. It was sold in 2004 for conversion to a house. This has brought about a big visual improvement. Mountain reservoir remains in use.

Whilst on the subject of water, sewerage comes to mind. The treatment works for most local sewage was and is at Shibden Head. Gradually sewers were laid to Queensbury, then up and down the A644 reaching Mountain about 1892. Drains from the houses had to be changed from a simple rubble drain to a proper gully-and-pipe and connected to the main sewer – at the householders expense. Property owners Bairstow (of North View, Mountain) and Paul Speak (concerning Montrose Place) both failed to comply until threatened with legal action.

PLACE NAMES AROUND THE MOUNTAIN

How place names came about, or how they've changed, as related by residents. Some plausible, some unlikely !

The names of some blocks of houses related to the property owners – for example, Bairstow's, Rushworth's, Parkinson's – and these names changed over the years as ownership changed, until street names and numbers became formalised from about 1877 onwards. Progress must have been slow because in 1901 Queensbury Council notes that 'Street nameplates and house numbers are to be provided'. A new nameplate cost 1/-.

Harmony Place – one story is that two households in the row had harmoniums. Certainly there was one. Another suggestion is that several residents sang in the Chapel choir, which is the more likely.

Glazier Road

Locally known as Glazner Road, it had, at that time, a row of 8 cottages along it (known as Glazier Row since 1850 and which had existed since at least 1840). However, the lane is marked as Tarn Lane on earlier plans. The Tarn, where the local lads went swimming, was filled by a spring, and became part of the Mill land. One tradition has it that the name Glazier is a corruption of Glacier, relating to the waterlogged nature of the fields there which froze over in winter to provide 'skating' for the locals in their work boots or clogs. It is more likely that an early inhabitant of the Row was a glazier and also a local character, though in the mid-1800s a glazier could also refer to a person who removed windows for burglary, a 'cat burglar', which gives us another possibility. The cottages were always considered 'inferior'.

Marble Place

This was a group of three houses, backing on to Speak's cricket field, and was where the boundary wall differs from the rest, being opposite the nearer end of Luddenden Place. Each house had a separate garden in front, but was through-by-light. It seems to have been re-built around 1867. Local legend tells us that the name is in some way associated with Akroyd House at Boothtown, Halifax. To digress briefly: Akroyd house was originally a relatively small gentleman's residence, built about 1800. Purchased by the Akroyd family in 1838, it was considerably extended in 1851 with the Marble Gallery, a room overlooking the gardens and for the display of Akroyd's collection of marble figures. Further construction in marble took place in 1867/68 by a contractor who imported Italian craftsmen as overlookers. Notwithstanding, local labour was also employed. One of the first tenants of the 'new' row at Mountain was Gilbert Wood, age 34, of Halifax. He probably lived in the far end house in this row of three, with his wife Ellen, two kids and mother-in-law. He was a monumental mason who presumably did some marble work at Akroyd House and hence the name and association. Mr Wood seems to have moved to Mountain from Dewsbury and then moved on as soon as the work was completed.

Marble Place was known locally as Tea Pot Row. Tea was usually mashed in the mug (there's an art to drinking tea made this way, using loose leaves not teabags !). But if any one of the three families was expecting visitors, the one Tea Pot in the row was borrowed for the occasion.

This property was owned by Speaks, sold in the 1940s and demolished in the 1950s.

Fascination Place

The name might not be as innocent as you might think. Still current in the mid-1800s, to 'fascinate' was 'the power to charm or harm' – which would indicate the likely dwelling of a witch or similar eccentric.

Jester Place and Luddenden Place

The block was erected in the late 1870s. The name Jester is sometimes wrongly given as Chester.

Local legend says it was so called because a Court Jester used to live there. And like so many old tales, there is an element of truth in it.

A somewhat confusing newspaper report of 1872 (so what's changed in newspapers?) tells of "the death in Queensbury of Mrs Wallett, the mother of the Queen's Jester, F W Wallett". We know that Frederick William Wallett, born in Hull 12/10/1808,   was the eldest of a large family – ultimately of 24 children! He became a performer and travelled England and America as a clown, with his own troupe or 'circus'. It is claimed in a pamphlet of 1901 that the troupe once performed in Queensbury, and that the joke about the Queens Head was attributed to him ("What was the greatest insult to the Queen by the inhabitants of Queenshead? That they not only cut her head off but they buried her!" when Queens Head became Queensbury). Performers such as he might take an assumed title of Court Jester or Queen's Jester (as he did). Although not a conferred title, he did once have audience with Queen Victoria at Windsor Castle (19/7/1844).   Was she amused, one asks? Wallett lived latterly in Nottinghamshire until his death on 13/3/1892.

However, in the late 1860s one of his many brothers (Henry) had come to live in Mountain at No 7 in the row of cottages on the south side of Mountain Road, block [3]. Henry had aspirations as an actor, which he later gave as his occupation, but when at Mountain he was simply a mason's labourer. He was 41 at the time, listed as married with three daughters, a son, and no wife with him. His mother also came to live in the area, being with Henry for a couple of years.   Doubtless the exploits of her famous son became broadcast and he might even have visited. Indeed, in 1871 'Wallett the Queen's Jester' appeared as top of the bill at Pullan's New Music Hall,

Brunswick Place, Bradford. When this Mrs Wallett died (10/11/1872, grave E30 in Queensbury churchyard – no headstone survives) aged 83, her address was given as Law Hill, Mountain. In the late 1870s Henry moved to Vignola Place, Clayton, where he died in 1892. Two of his daughters are known to have died in the area, Margaret in 1923 and Constance in 1930.

The original 'Jester' row was demolished in the 1870s and rebuilt by 1880 as back-to-backs, the south side becoming Jester Place. The north side became Luddenden Place (mis-spelled as Luddendon on the current name plate), probably on account of a family from Luddenden (between Halifax and Hebden Bridge) moving there and because Luddenden is such a funny name!

Mill Lane

The present Mill Lane runs from Snug Cottage to Moorside Place. It used to be called Mountain Road or Lane at which time Mill Lane is thought to have been from between Derwent/Fascination to Speak's gasworks.

Where Mountain Lane left the main road was the location referred to as t'Gas Lamp, perhaps indicating the sparsity of street lighting in the area.

The second row of cottages on the left (Fascination Place/Montrose Place) was known as 'Paul Row' (owned by Speaks). Likewise the Mill was known as 'Paul Meln'.

However, to return to the present Mill Lane. From Brighouse and Denholme Road to the Lodge/Mill Gates, locals called it Top Road. From there to Jester Place was The Plantation (trees on the left, courtesy of the Mill); and Luddenden Place to Old Guy (or some say Mill Gates to Old Guy) was the t' Lang Drag (the Long Drag), named after events in the Klondike gold rush of 1896: One notorious mountain pass, called Dead Horse Trail, was the Long Drag over the mountains often in atrocious wintry weather. Some Mountain folk had been prospectors there. Seen it, done it, got the T-shirt. In Mountain it is quite a daunting walk in winter, carrying your shopping along Mill Lane, with the prevailing wind blowing right at you !

California Row

This is also claimed by some to have been named in association with the Klondike Gold Rush. However, wrong country, wrong era ! In 1848 there had been the California Gold Rush, centred on Sacramento. California Row is known as that from before 1871, so the association (if any) is obviously with that Gold Rush, not the Klondike. Some credence must be given to this name origin, since adults born in England are listed as resident 'on the Cali', and having children with them born in America.

Old Guy Road

This runs from Brighouse and Denholme Road (opposite Pit Lane) as a dirt track to Moorside Place, whence it continues as a tarmac road towards Ambler Thorn. The long straight tarmac part is locally known as Sam Loine (Lane), after Sam Parkinson who lived at Micklemoss Farm from the 1830s to 1861. The dirt track part is known as Guy Nick. This is thought by some to be derived from Guy (a one-time resident) Snicket (a narrow thoroughfare). But consideration of old maps suggests otherwise. This lane was the boundary of Mountain End Farm lands. In an enclosure on the Mountain side of the lane on the top corner was a small dwelling called Boundary House (situated at the meeting point of Clayton, Thornton and Northowram boundaries) and corrupted to Bounder Hall; it was also called Guy House, after Guy Pearson who lived there in the mid 1700s. The narrow field below this dwelling (down to Brighouse and Denholme Road) is described in deeds as Gie (=Guy) Neck (= strip of land). Hence Guy Nick.

Mucky Lane

This was both the official and descriptive name for the road from Raggalds, passing Small Tail and to Charnock's (Sun Farm). Pronounced 'Mucky Loine', it had long been a problem in bad weather. Run-off from the moors at the top caused rutting down past the terrace of houses. At the bottom, the fields were often flooded, and hence the road too. The residents of adjacent houses and farms who used this road decided action was necessary, and "sin t'Council 'ed do nowt", decided to re-lay it themselves. It opened on 4/11/1871. The cost of materials (£75) was met by subscriptions from the locals, who also provided the labour. To celebrate, a procession formed at the Sun Inn and, led by 'the Junior Band', marched down to the

The commemorative monument on Perseverance Road, which stands about 6 feet tall, carries the wording:

PERSEVERANCE ROAD
OPENED NOVEMBER 4 1871
LOCAL BOARD
Jonathan Ramsden, James Briggs,
George Bairstow, Henry Charnock,
Jonas Shackleton, John Hoyle,
Phillip Mann, David Dawson,
Edward Charnock, Arthur Charnock,
Edwin Priestley,
Alfred Bairstow, Samuel Bairstow

bottom of Mucky Lane. The Chairman of the 'Local Board' (as they called themselves) Samuel Priestley declared the road open. Many then retired to dine at the Sun Inn. An inelegant monument to their perserverance stands at the roadside.

Above Perseverance Road is Soil Hill (also called Swill Hill or Swilling), mentioned since the 1300s. Its 'time of glory' was perhaps in 1803 when 'Charnock's on Swill Hill' was chosen as a beacon site in case of invasion by Napoleon.

Raggalds/Raggles

The area of Raggalds now includes Raggalds School, Travis Farm and Perseverance Road/Small Tail. The remaining pub (Raggalds) has also been known as Ye Old Raggalds Inn.

A 1999 view from near the site of California Row. In the foreground is the former Raggalds School, now with added stables. Right is Raggalds Inn with Raggalds 'village' behind. Centre distance is (Pit) Lane Bottom Farm. Striking up the hillside to the left is Perseverance Road, with part of World's End farm in front of Hartley Square just included on the left.

Raggalds probably derived from dialect 'Raggald' or 'Raggel' – a wicked or abandoned person; person of low character. This would indicate that the reputation of the area preceded its name ! By virtue of its remoteness and being an excellent vantage point, the area was renown for dubious or blatantly illegal activities. The approach of the Authorities could be known, with ample time to clear things away and disperse.

The Halifax Courier newspaper records many references, for example in December 1863: "Just before 8 am on the Sunday, a considerable number of men and women assembled at Raggalds to witness a prize fight between William Drake (known as Bill o'Jerrys) of Mountain and William Sutcliffe (known as Pilt o'Bill Huts) of Swill Hill, both colliers and married men. Sutcliffe's father was the referee. Poor aim prevented Sutcliffe from kicking Drake's brains out, and ultimately Drake throttled Sutcliffe into submission." William Drake – the census of 1861 shows a William Drake age 26 living at No. 18 on the Cali. His father Jeremiah lived in Pineberry cottages. The report continues: "Also on Sundays, betting on pitch-and-toss, and on pigeon flying, is common here." A call was made for the Constables of Northowram, Ovenden, Clayton and Thornton to act.

In September 1866 the same William Drake appeared before magistrates, having accused a Thornton man of assault. Both had been boozing and, since it seemed that Drake threw the first punch, the case was dismissed.

Another Halifax Courier report of 1863 regarding Raggalds: "Not more than 30 houses, but one old licensed house and 3 beershops. Nearer Queenshead, there are two beershops and one licensed house. At this place [Raggalds] is neither church nor chapel, and only one school. At Mountain close by (pop. 1000) neither church, chapel, nor Sunday School." At Raggalds "there occurs Sunday drinking, fighting and gambling. A paid lookout watches for strangers approaching." "Games played include pitch-and-toss, wrestling, throwing-stones-off-the-foot, highway bowling, pigeon flying, and shooting matches". Another correspondent the next week replied that there were only 600 residents in Mountain, that many attended church in Queenshead, or at Raggalds School which "was largely supported by a local manufacturer", and services and Sunday School were held there.

In the 1990s before enlargement took place, Raggalds pub was frequented by dealers in dubious substances and firearms, culminating with death by shooting of a customer and the jailing of the landlord.

The 'Dross Pen' at Raggalds – now an L-shaped wall opposite the Old Foresters - was the local road-making 'depot'. Stone rubble was dumped here from the quarries, to be broken up by 'a man with a light hammer on a long shaft'. The Council provided hammer and shafts. The man was paid 13 pence per ton. After laying, dross (iron smelting waste) was brought from Low Moor Ironworks, and spread over the sandstone giving a compact surface. This method of road surfacing had been in use for years in the area. In 1867 in the Council Minutes, we read of the price of dross from LMI rose to 3/- per ton (a ton being given as 22 cwt), and alternative suppliers or surfaces were being considered. The Pen was in use when the road through Mountain was widened and resurfaced in 1905 – a project to help alleviate unemployment.

When tarmacadam became the prevalent road surface, contractors were employed. Into the 1960s, the firm of Glossops is remembered for their use of steam wagons and steam rollers. The Dross Pen is still used for stabling machines when road maintenance is carried out.

Small Tail

This probably refers to the farm called Small Tail being out of line with the row on Perseverance Road, 'tail' being a straggly ending.

Travis

Travis has two equally possible origins. First 'Travis' as a variant of Traverse or Trevis(s) meaning a stall (partition) for animals. This could relate to some peculiar characteristic of the stalls at this farm but more likely is derived from the layout of the buildings at Travis House Farm. The barn is known as a laithe. At Travis House Farm this laithe and stalls were 'traverse', or across the living quarters rather than in line with them. Travis House Farm is indeed marked Traverse Farm, on a plan of 1850, and on the 1841 Census.

Travis Cottages yard. Young Clive Cockroft stands with his scooter. (L-R) a family friend, Clive's aunt and her son, all in their 'Sunday best'. The pump dominated the yard. Behind are the low-deckers which were demolished in the 1960s to make way for a garage and petrol station. (Clive Cockroft collection)

Secondly, we must look at the adjacent cottages (at present Travis Cottages, between Travis House and the garage). On most maps since 1853 this, and the present garage site, is all labelled as Travis or Travis House. Travis Cottages were built as two cottages and a barn, probably in the late 1700s. Called Black Carr Farm on deeds and documents in 1815, it was purchased by John and Thomas Crossley together with James Travis! James was a worsted spinner from Northowram. He sold his interest in

Black Carr in 1824. The farm remained Black Carr Farm until after 1900, being referred to as 'at Travis', after which it carried several incorrect titles. Perhaps James Travis at Travis was a coincidence ….?

The whole area is called Black Carr. On maps, Black Carr Farm is shown as the one just beyond Sandal Farm (Keelham Bar Farm from c.1930). But both Travis (Cottages) and Boggard Houses were each named Black Carr Farm on deeds.

Finally, a Travis Hill Farm appears on the 1881 Census, which is probably that now known as Raggalds Farm.

Boggard Houses and Trash Hall

Situated beyond Travis towards Keelham was Boggard Houses, originally a farm and cottage, derelict in the early 1900s and since obliterated. It was also known as Scrat Hall. Boggard and Scrat are both North England dialect terms for ghost/goblin/spirit. Towards Keelham on the opposite side of the main road was Trash Hall which was the next farm beyond Shay Farm. One might speculate that Trash is a contraction of Guytrash, a large black spirit dog, and often associated with Boggard territory. Indeed, in our area Guytrash sometimes meant the same as Boggard. Alternatively, 'trash' in the parlance of the time meant money or wealth in a rather derogatory sense of 'filthy money', perhaps relating to wealth obtained by devious means. Trash Hall was re-named Kellham Farm from the 1930s.

Hougomont

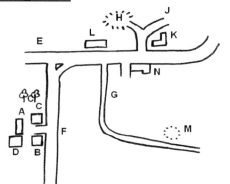

A – D See Text
E   Pit Lane
F   Low Lane
G   Track to Clough Farm
H   Old Quarry
J   Track to Nettle Hole Farm
K   Law Hill Farm
L   Low Well cottages
M   Old coal pit
N   Farm buildings

Plan is c. 1900

Situated on Low Lane, there were five single-room colliers dwellings (block A) in the 1700s. When the semi-detached cottages (block B) were built around 1812 the area became designated 'New Houses', and remained so on maps until the 1980s.

However, legend tells us that the cottages were named 'Hougomont' in 1815 in memory of the son (of the residents) who was a drummerboy and was killed in the Battle of Hougoumont in 1815. Unfortunately no 'rank and file' deaths are recorded with names, so this legend remains unsubstantiated.

To confuse matters further (block C) was built in 1854, and the residents planted fruit trees on the Pit Lane side. By the very early 1860s, these were bearing fruit. Not just this house but blocks A, B, and new block D acquired the colloquial name of 'Treacle Tree' (pronounced Traikle Tree). Our oldest interviewee, Miss Phyllis Gledhill, at the time of interview being aged 100, remembers her mother telling of "fruit trees at t'Traikle Tree. There were blackberries, apples, and pears (but very small pears)". Now, a type of pear tree was called the Late Treacle, and its fruit was used to make pear cider (Perry, 'Babycham'). This is likely the origin of the name. The fruit trees were still in existence at Hougomont until at least 1900. From the 1980s Hougomont has been acknowledged as the area name.

(Pit) Lane Bottom

Lane Top/Lane Bottom names are common, usually referring to where a lane, or side road, made a junction with a main road. (Pit) Lane Bottom, the farm opposite Sandal Farm seems to have no lane. However, when the Gin Pit and others on Soil Hill were in use the lane from there continued from where the bungalow is now at the top corner of Perseverance Road straight down to Lane Bottom Farm. This farm is now known as Willow Dene.

The Betty Field

This was where the reservoir was built, and does not refer to anyone called Betty (often wrongly quoted as Betty's Field). Its origin is probably from 'to betty about' being to fuss over or take excessive care of.

Banks Alarum/ Bank o'Larum

This name refers especially to the west side of Mountain Reservoir. The older folk pronounce it 'Banks Aleyrum', which provides a clue to its origin. Later folk tales claim the name Alarum refers to the stone tower at the Reservoir, and derives from the idea of a look-out point or beacon site. However, the beacon site was on Soil Hill, not here; and the stone tower supported a header tank for the water supply – nothing more glamorous !

An earlier folktale tells of a Russian Princess (or Jewess) who married an Englishman. They came to Mountain and she declared the view reminded her of the 'banks of the Larum', in her home area. Who was this person? Step forward Mary Klose.

Born Maria Amelia Kobetsky in 1841 at Bärslack, East Prussia and of a well-to-do family, she came to England around 1864, having married John Klose. His family was also from Prussia. It is likely that other members of John's family had already settled in London. Mary and John had a daughter Mary Amelia born in London in 1866. The family moved to Bradford, eventually settling at the newly-built 8 Barton Street, Horton around 1872/3.

John's trade was that of artificial flower maker – a job fraught with unhealthy production methods. Several children later, John died in 1877 of kidney failure, and dropsy, aged 52. His wife, a domestic servant with 4 children to support, moved to Littlemoor, Queensbury soon after. She may have been employed by one of the Foster's as a domestic. She shared a house at Littlemoor with William Bower, a wool sorter (which was a quite well-paid job), and it is likely that Mary married William in 1882. Daughter Mary worked at Black Dyke Mill, then became a domestic servant and is noted in lodgings at 10 Cunliffe Villas, Manningham in 1891.

Mary (senior) probably visited the reservoir area before the time of its construction (1889). She was most likely remembered because of being foreign. Incorrect transcription gives her place of birth as Berlick, Prussia. There is no such place, but we can see where the Russian association arose. However, Bärslack in East Prussia is near the river Alle. In Prussia at the time, areas of land were controlled by the gentry as hunting land, being known as 'Bannkreis'. The rounded slopes of the Calder Valley or the moorland towards Ogden must have stirred memories of over 30 years ago. Given the problems with translation, pronunciation and spelling, it seems likely that Mary said something like: "Der Blick von hier erinnert mich an den Bannkreis um die Alle (he)rum", describing the view towards Holmfield and Illingworth as 'a reminder of the hunting lands around the Alle valley.' Hence 'Banks Alle-rum' !

Thanks to colleague Rainer Buchwald of Germany for this logical explanation. His wife Heidrun just happened to be born in this part of East Prussia!

Roper Lane

This runs from Raggalds, past the old school, towards Ambler Thorn. In 1407, one 'John Roper, constable of Northowram, rented Shibden Mill' near Ambler Thorn. Roper Lane was named after him, 'tis said.

Clues (Clews) Moor – the swampy area from Sandal Farm to Law Hill – may be derived from the verb 'clew' – to guide through a mystery, that is guidance was needed to avoid the bogs. A more orthodox derivation would be 'close moor' since in the 1700s the central moor area was enclosed. And Law is likely the opposite – lawless, relating to the hill where a lookout was stationed to warn the Raggalds criminals of the approach of The Law.

A Miscellany of Other Local Names

Some names are obvious – Hillside Place, Mountain End, Heather Place, Moorside, Stone Street, Grand View. Montrose and Derwent are probably of patriotic origin.

New Park Road from near Pineberry to Russell Hall School, Queensbury, was originally Kitchen Lane, said to be named after Jack Kitchen. He was a local Baptist preacher in the late 1700s. The road was renamed in 1905, with reference to the new park at the top.

Fox Hill was a row of two cottages and a farmhouse just below the northern corner boundary of Foxhill School. They survived until the 1920s.

Thornton Road (Queensbury), sometimes noted as Thornton Street, was locally known as Second Hill. If proceeding from West Scholes, the route was: Carter Lane, Sharp Hill and Second Hill (which was from Airedale View to the A647).

From Foxhill School a track runs down to Carter Lane, being called Harp Lane. There is a high stone wall on the right. Follow the wall and you'll arrive back at Hill Top on the main road, having passed Well Heads (or Wells Head) Farm, The uphill part is known locally as Back Lane but is actually a continuation of Harp Lane. If you study a map, Harp Lane plus the main road is a harp shape.

Blind Lane, (pronounced with a short 'i') is a bridleway at the side of Pickering Farm, leading down to Lane Side. It is suggested that Blind is in the context of drunkenness – rather than going straight, it winds from side to side, as if drunk. Blind Lane used to be a main bridleway down to West Scholes. Low Lane was simply known as 'on to Lane Side'.

Heading in the same direction is Catsteps, the snicket which runs from the side of Mountain Co-op down to Low Lane. The steps at the bottom, which are small and irregular, have to be negotiated with the care and agility of a cat.

At Raggalds, Farside Farm (Green Lane) was World's End. Charnock Farm (Soil Hill) was the Gin Pit, the Sun or Sun Farm.

"There's no roads on t'Mountain" I've often been told. It's a local joke amongst the older members of the community, meaning all the street names are something other than Road. The main road is conveniently forgotten. Glazier Road is Glazier Row or Tarn Lane, Old Guy Road is Sam Lane or Guy Nick. Everywhere else is Place, Row, Lane, Terrace, Street, and Mountain Lane was considered just that (for the purpose of the joke) rather than the colloquial Top Road !

BREWERIES & PUBS

In early times 'farmhouse breweries' were quite common, where a farming family would brew ale and sell it, to travellers or locals, from their kitchen.

Real Breweries, Real Ale !

Daniel Fielding & Son

Originally at Saddle Hall Farm, Bradshaw 1860-1870, then near Bradshaw Row 1870-1894 (Beerhouse and Brewery), then White Castle, Green Lane, Bradshaw 1894-1961. Taken over and closed by Webster's. Everything in the brewery was left complete and in immaculate condition – it was hoped to turn it into a museum but Webster's sold it for conversion to housing in the 1990s.

A drawing of White Castle Brewery appeared on Fielding's letterheads

Members of the Cockroft family with friends and Jack the dog use White Castle Brewery as a backdrop in 1948. A Fieldings horse dray is parked on the left.   (Clive Cockroft Collection)

Bradshaw Row, formerly Colliers Row (one of several in the area) is on a track midway from Bradshaw Lane via Brandy Hall, to Taylor Lane. Alternatively, go from Bonnet Hall in Green Lane, past Bridle Hall and Saddle Hall, and the Brewery was next.

Albion (Hardy's)

Situated at Fall Bottom, Clayton, 1869-about 1930. The Hardy family lived at nearby Cresswell House, and the business was in Joseph's name. The brewery, which was close to Fall Bottom Pit became a fat refinery in 1932 but has since been demolished.

Ramsden and Jackson

Situated at Bradshaw Lane and run by the Jackson family 1871-1908 (approximate dates).

Joseph Stocks & Co

The oldest in the area, founded about 1790, part of the Stocks 'empire' of quarries, pits and other activities. Latterly situated at Shibden Head Brewery, Brewery Lane near Catherine Slack and taken over by Webster's in 1933. The buildings were demolished in the 1970s.

Briggs Brothers

Briggs, like most other breweries, produced both ale and porter. This drawing on their bill-head is a good representation of their building, the tower and chimney of which were lowered one storey by Fearnley's. The surroundings are wildly fanciful !

Originally a farmhouse brewery, situated at the first block of buildings (West Scholes House or "Briggs Villa") below the later brewery site and run by John Briggs from around 1840 until 1866; then run by others of the family and by Haley Briggs from 1883. The new premises known as Clayton Brewery was run as Briggs Brothers from 1887. The Briggs family were also licensees of West Scholes Gate Inn, later The Junction.

The brewery ceased production about 1902 with Samuel Briggs shown as the last operator. The building then became West Scholes Mill, being greatly extended for Moquette production.

PUBS

With brewery owners if known and applicable, and status in 2001.

Beyond Raggalds

GRAY HORSE: Taylor Lane (Stocks) **Private House.**

OLD GIN PIT/SUN: Soil Hill. A beer house. **Private House variously 'Charnocks' or 'Sun Farm'.**

At Raggalds

COLLIERS/FORESTERS: (Stocks) **Private House**

RAGGALDS INN: (Stocks) **Pub**

TRAVELLERS INN: A beer house, probably in the row of cottages where the garage at Travis now stands. No record of its existence after 1861. **Cottages demolished.**

At Mountain

(MOUNTAIN) EAGLE: Built and opened as a pub in late 1861. (Fieldings) **Pub 'Mad Ma Jones'.**

FLEECE: (Stocks) **Fin Inn private club**

PINEBERRY: (Stocks) **Pub**

Beyond Mountain towards Queensbury

HILL TOP WORKING MENS CLUB: Situated half way between Hill Top Farm and 2 & 4 Hill Top. Formerly David Knowles' house, it became a WMC in the early 1900's then a woodyard post WWII, **Demolished c. 1960.**

DELVERS ARMS: It was located at the roadside, being at the road end of a short terrace by the driveway to Well Heads Farm. It was also known as the Quarry Arms. Closed 1907. **Demolished.**

SPORTSMAN: The second terrace house from Mountain in Small Page Row. Also known as the Black Dog. Closed 1907. **Private House.**

SUN: Built for railway navvies, around 1875. Closed 1907. Working Men's Club from 1908. Currently Queensbury Music Centre, and seriously dilapidated. Beyond this point was considered to be Queensbury area by Mountain folk. **Private Rooms.**

WHITE HORSE: It was the end property on the main road, immediately before Thornton Road Queensbury in the row known as Ambler's Buildings. Closed 1907. **Demolished.**

FRIENDLY INN: Opposite the White Horse site, at the end of Small Page. Closed 1907. *Shop.*

West Scholes/Yews Green

THE JUNCTION: West Scholes. On the census of 1841, it was known as West Scholes Gate Inn. It was listed in the 1857 Trade Directory as Hare and Hounds, but West Scholes Gate Inn again in 1871, and became The Junction Hotel around 1890. Two attached cottages on the West Scholes side were demolished in the late 1800s. Most times considered a 'decent pub'. (Briggs). *Pub.*

GREEN DRAGON: Cockin Lane. Green Dragon Farm, now Meadowcroft. Many locals claim it was the Blue Dragon. It adjoined Cockin Farm. Beer house, pre-1870 to early 1900s. *Private House.*

THORNTREE INN: At the junction of Low Lane and Cockin Lane, Fall Bottom. (Albion). *Private House.*

Memories of Pubs of Yesteryear

THE GRAY HORSE, off Taylor Lane, Soil Hill, was 'already established' in 1871 and was essentially an 'Ale Kitchen' – a tap room attached to a farm. In the 1930s locals remember a gypsy caravan long residing in the yard. The final landlord recalls that he kept the pub: The pub didn't keep him ! Due to poor trade, it closed 29/1/1941.

Like many farm ale kitchens, the accommodation at the Gray Horse was unpretentious. At least the privy was 'convenient' ! Note the stepping stones across the mire.

(R Hunter collection)

THE GIN PIT (or Old Gin Pit) building on Soil Hill had been erected as a farm 'of some importance' by James Charnock in 1739, being known as 'Charnocks'. It was also established as a pub by 1845, when mine host was Titus Holmes, and described in 1858 as 'an old established inn'. It was renamed 'The Sun' about 1880 until it closed in 1906. Reverting to a farm only, it was Sun Farm until the 1990s when it became 'Charnocks' once again. Like the Grey Horse, its main patrons would have been the delvers/quarry-men from Soil Hill. It was known as the Gin Pit because of the horse gin at the nearby coal pit in the S-W corner of the field below the farm, though this had closed before 1850.

THE FORESTERS, on the main road at Raggalds, was originally the Colliers on account of the coal pits adjacent and to the rear at Nettle Hole. Already established by 1841, when Joseph Mann was licensee, living on the premises. Still licensee, he moved to Clog Row, then to Smithy Hill, and the pub's name was changed for no logical reason to Foresters Arms (or Old Foresters) in the 1860s. It closed 31/12/34, was bought by Albert Briggs of Travis Cottages, refurbished as a private house and reoccupied in 1936. Presently named 'The Old Foresters'.

The Colliers, better known as The Old Foresters.
The track to the coal pits ran on the left of the building

RAGGALDS INN (Ye Old Raggalds Inn) was already established in 1841. It is mentioned elsewhere for its notoriety. In the 1930s a garage-type building attached to it had a big sliding door, and provided one-room rented living space for a local gent.

At Raggalds, the Foresters and the Raggalds Inn were in different districts (the boundary being along the road) and there was a half hour difference in licensing hours. The police were very keen, and you had to ensure you had no drink with you if you staggered across the road from the late pub!

A 1963 view showing the L-shape of Raggalds. The entrance is the porch in the centre. (M Bentley collection)

Raggalds Inn c. 1967 taken from the Dross Pen. The building in the foreground once provided accommodation for a local gentleman. At one time a large sign on the end of the pub advertised: 'White Pedigree Boar at stud'. On the skyline to the left is Mountain Mill chimney. Extreme left is the dark shape of Mount Pleasant, with the chimney pots of Fascination Place above.
On the skyline to the right is California Row
(R Hunter Collection)

At **THE FLEECE,** one landlord was Joe Hoyle. It was dubbed "Happy Joe's" since he was a "reet miserable sod". He'd often argue with customers, and if they annoyed him he'd put the towels over the pumps and close !

Early licensees of the Fleece were Robert Foster in 1841 and Martha Foster in 1851 – members of the Foster family of Black Dyke Mills. Before being taken over by Stocks, it had its own brewhouse across the yard behind the pub.

Before WW II there was a piano in the pub, and Sunday nights was sing-song time (presumably after Chapel).

The kitchen was equipped with hard fixed seats and was where the women gathered before the days when they were allowed into the bar.

1999. The Fin Inn (Bradford Sub Aqua Club), formerly The Fleece, still showing the 'Refreshments' sign of over 40 years ago painted on the wall. Cottages on the left are numbers 19, 21 and 23 Mountain. Note the 'stone runners'.

The Best Room (lounge) was on the left, the bar ahead, and the Tap Room nearest the Institute. The landlord's accommodation was above, with use of the pub kitchen.

Mr and Mrs Turnpenny took over from Happy Joe and were licensees in the 1950s/early 60s. Food such as Pies, Fish and Chips, and other dishes was regularly provided on a Sunday. At Christmas, dinners (lunches) were available.

A woman, on her way home with tripe for her husband's tea, called in for a few drinks at the Fleece. Somehow when she paid a visit to the toilet the tripe fell into the loo. She dutifully fished it out, swilled it off and took it home. Presumably her husband never noticed !

In 1959 Kirks of Skipton were engaged to cover Mountain reservoir. That summer was very hot, even in the early morning, and workmen paid frequent visits to the pub. The foreman knew where to find them, and they'd try to escape through the kitchen !

One of the bar games played there was 'Bull Ring'. A bull's nose-ring was attached to a cord. A hook was on the wall. The aim was to throw the ring on to the hook – the cord was to pull back misses without having to bend down.

THE EAGLE INN (Mountain Eagle). Purpose-built in the 1860s, it was described in 1890 as being situated at 1158 feet above sea level, and having an Alpine-style signboard.

On 25 May 1871, the Halifax Courier reports, navvies employed by Bradford Corporation Waterworks entered the Eagle and 'demanded liquor'. They were refused, the landlord was threatened with a knife and in the ensuing scuffle his young daughter was stabbed (though not fatally). The assailant, John Parker, was pursued to the Fleece, and apprehended. He was subsequently jailed for 4 months.

The interior was fairly basic. The Tap Room was to the left, with a flagged floor and spittoons. The Best Room (Lounge) was to the right and equipped with a 3-piece suite in the late 1940s.

The Mountain Eagle c. 1908 when Job Taylor, seen posing in the doorway, was licensee

In the 1990s The Eagle became Mad Ma Jones'. Perhaps not the best of names but the home-made food was simple and really worth a visit. A beer garden was added, but the pub closed in 2003. In 2005 the building to the rear was demolished, and the site of the old pump obliterated. Townhouses built there are named Weavers Court.

Left: The famous buttress at the back of the Eagle, in place for over 100 years! It is supporting a building of about 1814, part of the original Fold.

Below: The last years of the Eagle as Mad Ma Jones'. A lean-to has been added to provide a side entrance and wheelchair access.

The cottages of Back Fold (Warehams Fold 1851 or Wainhouse Fold 1861, prior to the construction of The Eagle) were attached and to the right where the cars stand. The Fleece can be seen on the far right. Off-picture to the left of the white van was the site of the pump house, associated with Langdrake's Mangle.

THE PINEBERRY was 'an established beer house' by 1842 when it was acquired by Stocks Brewery.

The Pineberry, a former farmhouse. To the right is Foxhill School.

Prior to 1830 (when licensing was introduced) there were many 'beershops' or beer houses where ale could be purchased and drunk – sometimes with food available – being simply a room in a farm or house. Originally built as a farm (being the half of the property nearer Queensbury) two further additions have been made. It remained a beer house until 1962 when a full licence was obtained – the last beer house in our area.

In 1963 Webster's bought out Fielding's Brewery, having already taken over Stocks. This meant that Webster's owned Raggalds, the Eagle, the Fleece and the Pineberry. The licensee at the Pineberry, Joshua Wood, was having problems running it (he had a full time job as well) so Webster's offered it to the Turnpennys at the Fleece, who accepted, and the Fleece was closed on 10 April 1963. The Pineberry was revamped that autumn – much to the discomfort of the new licensees, since the weather was cold then and structural work was called for, creating voids through which the winds blew. Afterwards catering was provided, and the Pineberry became established as the meeting place for farmers coming over from Denholme and Thornton on a weekend. It was also a venue for Queensbury Rugby Club, and Yews Green and Union Croft Cricket clubs.

And finally one item rarely mentioned: Queensbury Council meeting of July 3rd, 1889: "A Petition in favour of the closing of Public Houses on Sundays was submitted ..... [by Chairman Paul Speak and Mr Briggs] ...... and unanimously resolved on the motion ..... that it be not entertained." Phew!

TRANSPORT: BUSES

Pre- WW II, Mountain was served by two bus services. One was an hourly service from Dewsbury/Brighouse via Queensbury, Mountain, Keelham and to Keighley by Yorkshire Woollen/West Riding. It was cut back to Cullingworth in the 1950s, abandoned around 1960, and briefly revived as Dewsbury-Raggalds by Yorkshire Woollen in the 1980s, using a Yorkshire Traction bus on lay-over in Dewsbury.

The other service was introduced in the 1920s by Halifax company Hebble. It was a rambling route 11, which required only one vehicle. From the terminus at Raggalds, it proceeded through Mountain to Queensbury via Chapel Street. It performed a U-turn or 3-point turn at The Granby pub then headed to Clayton via Baldwin Lane; next Low Lane and Chat Hill to Thornton (Wellington) then via West Lane, Black Dyke Lane and Old Allan Road to Hare Croft, Wilsden Station, then to Wilsden, and Duckworth Lane via Sandy Lane. In February 1950 road subsidence at Egypt Quarry caused Black Dyke Lane to be closed, and the 11 was diverted via Ten Yards Lane and Tewitt Lane. This proved impractical and was discontinued in April 1951. The service was revised to run as before, Raggalds to Thornton (Wellington) then via the B6145, along Rhodesway/ Pearson Lane/ Duckworth Lane/ Little Lane via Sandy Lane to Wilsden and Hare Croft (Wilsden Station). The 1½ mile trip from Thornton to Hare Croft now became over 7 miles via Duckworth Lane. It ran hourly from 1315 pm until late evening. By 1957 only one Hebble bus a day served Mountain and Raggalds, being the 2153 from Duckworth Lane, 2235 from Raggalds. Four other journeys ran from Queensbury to Hare Croft, the first of the day being 1430 then every 2 hours.

In 1963 the service was revised to run Queensbury – Clayton – Thornton, then a loop round West Lane/ Hill Top Road/ Half Acre Lane/ Back Heights Lane/ Lower Heights Road/ Spring Holes Lane/ West Lane, running clockwise from Queensbury and anticlockwise to Queensbury, then to Duckworth Lane and Hare Croft as before.

The service was known in Mountain as the Wilsden Flyer. Although many remember the Hebble service on the Mountain-Queensbury-Clayton-Thornton section, which was most used by Mountain folk, beyond Thornton seems a mystery area. The route has been 'remembered' variously as 'to Allerton', 'to Bradford', 'to Bingley', and even 'to Five Lane Ends'!

The 11 was an interesting route, hilly and featuring many narrow country roads. It was latterly worked by single-deck buses of the AEC or Leyland type, rear entrance, with dark varnished wood interiors; and AEC Reliance or Regal front entrance types.

When the Queensbury railway closed to passengers in 1955, it was a requirement that various 'replacement' bus services be introduced. This involved Bradford Corporation (Clayton to Bradford via Great Horton), West

Yorkshire, Yorkshire, and Hebble. Routes were subsidised for up to three years by the British Transport Commission. Some services provided only one or two journeys per day (weekdays only) which hardly constituted 'replacement' for the trains.

In our area Hebble instituted service 10, referred to by locals and Hebble alike as the Clayton Circular even though not all journeys (Monday to Saturday) actually completed the circuit, which was Clayton Towngate-Yews Green-Queensbury Stags Head-Clayton Towngate. One vehicle was required for the service: In the morning it departed Yews Green 0630 – School Green Hotel 0635 – Yews Green 0645 (reverse) and 10 minutes layover – 0655 via Low Lane to Clayton 0703. Then two circulars 0715 Clayton – Queensbury Stags Head 0724 – via Carter Lane to Yews Green 0729 – via Cocking Lane and Low Lane to Clayton 0737. This was then repeated at 0745, arriving back to 0807. Then a final return trip to Yews Green (reverse) with a 10 minutes layover, finishing at Clayton at 0833.

In the evening, again with one vehicle, service began at Clayton 1616 – Yews Green (reverse) – School Green Hotel – Clayton 1634 – Yews Green – Queensbury – Clayton – Yews Green (reverse) – School Green – Yews Green – Queensbury – Clayton 1809, with a final trip at 1820 to Yews Green (reverse) – Clayton arriving 1838. By 1956 the only alteration was the final journey which ran via School Green on the return, by omitting the previous five minutes standing at Yews Green. This timetable remained thus until the subsidy ran out and the route was abandoned at the end of September 1958.

Incidentally, Hebble also operated an hourly Bradford-Queensbury-Halifax through service. Bradford and Halifax Corporations were allowed to operate to Queensbury only (in the days before the deregulation fiascos!) since their buses were simply 'tramway replacements'.

In 1971 Hebble ceased to be and the Bradford-Queensbury-Halifax through services were taken over by Halifax Corporation (later Metro/Firstbus), who also (in 1970) introduced service 26, Halifax – Bradshaw – Raggalds – Mountain – Queensbury – Shelf, providing once again a bus for Mountain. West Yorkshire ran a (generally empty) Bradford–Queensbury – Mountain – Denholme – Cullingworth – Haworth service for a few months.

Mountain had a coach company – briefly! – run by Greoge Feather who rented Micklemoss Farm. He operated a trucking business and sought to move in to coaching. In 1950 he acquired the company Westercroft of Northowram, together with its two coaches in orange and cream livery which was retained along with the name. According to their excursion licence terms, they commenced journeys from Micklemoss Farm, with additional pick-up points at Speak Institute and Chapel Street, Queensbury. In 1952 the coaching business transferred to a garage at Ambler Thorn.

Yorkshire Traction bus 535 stands at Raggalds, showing '278 Queensbury' since 'Raggalds' was not on their blinds. The service ran from here to Dewsbury and was a brief revival in the late 1970s of a previous service. Mountain is on the skyline behind. (Photo: Keith Jenkinson)

The Raggalds terminus of Hebble route 11 to Duckworth Lane and Wilsden Hare Croft. Here Leyland HD 6610 stands opposite Raggalds Inn, with Black Carr Terrace behind her. (Photo: Don Akrigg)

Queensbury crossroads, with a Yorkshire Woollen bus on the Dewsbury-Cullingworth service disappearing up Albert Road c. 1956. (Commercial Postcard)

Hebble NCP 383 prepares to turn opposite The Granby in Queensbury, for the return journey on route 11 to Harecroft. 1966. (Photo: Philip Tordoff)

TRANSPORT: RAILWAYS

From various fledgling schemes to link Bradford and Halifax, powers passed to the Great Northern Railway and construction of the line from Bradford to Queensbury and to Halifax and Keighley commenced in 1872. By 1878 the line was opened to Thornton via Queensbury, with 4 return trips Thornton to Bradford, and 2 from Thornton to Laisterdyke, each weekday. In 1879 the line from Halifax to Bradford via Queensbury opened.

The Bradford/Halifax/Keighley line came nowhere near Mountain – nor to Queensbury for that matter ! The station called Queensbury was some 350 feet below and a good half mile distant from the village, initially with only a footpath access. However, inhabitants of Yews Green/West Scholes had only a short, fairly level walk to the station, which opened in 1880, providing the fastest link for them to any of the three main towns. Prior to Queensbury station opening, passenger trains were running through. Passengers from Halifax wishing to proceed towards Thornton had to change at Clayton.

Page from a pocket timetable of December 1900 (published monthly)

Until 1889, Queensbury station consisted of six bare platforms. In 1889/90 the GNR added waiting rooms, and made other improvements. Bricks were acquired from Whitehead's, it is said. The timetable shows some 60 trains a day calling at Queensbury, the first being around 0515, the last around 2345. There was a much reduced service of about 20 trains on a Sunday. Being a triangular station, Queensbury was well-suited for change of train, and while this usually involved a three-or-four-minutes dash from one platform to another, there were occasions on Sundays when you had to wait over an hour for a connection – a mind-deadening prospect ! On Saturdays, late evening stops were made at some stations not open on other evenings. Occasional services ran Halifax to Leeds via Queensbury, and vice-versa, avoiding Bradford by joining the Bradford-Leeds line at St Dunstans which was a triangular junction but with platforms on two sides only. There were a few 'fast' trains which called only at stations before Queensbury or after Queensbury, but not both. Normal journey times were around 20 minutes from Queensbury to Bradford or to Keighley and about 15 minutes to Halifax.

In the 1880s and 1890s the route was used for excursions from Bradford and Halifax to Keighley and beyond, many of which (if they stopped anywhere on this section) called at stations except Queensbury ! A poster for the type of excursion reads as follows:

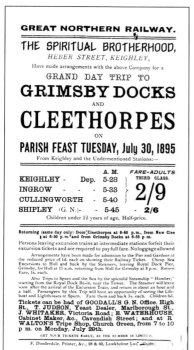

GREAT NORTHERN RAILWAY
THE SPIRITUAL BROTHERHOOD
Heber Street, Keighley
Have made arrangements with the above Company for a
GRAND DAY TRIP TO
GRIMSBY DOCKS
And
CLEETHORPES
On
Parish Feast Tuesday, July 30, 1895

Keighley depart	5.28 am
Ingrow	5.33 am
Cullingworth	5.40 am
Shipley (GN)	5.45 am

The fare was 2/9d return (2/6d from Shipley) No luggage was allowed. The return train left New Cleethorpes at 6.50 pm; Grimsby Docks at 6.55 pm.

Actually there were two separate trains – one from the old (Great Northern) Shipley station, routed via Eccleshill to Laisterdyke. The other from Keighley via Queensbury to Laisterdyke, where the two portions were formed into one train.

An interesting proposal, supported by Queensbury Council, was tabled in 1890 for the continuation of the line from Cullingworth to Preston ! The GNR went so far as to gain an Act of Parliament, and purchase some land, before the idea fizzled out.

From the end of 1938 until after the war there were no passenger services on Sundays. There was a brief upsurge in services just after the war, with around 60 passenger trains a day stopping at Queensbury and a restored Sunday service. By 1948 most of the through Halifax/Keighley trains ceased, with passengers having to change at Queensbury, and the Queensbury Line was one of many axed in the 1950s. It closed to passengers on 21 May 1955. Queensbury Tunnel closed a year later.

There are two funicular (cable-worked) mineral tramways associated with Queensbury station.

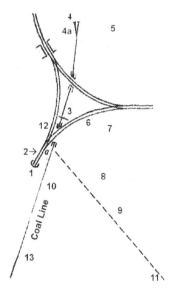

1. Queensbury Tunnel
2. Signal Box, South Junction
3. Footbridge over coal line
4. Coal Mine
4a. Sidings, with junction on the roadway at Hole Bottom
5. Whiteheads Fireclay Works
6. Goods yard
7. Willow Hall Farm
8. Clayton Head Farm
9. Intended line over Station Road (buttresses remain)
10. New Pit
11. To former quarry at Sandbeds (behind Sunny Bank)
12. Bridle Stile cottages
13. To coal yard (Sharket Head)

Pre-dating the arrival of the Great Northern was a line from Sharket Head (off Thornton Road, Queensbury) to Hole Bottom. The land was leased from William Foster 'and others' by Briggs and the tramway used to transport coal from their Hole Bottom Pit (which opened in the 1860s) to Queensbury. Two sides of Queensbury station had to be bridged over it. On the north side, the tramway passed under the western arch of the two main arches. The gradient was variable, climbing almost 400 feet in about 2800 feet. The steepest part was at the top. On the 1893 map, the cable track is shown ending in two sidings as it crossed the road at Hole Bottom by the beck. This indicates that there were probably two tramway wagons, the cable being transferred from one to the other at Hole Bottom. Corves could be run directly from the shaft on to a smooth-surface platform on a level with the flat of the tramway wagon, and loaded on, several at a time and secured. Where the line curved as it passed under the GN lines, there were a few vertical rollers to guide the cable round the curve. Wooden sleepers were used, and it was of 4 feet gauge. Known as 'the Coal Incline', or 'the Truck

Line', some claim that there was a proposal that it be joined to the mainline railway, though it is hard to imagine why!

There is a strong traditional tale that the tramway wagon had small wheels at the top end and large at the lower end, to give a level carrying platform. While this may be the case on constant gradient inclines, one cannot imagine such a system on this variable incline, though no photo has been found of the tramway wagon.

It has been assumed that the corves would have flangeless wheels, to make manoeuvring simpler, though flanged wheels could have been used. Both systems were in use in our area.

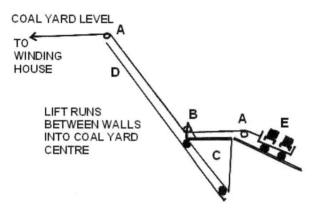

Coal Yard Lift *(Possible Method)*

A	Roller to carry the cable of the tramway wagon
B	As (A) but fixed to the transporter.
C	Transporter – 4 wheels on its own track. 4-foot gauge rails on top.
D	Track for transporter.
E	Tramway wagon with corves.

At the top of the incline was Sharket Head Coal Yard Lift. (O.S. map 1893). To avoid very extensive earthworks, the tramway followed the contours of the hillside, but here a rise of 15 to 20 feet was required to the coal yard level, with a gradient of about 1 in 2. The lift was a separate track, but in line with the tramway. No records of the system have been found but the simplest method would be for the loaded tramway wagon to run on to a transporter wagon (or lift) on the 1 in 2, and, using the cable still on the tramway wagon, haul the transporter to the top of its track [D] so that the corves (still on the tramway wagon) were level with the smooth coal yard platform and could be pushed off. The lift might have been bolted down when in the lower position. The lift transporter could be the one remembered with the small and large wheels.

The Hole Bottom pit [4] closed in 1893. The tramway was lifted to South Box serving New Pit [10] until 1913. It is said to have existed into the 1920s, possibly to the 1930s.

The other line has an element of mystery about it. Right from the opening of Queensbury station, access from Queensbury was by a footpath only. Vehicular traffic was obliged to go via Yews Green.

Station Road, Queensbury, below Greenland Farm. The substantial buttresses are all that remain of the Station to Sandbeds tramway.

Various proposals were considered, one being in 1887 when the Queensbury Co-operative Society 'and other tradesmen' petitioned the Council 'to devise some steam-powered means of transport for goods and passengers'. A study group was set up. In 1889 plans for a road link (Station Road) were drawn up. This resulted in haggling between the Council, the Railway and even Clayton Council (part of the road was within their area) as to who should pay for what. Clayton Council laughed the idea (of contributing) out of the Chamber. However, in 1889/90 the road was constructed by the Great Northern Railway. The surface was compacted red and grey granite ballast. The gradient is around 10%. Gas lamps were made by John Berry, Ironfounders of New Bank, Halifax and two of the original standards can still be seen along Station Road, just below Greenland Farm.

But the idea of a funicular was not dead. Two substantial buttresses were included to carry a line over Station Road, and a mining map, dated 1902 but drawn several years earlier, shows a timber or girder span in place. The line would have run from Queensbury South signalbox to the area now called Sunny Bank, (a former stone quarry) in a straight line. The length of the line would have been just over 1800 feet at a fairly constant grade of about 1 in 6. It was never completed.

There is a local legend that Foster's (who were probably behind the intended tramway since it was routed on land owned by them), planned a line in a tunnel from Queensbury station direct to their Black Dyke Mill, for coal supplies. How the legend arose was probably through Foster's plan of 1892 'to make a tramway under or across Brighouse and Denholmegate Road near to Black Dike Mill, to connect two parts of their property', a proposal which was approved by the Council. The intention of coal transport for Foster's, using the incline tramway, probably was true. Foster's Mountain End pit was about to close (1891) so an alternative source of coal was required. One option was coal brought by rail. It would have been possible (via a wagon turntable) to put standard railway wagons of 6- to 8-tons capacity directly on to the intended tramway, or to use a transporter wagon on the tramway, and haul them up to Sandbeds one at a time. From there, coal could be transferred to road transport, though it would have been possible (but expensive) to lay a standard gauge line along the roads to Black Dyke Mill boiler house, with horse- or locomotive-haulage. An interesting layout would have been created when Bradford trams arrived a few years later!

It is noted on the OS map (revised issue 1908) that earthworks have been created since 1892, joining Queensbury goods yard to Briggs tramway at South Box. This could have been either to use Briggs tramway or to lay a track to the proposed new funicular, the latter seeming more likely.

The GN-Waggonway connection, proposed in 1893 and mentioned earlier, most likely referred to this funicular, not the existing one of Briggs.

The Great Northern Queensbury lines carried considerable and varied freight traffic, and most stations had a decent sized goods yard – except Queensbury which had only 3 sidings at its best. The Queensbury Co-op coal yard was located here. In early 1885 the fireclay works at High Birks (Morton's) had its own sidings laid out, with a pick-up service once a day if required. To operate this, the signal lad from Queensbury would travel on the train from Queensbury to the siding. There he had to remove the padlock from the points to change them. The train reversed in with coal deliveries or empties to one of two sidings parallel to the main line. Wagons waited on the other siding for despatch. There was a siding into the works yard which was worked by steam winch, and also a head-shunt. The loaded wagons were hauled out to Thornton which was the nearest place for the engine to run round them if they were destined for Bradford or Halifax. The signal lad re-set and padlocked the points then had to walk back to Queensbury station – not the pleasantest of prospects in winter ! The sidings were removed in 1965.

Thornton Fireclay, adjacent to the Thornton/Keelham road, had sidings from 1929 to 1947, joining the main line at Thornton station. After closure, the brickworks became Naylor Myers builders merchants. Some narrow gauge track was visible in the yard until 1999. Opposite the site was Shawl Mill, demolished in 2002. On the Thornton side of the brickworks was Thornton Colliery (opposite Albion Mill).

Although adjacent to the railway line, Whitehead's Fireclay Works at Hole Bottom had no rail connection.

In 1956 the section Queensbury-Holmfield was closed, and by 1965 the Horton to Thornton section was closed (the Keighley end of the line had also gone). At Queensbury the stationmaster's house remains but little else is intact. The cutting to the Clayton tunnel, and the area within the triangle of the former platforms, have been filled. The high bridge over the road at Hole Bottom remains. The bridge over Cockin Lane was removed in the 1990s, and the Morton's brickworks area has been filled. Thornton Viaduct re-opened as a cycleway in 2008. The original footbridge near Morton's was removed and replaced with another after the railway closed. The passenger walkway from Brow Lane to the station is still evident but the tiled underpass is buried. Bridle Stile cottages, shown looking smart and white in many photos of Queensbury Station, have been demolished. The viaduct carrying the Thornton-Bradford platforms (a listed structure) was demolished without consent, the stone being sold and, as the owner allegedly said, the sale of the stone far outweighed the fine for being a bad boy ! The cutting to Cockin Lane has been filled. From 2007 the Sustrans route passes along it.

During operations for Sustrans at Queensbury station, a gravestone was found, having been dumped as landfill from a site thought to be in Clayton. Ironically, it relates to one John Dalby (1823-1893) and his wife. It states that he had 'upwards of 40 years in the service of the Midland Railway Co'. Ironic because Queensbury was Great Northern, not Midland territory!

Coal Incline route

Dating from 1955, a view from the centre of Queensbury triangle, where a siding was created to dump ash from Bradford loco sheds. Steam rises from the first vent of Queensbury tunnel. The route of the coal tramway can be clearly seen, heading for Sharket Head on the skyline. (Photo: Peter Sunderland)

About two-thirds of the way up the incline was New Pit, which opened when Hole Bottom closed. The tramway diverted at New Pit on to this levelled area (above right) for loading corves. The shaft was on the right near the loading platform.

The coal tramway passed under the main line near Queensbury South signal box, then under the viaduct beyond. Seen in 1980. (See photo of Queensbury station on the next page.)

The same area seen in 1889/90 after Station Rd had opened. The lattice footbridge is in the original 'high' position. The coal tramway is in use. The first roller on the tramway is vertical, to guide the cable round the curve, and is adjacent to a normal horizontal roller. (R Hunter Collection)

A view of about 1904. The lattice footbridge, is now below platform level and links to the subway crossing under the main line on the left. (Graham Hall collection)

The disused railway bridge over Cockin Lane 1992, shortly before demolition. With only 11 feet clearance it was often a problem for HGV drivers who ignored the advance warning signs ! Hebble single-deckers just fit.
(Photo: David Shepherd)

Above:
A 1955 view of an unidentified tank loco with a regular Keighley-Bradford two-coach train leaving Queensbury station. On the skyline, left of the two telegraph poles, is Mountain Mill chimney. To their right, the Institute, Evelyn Place, West Royd and Harmony Place are visible.
(Photo: Peter Sunderland)

Left:
The entrance to Queensbury tunnel, 1955. On the skyline (left) is Sharket Head. (Photo: Peter Sunderland)

Between Clayton Tunnel and Queensbury Station was this accommodation bridge, seen here in 1995. The cutting has since been filled but the bridge remains. (Photo: David Shepherd)

The bricked-up Clayton tunnel 1995. Most of the cutting has since been filled. (Photo: David Shepherd)

THE NAVVY HOUSES

These were built around 1873-75 for the navvies who were boring Queensbury tunnel. They occupied the area where Goodwin House now stands. They were intended to last for 'as long as the job took' – but in fact were not condemned until 1957 (demolished 1961) and actually outlasted the part of the railway which had been the reason for their erection, since the Queensbury-Holmfield section closed in 1956 ! The 'recreational pub' for the navvies still survives as the Queensbury Music Centre. In the row of old cottages fronting the Navvy Houses was the Sportsman beerhouse, being part of Small Page Row, known locally as Slave Row, which pre-dates the Navvy Houses so it is no reflection on the Great Northern Railway as an employer ! 'Slave Row' was owned by David Knowles, one-time owner of the uncompleted Highfield Mill Queensbury, and employer of hand-loom weavers. The latter, who lived in the properties owned by him at Small Page, were paid in goods from his store on Chapel Street.

The Navvy Houses, unlike the more usual accommodation of temporary shacks, were stone-built like most mill workers' houses. Each had a cellar; a small cellar-head kitchen and a living-room, all stone-flagged; stone stairs led to a first floor bedroom, with wooden stairs to the attic or 'garret'.

There were three rows of back-to-backs. The road at the back of Slave Row being Railway Street; then Northern Street and Great Street; and Oakley Street (often shown as Darley Street on plans) named after the GNR director Henry Oakley. Mid-way along each of the rows was a ginnel, from one road to the next. There were 44 houses in all.

By 1881 only four or five were still occupied by GNR employees. Of the rest, 11 were empty.

For some reason, later inhabitants of the Navvy Houses tended to consider themselves to be of Mountain rather than of Queensbury, possibly because several Mountain families moved there after the navvies left.

The Nessy

Most houses of the era had an outside lavatory, originally often without water. Several houses shared one lavatory. You had to plan your visit, particularly in bad weather or if you were part of a big family! Some had a family nessy – three holes/seats side-by-side, as at the Navvy Houses. The lavatories were usually stone built, with flagged floor, one large slab of stone for the roof, and no window. The wooden seats and fronts were generally kept well scrubbed, and each seat might have a hinged lid. If fitted, the water tank, with a pull chain, was above. The walls would be lime washed twice a year. There were no toilet rolls, just squares of torn newspaper fixed on a nail inside the door which also provided reading material if motions were slow ! In the dark, a candle or hurricane lamp was useful, there being no fitted lights.

EDUCATION

Anecdotes in this section are in part taken from the school log books of Raggalds and Foxhill schools, with thanks for the kind assistance of the head teacher Andy Bleasdale. Some names have been omitted by way of confidentiality !

In the 1830/40 period, knowledge of what was happening outside your town was gained through newspapers, which might appear once a week. Several working men who were sufficiently interested might contribute to buy a paper then to be read aloud by the literate ones to the group on a Saturday night. The less fortunate could only experience 'news' by word of mouth.

Mention is made of a small school 'at Mountain' (actually Mucky Lane) in about 1820, run by John Briggs. It was probably the same establishment attended by John Bates. There were a few such educationalists in the area, and later we hear of Dame schools run by ladies for young children at both Yews Green and on the Mountain. In 1851 the school at Raggalds was opened to serve Mountain, Raggalds and surrounding area. It was built on a site marked Hop Houses on early maps. Hop Houses were three cottages, of which only one was occupied by 1841. The land was gifted in 1851 by the owner, Michael Stocks of Shibden Hall, Northowram. Hop Houses were demolished and the school built on/near this site using some materials from them. There was two-storey accommodation at the road end which was the schoolmaster's house. The rest consisted of one room 42' x 24' (which could be divided into two), with a gallery at the far end. Outside toilets (earth closets) were provided. The commemorative stone, now in the outer wall, was originally above the school-room (centre) door. Operating for 47 years as a school, it was governed by a body of 3 and chaired by Paul Speak until it was taken over by the Local Board (1892-98). In the early years it was referred to as Raggalds Inn Church School.

The school was grant assisted, with pupils paying 2d to 4d per week. The three R's were taught, together with needlework for the girls. In later years cookery, gardening, joinery and singing were added. Most written work was done on slates. Children under 10 (later raised to under 12), were supposed to receive full-time education, and those 10-12 (called half timers) should have the equivalent of at least 3 full school days per week. However, financial pressures being what they were, absenteeism was common – either because the children were 'helping out at home' or were actually employed in the Mill or pits. Technically for a child to work part-time, a certificate had to be issued by the school, stating the child's age. This didn't please all employers, Speaks included, and resulted in confrontations. Even so, Speaks continued to be benefactors of the school. From 1865 Nancy Speak provided a Whit Treat for children of Raggalds school. There were games organised, and food which included 'nuts and raisins' – presumably a delicacy – and a concert. At Christmas she provided a Christmas tree.

Raggalds School, when in use as a joiner's shop by George Glew. The headmaster's house was at the left hand end. (R Hunter collection)

Heating in the school room was provided by a fireplace and a single coal-burning stove, fuelled courtesy of Speak's Mill (if they had enough to spare!). At times in winter, it was said to be so cold that 'the ink froze in the inkwells', and that 'the temperature in the classrooms is several degrees below freezing point'.

Most of the children who attended Raggalds school were not academically bright. But what they lacked in this area of ability, they more than compensated for in their awareness and knowledge of subjects such as mining, quarrying, pottery (there being 3 potteries in the area), well-making, farming and country lore, subjects of which the academic 'townie' children would be ignorant.

Discipline was strict, but some variety was introduced with occasional visiting speakers – records tell of lantern slide talks, a puppet show, a conjuror, and a lady who brought along preserved frogs legs to illustrate her lecture !

Teaching was done by the 'head master', his wife (for the infants and for girlie subjects like sewing), an assistant (sometimes) and by older pupils teaching younger ones – a useful system if closely controlled, as it was by the headmaster who arranged to take his class in the gallery so he could keep a constant eye and ear on things.

There is no record of teaching staff from when the school opened (in November 1851) until 1861. Then Joseph Frederick Durick (54) was head, teaching Reading, Writing and Grammar. His wife Catherine (58), and his daughter Ellen Jane (23) both taught Knitting and Sewing. In this year it is noted also that "chimney sweeps using boys to climb in chimneys to sweep them is now rare in the district".

In 1871 John (31) and Susannah Halliday were running the school. In 1881 it was Thomas and Elizabeth Singleton, both 29 years of age.

Around 1890 Mary Inglet was schoolmistress with 4 live-in scholars, and John Battersby a retired carpenter in his 70's also lived there (caretaker?). He was partial to his ale and one of the pupils was required to go for supplies, sometimes four times a day, from the Raggalds Inn.

Prior to the Queensbury Local Board taking over, reports on accommodation were prepared. One comment was the need for a separate room for infants; provision of a cloakroom; and "the fireplace needs repair and a guard – it is unusable". The school was closed from 23/12/1891 until 10/10/1892 when the Local Board took over.

Raggalds schoolhouse served not only for the education of the young but also as a night school and chapel. Even before the school opened, it was consecrated in early November 1851. By the end of November, it opened for education, and we are told of Sunday School attendance being 120, day school 65, and night school 'for young men' being 55.

Having left education as soon as possible to get a job, quite a lot of people wished to 'improve themselves' in later years. Locally this was at night school, as mentioned at Raggalds, and also for some years around 1870 at one of the old cottages on the north side of Mountain Lane, and probably supported by Speaks.

Initially, Raggalds was the only place of worship in the Mountain area – the chapel in Mountain was not built until 1866/7, although religious meetings had been held in a rented room there for a few years beforehand. However, services were transferred to the chapel, and we are told that in 1870 the school inspectors asked for the removal of the pulpit and a pew, to make more room for students at Raggalds School.

School holidays were far fewer than today and were according to the whims of the School Board. We read that in 1865, for example, the Christmas break was 22 December to 7 January, but the only other official holidays were Good Friday to Easter Tuesday, Whitsuntide Monday and Tuesday, a week in July for the summer holidays, and 3 days in September for the Queensbury Fair. However, even full-time pupils had other time off if necessary for helping with family crises, or for seasonal work (eg haymaking), though this was frowned upon by the Board. This practice survived into the 1900s at Foxhill.

Also in 1865 we read that the headmaster's basic pay was £21. 9s. 0d per year, and he was also expected to lend a hand with building maintenance.

The school catered for children from the Mountain, and all the adjoining areas. Maximum enrolment was in 1877 with over 280 pupils, though many were part-timers.

Speaks played a large part in school affairs – sometimes in confrontation, but usually as benefactors. In the Head's log of June 1897, with closure less than a year away, we read: "The children, in connection with the school, having been invited to coffee and buns at Laurel Bank, Holmfield by Paul Speak Esq, tomorrow Saturday June 26. I have devoted the singing lesson to practising special hymns printed for the occasion."

Accommodation having been long considered unacceptable, Raggalds school closed on 17 March 1898. Books and equipment were transferred the next day to the new Foxhill school, which opened to pupils on Monday 21 March. It is the highest altitude Education Board school in England and is said to have been the first building in the area to have been built incorporating double glazing. There was central heating also. The assembly hall at Foxhill was larger than the whole of Raggalds school. The dimensions given for Foxhill were – Upper school: Hall 52 feet x 20 feet, 4 classrooms each 20 feet x 20 feet. Infants school: Two rooms one 35 feet x 20 feet and one 20 feet x 16 feet. It was intended to accommodate over 300 pupils, though a maximum of around 250 was recorded. By 1928 registration was down to just over 100. Despite 'modern' amenities, the children still wrote on slates for the first years of the 20th century.

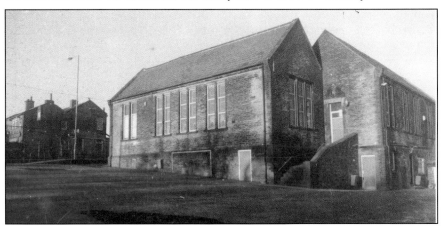

Foxhill School as original. The basement of the right-hand building became the dining room in 1901. The Pineberry pub can be seen on the left.

In 1899 the school asked the Council to provide setts and to create a road crossing at Fox Hill – the road surface was still dross. At the time, traffic did not warrant a 'Lollipop Lady'!

In 1901, a dining room was provided under the school (in what were the cellars) since many pupils travelled too far (on foot, of course) to go home for lunch. However, they had to provide their own food until 1908 when a free lunch was provided for those 'most needy', which accounted for quite a lot of Foxhill pupils ! In 1911, we read of 268 hot meals being provided over a three-day period. Meat and potato pie, followed by rice pudding, seems to have been the regular lunch.

The head teacher in the first years of 1900 was John Hall. He is remembered for caning kids who arrived with muddy shoes – so the children from places like West Scholes had to be extra careful.

The efforts of the school to assist the poorest pupils went so far as to organise a concert (in February 1912), the proceeds of which (over £4) went to provide 'clogs, stockings and soup' for some 14 needy children.

A very posed classroom photo, Foxhill 1910. Note the tiled walls and massive central heating pipes. On the wall is a picture of George V and Queen Mary, and a picture of an Indian elephant. There is a large class timetable and a nursery rhyme roll chart. On the blackboard is 'Father Mother and Baby Bear go for a walk'. There is a Union flag; and pennants and link-and- twist decorations probably made by the children.
(Fred Jagger Collection)

The regime at Raggalds and especially Foxhill seems to have been firm but with the best interests of the children in mind. Many kids came from poor families – feeding and clothing them might be a problem – but there was no excuse for being dirty ! We read of kids being excluded because of 'verminous infection'. And frequent reports such as: "I excluded F.B. at noon on the grounds of filthy underclothing. Her vest and thin cotton frock (her only upper garments) were in a shocking condition." "Several complaints having been received of objectionable smells arising from the clothing of R.W., I excluded him. This is the second time within a fortnight."

In 1912 was the Miners Strike. From March 18th, the half-time children employed at Speak's began attending school full-time because the mill (like many others) had to close for lack of coal. To help with the hardships (no work = no pay) the school took it upon itself to provide dinners for the children most in need – this had been approved by the Board of Education as 14, but now rose to 82. In addition to the 'soup and bread', there was now 'currant and rice pudding'. This might have been the only hot meal some kids received. Extra plates were borrowed from the Hall of Freedom in Queensbury. Nancy Speak must have played some part in the provisions since "a vote of thanks (was sent from the school) to Mrs Speak for her generosity in providing meals to the children ...."

In 2000, construction began on an addition to the Queensbury side of the school, which roughly doubled its size.

In a later period, a few parents arranged for their children to have lunch at The Pineberry, before school dinners were the norm. One ex-schoolgirl remembers: "There were five of us. Lunches, which were substantial and varied, cost 2/6d per week. Afterwards we were allowed to pull beer – though not for us, of course."

Extra classrooms were erected in the school playgrounds in 1955, and more in 1960. These Portacabin-type structures are peculiarly referred to as 'External Terrapins'. Toilets inside the main building were provided in 1960.

It's pleasing to note that the fox has returned to Foxhill, as shown on the commemorative stone in the gable of the new building. Pupil figures are again around 250, with an annual intake of about 30.

Foxhill class photo 1905. Phyllis Gledhill is on the back row, second from the left. Isn't everyone smart ! John Hall was headmaster, having previously been at Raggalds School. (Phyllis Gledhill Collection)

Foxhill Infants class photo 1921. Standards of dress have dropped drastically ! George Smith is head teacher, Mrs Riley the infants teacher. Another Mr Smith, one Charles Henry Micklethwaite, became Head in 1947. He is remembered for writing verse in pupils books as comments on their work. (Fred Jagger Collection)

RECREATION

Knur and Spell

This was a popular game in the North of England, and has many variations. It seems to have several features in common with the early (1800s) style of golf. Knur and Spell is still played at certain pubs in Yorkshire, Lancashire and Durham.

The knur is a sphere of about 3 to 4 cm diameter. Traditionally of wood, it was more commonly made of fired clay. The spell is a spring mechanism which launches the knur into the air, to be struck with the club or bat. A club was a long stick (about 1 metre) with a block attached at the end, to give a better chance of a hit ! A bat was shorter, cylindrical, with a flattened striking face. Often a pick-axe handle with a striking face lashed on, the best face being made of hollin (holly) wood. The holly was cut to size then compressed for several days in a (cheese) press, before being attached to the handle. Holly treated thus was regarded as especially 'bouncy', giving greater striking power. The player used the bat or club to release the spring on the spell, then struck the Knur when it shot vertically in the air. He might adopt a golfer's stance, with arms stretched for greatest club-head velocity.

An alternative to the spell, and used for impromptu games, was a gallows, also known as a sling or a pin. This was a vertical support with an arm from which a looped string was suspended. The knur was balanced in the loop, at a height of about 80 cm from the ground, and was struck in this position.

There are two main variants of scoring – Scores (also called laiking) and Long Knock (also called striking). Sometimes the two were combined. In Scores there may be several players, or teams. A large field is marked out in arcs at intervals of 20 yards from the spell position. Each player takes turns to hit the knur, and the total number of turns (or rises, or cuts) may be 20 or 30 for each player or team. The scores are measured in units of 20 yards – thus a score of 3 means the knur has gone 20 x 3 yards – approximately 55 metres. The player or team with the highest total wins. Since the knur is small, assistants called doggers are positioned in the field to watch where the knur lands. If the knur fails to make it into the first arc, that is a nil score, since second strikes are not allowed except for a broken knur. A total is expressed as so many score off so many rises (eg 200 score off 20 rises).

In Long Knock (striking) there may be only two players. The aim is to make the longest single hit. Each player might have, say, five rises; then the other player has the same. This might be repeated several times, but only the longest hit counts. The player may be required to locate his own knur, there being a time limit for this, and failure means a nil score for that shot. Long Knock is measured accurately (in feet and inches) within a score arc.

Thus a Knock of 18 score 37 feet 8 inches (giving a total of about 125 metres) is the likely record set in 1906 by Fred Mount of Claremont, Halifax.

Knur and Spell contests attracted big crowds – and big wagers ! In 1854 we hear of a contest at Wibsey between William Sutcliffe of Midgley and Joseph Coward playing Long Knock for a purse of £100. On the 2nd of May 1859 we are told of crowds of up to 10,000 (maybe an overstatement!) attending Wibsey, this time to see William Sutcliffe (the same person but now of Mountain and described as Bill o' t'Mount) versus J. Jagger of Wibsey. This was a Laiking contest wherein each player had six sets each of five rises. The total score was averaged over the number of rises – Bill put in the best average in history with 12.5 score over the 30 rises (an average still unbeaten) and won £20.

It is probable that this William Sutcliffe was the same who was involved in a prize-fight at Raggalds in late 1863, as mentioned elsewhere. His son, Fred (known as Fred o' Pilts) was likewise a champion bare-fist fighter and Knur and Spell player.

Another champion player, who also made Spells to sell, was Tom Bartle Brooks of Mountain. Born in 1872, he was still playing in 1950 !

Arra (Arrow) Throwing

Although played by children, it was also a serious, competitive adult sport. (For details see the book by R. Payne-Gallway 'The Crossbow'). The arrow would be about 30 inches long, or less if you couldn't find a suitable stick ! Hazelwood was preferred. A string was knotted at one end and held by a shallow groove at the rear of the arrow. The other end was tied or wrapped around the index finger so that it would be taut when the arrow was held about a third of the length back from the tip. As you threw it, the index finger was flicked, giving much greater impetus. A champion thrower could achieve over 300 yards, it is claimed.

Mountain Trails – dog coursing, pre-World War I

The trail-ligger (a man with a sack of aniseed to mark the route with a scent for the dogs to follow cross country) set off, all the other participants going 'for a sup'. The trail-ligger would run, taking a route of about an hour (about 4 miles). The route was designed to be visible throughout from Mountain. The ligger then 'went for a sup' as well, and about 40 minutes later the dogs were released, and bets were made for the winners. The local pubs had paintings of the champion dogs hanging on the walls.

So enthusiastic were some dog owners that they put the animal before wife and kids, with the dogs being better fed and attended to. Mountain-bred dogs were renowned for their speed and endurance, being recognised even over the border into Lancashire. They rarely changed owners.

Whippet Racing

Although a simple activity, there were whippet breeders in the area, and the sport was taken seriously. The dogs would be lined up across the starting line, held on the leash. The marker would hold a flag or cloth at a distance in front of them to get their attention then run off with it – and presumably drop it and get out of the way when the dogs were released ! Their owners were at the finish to catch them. Whippet racing was popular in this area in the 1900-1920 period.

Pigeon Shooting

From the late 1870s, this 'sport' involved releasing live pigeons, one at a time, the intention (which involved serious betting) was to kill as many as possible in a pre-determined range and with as few shots as possible.

Pigeon Racing

Meetings of owners were held at the Eagle. The direction of flight was chosen randomly by spinning an indicator and the pigeons were then taken a decided distance (a couple of miles) in that direction and released. Bets were made on the time taken to home. Two special (that is, accurate) clocks were bought from Fattorinis of Bradford. One went with the releaser, to note that time. The other stayed at Mountain to clock the birds as they flew in. This sport was active up to World War II.

Street Bowls/Highway Bowls

This was played with roughly shaped discs of stone about 1" thick by 3" or 4" diameter, used instead of balls. A length of road or track was chosen and one version of the game was to see who could roll their discs along it with the least number of 'throws'.

Other Activities

The Eagle played host to Lark Singing contests, the birds being specially 'trained' for this. How scoring was done is uncertain, but presumably related to how many notes a bird sang in a given time, or for how long they sang continuously. We hear of one in 1872, where Samuel Dean of Mountain was 3rd, with his lark scoring 'four of a round, six-and-a-half a time'. Before a contest, the birds were fed mealworms. Lads would be paid 1d for 20, which they caught around Rodney Dock. Some lads kept "a gurt pot full on 'em at 'ome" , in readiness.

Various games involving tossing or throwing were subjects for pub gambling. And, at Raggalds, prize fighting was popular, and dog fights were sometimes held.

Games for Kids

In common with children's games everywhere, certain principles were involved (such as running and chasing, throwing and catching) though rules varied on whim, and game names varied with locality.

The girls favoured skipping, and battledore and shuttlecock. The boys liked ball games, using an inflated sheep's bladder.

Piggy was similar to Tin Can Squat. A stick was hit in the air with a bat. The first child to retrieve it was 'It' (the seeker) and everyone else had to run and hide while the seeker wasn't looking. Another Hide and Seek game was 'Hare's in the Hollow'. This was played in the fields. The seeker set off at a signal given by those hiding – "Hare's in the hollow but I'll not follow until you blow your horn".

A game of leap-frog also had a rhyme accompaniment: "Hinkum Jinkum Jerrimun Buck. How many horns do I cock up?"

A chasing game was 'Run, sheep, run' which involved the one who was 'It' to cause the others (the sheep) to run into a particular segment of the field where they were 'penned'.

'Tip Cat' was probably modelled on Knur and Spell. A short wedge-shaped or pointed stick is balanced on a stone or stick so that when one end is hit downwards with a bat it spirals into the air where it is again struck with the bat to see how far it will go. Alternatively (and less dangerous !), the second strike was omitted – just to see how far the spiralling stick will go.

'Duck-on-the-Peak', or 'Duck Stones' involved a small pile of stones with the Duck (target) stone on top. A circle about 6 feet in diameter was marked around it. Standing outside this circle, the object was to throw stones to be the first to knock off the Duck.

THE CO-OP GALA IN THE 1930s

For many years the Queensbury & District Co-operative Society organised a gala, in the month of June. This was centred at the Gala Field which was near their bakery at Hill Top. Each branch within the area was expected to supply a 'float' (a wagonette or other decorated vehicle). Sowerby Bridge Co-op was invited to attend each year, as was Great Horton Co-op. The Queensbury Ambulance Brigade also joined in. All assembled at the Granby Fields then did a tour of Queensbury (passing the main shop, of course) and to the Gala Field for entertainment and games.

To get people to and from the Gala, a bus was sometimes hired, picking up from the outlying Bradshaw and Shelf branches, to ferry children (no mention of adults !) to the field for 2 pm, and back home about 7.30 pm. In 1934 the society's own motor wagons (a Bedford 3-ton, and a 20 cwt) provided this service.

Admission to the field was by ticket – around 1200 were printed. Ice Cream vendors were admitted, being charged 2/6d for a pitch. Covered accommodation – necessary for some events - usually consisted of a Marquee, a couple of tents, and a Dutch barn with a fresh coat of paint.

Free buns were distributed to the kids, and this seemed to cause considerable dispute within the committee. Initially they were handed out at the gates. The next year a hamper was placed by each Branch's display, supervised by each Branch Director. Then the buns were deemed too large, and from 1936 a smaller size was ordered 'to avoid waste'. Tea was also on offer but you had to have your own tin mug with you !

There were entertainers but for most folk the real entertainment was the competitions, with something for every age group. For example, we read of:

A Baby Show; Skipping Race; Two-legged Race; Tyre Race; Wheelbarrow Race; Egg and Spoon Race (using a pot knur rather than an expensive egg); a Baking Competition with 'prizes to be provided by Sowerby Bridge Co-op'; the Best Fancy Dress (Prize £1); Best Comic Dress (Prize 10/-); Guess the Weight of a Pork Pie (Prize: the Pie); Guess the Weight of a Bag of Coal (Prize: the coal); Shoe Cleaning competition (shoes were provided); and Co-op vouchers for 2/6d presented to the oldest lady and oldest gentleman there. Non-perishable prizes might be displayed for a few days in the Queensbury Co-op window, with a card showing the winner's name.

Each year the Committee drew up a list of requirements for the Gala, and for several years the first item was 'Revolver and Bullets'! Was it a starting pistol, or a means of crowd control? Another regular item was 'Sawdust for Dressing Rooms'. The Gala continued into the 1950s.

RAGGALDS

This area, around the junction of the A644, Roper Lane, Green Lane and Perseverance Road, has changed little over two centuries. The remains of several coal pits can still be seen; many of the farms and cottages are as they were externally, except for minor alterations. The brewery buildings of White Castle remain, now as private houses. The school building is extant currently known as Moss House; most beerhouses remain as private houses; and Raggalds Inn remains thus, though greatly extended.

The adjacent area of Swilling Hill (Soil Hill) was mentioned in writings of 1369 as being tenanted, but little is known of Raggalds until the 1700s, when the Charnock family was established in the area, erecting Charnocks farmhouse in 1739. Farming, quarrying and mining were the main activities – manufacturing never appeared here. The road from Queensbury to Denholme was well used and was mettled as a turnpike from about 1821. In 1841 there is mention of "William Turton, Barkeeper, at Raggles", situated at the end of Clog Row. Again we have Samuel Garth, Tolltaker, in 1861. In November 1864, it ceased to be a turnpike road.

In 1871, Mucky Lane was made up for the benefit of Soil Hill and Small Tail residents and was renamed Perseverance Road.

About half way along the row of cottages on Perseverance Road was a shop. The property is now a private house, decorated with stone heads. Further down, a gap in the row gives access to Small Tail Farm. Opposite, a track leads to Hartley Square and Black Castle Farm. Half way between these two farms some ruins mark the site of Far Shugden Farm which predates them considerably. The track continues to Taylor Lane.

The three houses now at the bottom end of Perseverance Road, numbers 5, 6 and 7, were known as the Club Houses, built as a unit by three families who clubbed together their money.

Further down were cottages Nos 1-4 in one block in the small triangle now the garden of number 5. The remaining evidence of these consists of two domestic wells, all other traces having disappeared by 1890. Most likely they were four single-room low-decker cottages facing the road, each with a small yard, typical of the late 1700s and inhabited by farm labourers, coal miners or delvers. In the early 1800s, three were made into one and occupied by school teacher John Briggs in the 1820s-1840s period.

For liquid refreshments, the Raggalds and the Foresters were well-established. There was a third beerhouse in the area around the road junction. Mentioned as Travellers Inn in 1841, run by Thomas Sharp, it continued (unnamed in the census) under John Jagger (1851) and Lewis Balmforth (1861), after which it presumably closed. It seems to have been between Foresters and Travis – which would indicate in the row of low-deckers, formerly on the garage site.

Another establishment for non-alcoholic refreshment was the Willowdene tearoom, at Lane Bottom (now Willow Dene) Farm. It was constructed in the 1930s. In 1943 the farm was purchased by the Leedale family, who lived there until 1947.

The tearoom was a wooden structure with a tar-felt roof, built at the back of the farmhouse kitchen and joined to it with a short covered passage with a couple of steps down to the café. It has been variously described as like an old bus, like a cricket pavilion, and like a Butlin's chalet. It was painted green. There was access up a few wooden steps, to double doors, from the cinder lay-by adjacent to the road and a flagged-over ditch.

In the café were half-a-dozen tables with oilcloth covers. Mrs Leedale was in charge, assisted by husband and eldest son David. At weekends, friends and relatives helped out. During the week, most customers were lorry drivers and reps. Sandwiches, egg and chips, and home-made cakes were served, with the expected large mugs of tea. The attached smallholding provided most of the food served. At weekends trade greatly increased. David was put outside to sell pop to the cyclists and walkers. Inside the speciality was chicken salad – chicken was a luxury for townies in the war years. The locals called Willowdene "t'chicken-and-pie oyl". After Leedale's left, the café continued for a few years before Sandal Farm began serving food.

Beyond Travis was Boggard Houses, or Scrat Hall. Go to the gate immediately after the first field beyond Travis. Through the gate, follow the wall (on your right) until the land slopes down. On the left is an old coal pit. Although the pit closed before 1850, the abandoned pitside building and the office at the roadside remained for another hundred years! Ahead a sunken track is obvious. Boggard House boundary is marked by two massive gateposts. These, standing five feet above ground and about eight feet apart, are each single blocks. Their shape is unusual, being plain cylindrical but with the outer curve flattened (major axis about 18" and minor axis about 16"), and with a flat top. The right hand one carried two iron brackets (gate hinge pegs), the left hand one had the sneck. The house was down and to the left of the gateway, but the land has been levelled so no evidence is visible.

Boggard Houses was listed on the 1841 Census with the principal occupant being John Whitaker, farmer, and family who were probably the original residents. Also known as Black Carr Farm, it consisted of a house, barn, stable and cottage, together with fields named Little Ing, Great Ing, Croney (potato field), High, Croft, 4-days' Work, and 2-days' Work, totalling 18 acres. It was purchased by Paul Speak and occupied (in 1880) by Joseph Pollard. By 1891 the property had become Scrat Hall, occupied by one Ben Sugden and family, joiner and farmer. After this time, it seems to have been abandoned. It is known to have existed as derelict into the very early 1900s (see Ghosts 'n' Beasties).

The massive gateposts at Boggard House, as you entered Boggard lands.

Proceeding towards Keelham, Shay Farm (Grade II listed) stands back on the left. It dates from the early/mid 1700s. Next is Trash Hall, renamed Keelham Farm and later rebuilt, with Far Shay Farm up the hillside. This part of Soil Hill is often called Keelham Hill or Thornton Moor, and Shay is a local variant of Shaw – an area of woodland, now distinctly lacking trees!

Farming families in this area recall horse-drawn sledges being used in the fields until after WW II, because of the boggy nature of the land.

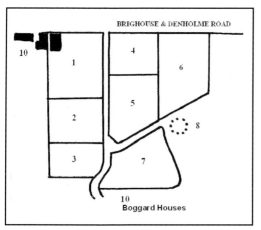

Land belonging to Travis House Farm until 1965, after which only the Ing remained with the house.

1. Ing/Travis House Farm
2. Middle Field
3. Low Field
4. Upper Pit Field
5. Lower Pit Field
6. Rough
7. Black Field
8. Coal Pit, not belonging to Travis House
10. Cottages and farm, not belonging to Travis House

Travis House farmhouse was probably built around 1830. In 1837 the whole farm was sold by Mary Horsman to Arthur Robinson who leased it to Henry Charnock, farmer, of the Soil Hill Charnock family. Another Charnock lived in one of the attached cottages. Henry was tenant for over 30 years.

Although no properties existed at the time of the 1779 enclosures, the area 'Travis' came to include The House, the farmhouse and barn next door (now Travis Cottages), and the adjacent row of low-deckers.

Travis. Furthest from the camera is Travis House Farm, painted white, with Lane Bottom Farm (also white) in the far distance. Nearest are Travis Cottages. The low-deckers occupied the carpark in the foreground. On maps, the whole group is usually lumped together as Travis House.

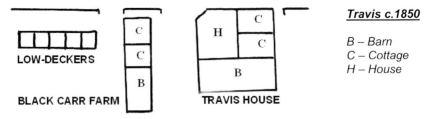

The area from Travis to Keelham Hall was known as Black Carr. Several farms in the area were known as 'Black Carr Farm', with Travis Cottages being one of them. In 1779 William Pearson (probably a relative of Guy Pearson who owned Boundary House at Mountain), "added 7½ acres to his land" which, with the addition of buildings, became Black Carr Farm. It was referred to (in the deeds) as 'Black Carr Farm at Travis' in 1894; and in 1919 as 'Travis Farm'. The row of four one-room low-deckers was in the same ownership, with a fifth added-on structure at the Black Carr Farm end used for non-domestic purposes. Having been built in the late 1700s, before 1840 the four low-deckers had been converted into two. One became a beer house called 'The Travellers' from around 1840 to 1864. The row was demolished in 1963.

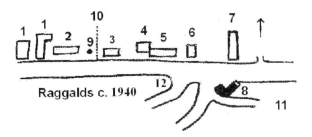

Raggalds c. 1940

1. Travis House Farm/Travis Cottages
2. Travellers Inn: One of 4 low-deckers demolished c. 1960 for petrol station.
3. Colliers Inn pre 1860. Foresters Arms to 1934, then private house 'Old Foresters'
4. Smithy Hill. Cottage, now 2 semis.
5. Smithy Hill: 3 Low-deckers; 2 in 1950s. Now one.
6. Black Carr Terrace: Originally a pair of semis with 2 cellar dwellings. Later 2 semis. Now 1 dwelling.
7. Clog Row: 5 low-deckers plus one 2-storey at the road end. Demolished by 1930.
8. Raggalds Inn: Much extended in the 1980s.
9. Old coal pit. Disused by 1860.
10. Track to Nettle Hole coal pit. Disused by 1900.
11. Hop Houses. Later site of Raggalds School. From 1900 commercial/domestic uses.
12. The site of the 'Dross Pen' used for road-making materials.

Next towards Mountain is the former Colliers/Foresters Inn. Locals remember that the cellar would flood to such a depth that the kids could float around in a tin bath ! Next along is a two-storey house (Nos. 27/29) which was probably built in the early 1900s on the site of pre-1850 cottages. The adjoining low-deckers 31/33 were, until around 1900, 3 cottages. Each had one room, about 15 feet square, with door and window facing the road; a fireplace on one side; a 'shut-up' bed; and a door at the back into a 'scullery' – a storage space with a sloping roof only high enough to stand by the door. The middle one had, in the 1840s, been used by a blacksmith, hence the name Smithy Hill by which these houses are sometimes known. By the time house numbering was introduced, the far cottage was 31, and the other two had become one dwelling, 33. For many years Elizabeth Sutcliffe lived at 31. Right up to the 1950s, her one-roomed cottage retained an original 'shut-up' bed. And Elizabeth was terrified of having gas, electricity or even mains water in her house – she used the outside well and had a coal range for heat and cooking.

Next is a two storey semi 35/37 built around 1843 by John (or James) Holmes, and formerly known as Black Carr Terrace, at which time it was divided into 4 dwellings – there are two doors facing away from Mountain, and two for 'cellar apartments' facing Mountain. It remained as 4 (nominal) dwellings until around 1900, when the cellar accommodation was abandoned. The house, sometimes known as Hollins Rough or Smithy Field, was latterly known as Cluesmoor House. The property is symmetrical on a face (ie the placing of windows and doors) except for a coal grate on the road side and an off-set basement window on the opposite side.

In 1844 John Briggs, age 54, a Thornton School master, lived here – quite a walk to work each day! He had lived at Mucky Lane until a year or so before, where he gave private tuition at his home.

Finally a row at a right angle to the road, being a two-storey plus 5 low-deckers, all opening to a yard on the Mountain side, and known as Clog Row or Clog Street, and colloquially as Creddle 'Ead (Cradle Head) because of the outline shape of the block. Not to be confused with 'Creddle House' at Cragg Lane, Keelham, where the shape of the roof is like an upturned crib, and whose official name is Oats Royd. The low-deckers were referred to as "Low rahmdens" (low roomed ones). Two-storey cottages were termed "cham'er 'eights" – chamber heights, the bed chamber being high on the first floor.

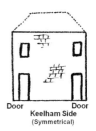
Door   Door
Keelham Side
(Symmetrical)

Door   Door
Mountain Side
(Symmetrical)

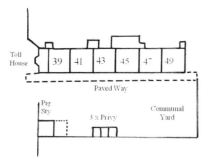

Clog Row. The toll house faced the turnpike road. The row was also known as Cradle (or Creddle) Head. It was built pre 1820.

Clog Row carried the numbers 39 to 49 (odds) from the road end. A paved footpath fronted the cottages. Opposite them (Mountain side) was a communal yard with 3 privies half way along, and a pig sty at the road end. In the days of the road being a turnpike, the tollkeeper's office was adjoining number 39, with its 'typical' bay window. No. 39 was listed as Raggles Bar, and 41 to 49 as Clog Street. The row was demolished around 1930.

Originally Clog Row was simply 'Raggles', but became Clog Row by virtue of William Dean, clogger, resident there in 1841. He and his son, also a clogger, moved to Mountain in the late 1840s.

Our contributor Rennie Briggs (1902-2001) was born at Raggalds (now Number 35). Around 1930 Rennie's family moved to the Cali and gypsies took over the Raggalds house. They, the Smith family, are remembered as being very noisy and usually yelling at one another as they walked to the Mountain, or down Lane Side where a married niece lived. Four daughters remained at home: Martha, who sold lace; Maggie, considered a good worker at Speak's Mill; Ann, the only one who could read; and Ellen, the youngest, who liked furs, gold earrings and gypsy bangles, but who was considered to be 'not all there'. She was known as 'the fancy one', and had a 'certain following' of local youths. Ellen also worked at Speak's for a while. The Smiths lived there from around 1932 to 1965. The grandfather (Bill) didn't live in the house – he had his vardo (caravan) in the field by the house. When he died, it and his possessions were burnt in the traditional fashion.

(Above) Black Carr Terrace as original, and (below) during alterations which raised the roof ! A single-storey extension has been added since

Charnocks

In the 1700s, the area on the Raggalds side of Soil Hill was known as 'Charnocks', referring to the family who occupied it. The farm Charnocks (Sun Farm) has a date stone of 1739.

World's End farm in 1996. Hartley Square is behind (left), Perseverance Rd (right).

The Charnock family farmed the land from then until the 1900s. However from the early 1800s until 1906 there was a beer house at the farm, originally called 'The Gin Pit' and latterly 'The (Rising) Sun'. The main family group seems to have moved to World's End in the early 1800s, with William as head of the house. On his death in the 1840s, the property passed to his son (also William), who lived there for more than 50 years. The name of World's End was changed to 'Farsides', around 1900.

Looking across the dewpond on Soil Hill, 1999, showing animal access corridor.

On Soil Hill top, beyond the new reservoir, is a dewpond and remains of a barn. The dewpond, which collected water from a spring and the frequent cloud covering and provided for cattle, is surrounded by a circle of upright stone slabs with a narrowing entrance allowing cattle to drink one at a time, but not fall in. It was probably constructed in the mid or late 1800s, perhaps using a filled-in pit. The altitude of Soil (Swilling) Hill is given as 1320 feet.

An unusual visitor at Raggalds! In May 2007 a Sea Harrier jet fighter arrived in kit form at Raggalds Farm. It was re-assembled in June, then disappeared again in October. In 2008, two planes were 'based' behind the farmhouse. It seems that the owner of the farm ran a business called Jet Art, recycling bits of planes, or whole jets, as ' ornamental items'.

HOUGOMONT and LAW HILL

Hougomont, this isolated group of buildings situated on Low Lane, Mountain, has many stories associated with it. It may be the site of a very old dwelling, since a supposed Celtic stone head was excavated a few years ago on the site of block [D]. In the 1770s a row of 5 single-roomed miners cottages was already there [A], serving the nearby pits. A 'semi' of two two-storey cottages was there by about 1812 [B]. A communal well supplied the water.

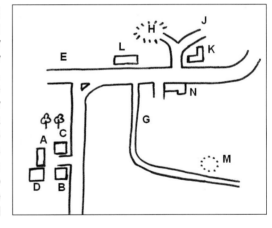

In 1854, Simon and Martha Mann had cottage [C] built, together with a garden with fruit trees. This was later converted by a Mr Swithenbank to two dwellings, one with inside coal cellar/outside pump, the other with an outside coal bunker and inside pump. In 1864 a final pair of cottages [D] were built. The area was called New Houses on maps. It is now Hougomont. The local name (c. 1860 onwards) was Traikle Tree. (See Place Names.)

In 1999, the colliers cottages were being used as store sheds and garages. The colliers cottage adjacent to [D] had been least altered, and an idea of living conditions can be realised. The stone roof slates rest on exposed beams – plenty of daylight can be seen through the slates. The floor is flagged, though compacted earth was quite common. At the front, a 3 feet wide door is in the right corner. On the back wall, a window. On the left wall, centrally placed, a large stone fireplace, 5 feet wide. In the back left corner, was the (double) shut up bed, about 4 feet wide for Mum and Dad Anyone else slept on the floor! The room is 15 feet front-to-back and 12 feet wide. Water was from a well outside, said to be still usable with the water level at 12 feet, and a depth of 25 feet. There is also a communal stone washing-trough. The two-storey cottages each had their own pump or well.

Block [B] has been completely re-built (nos. 5 and 7). It had become too dilapidated, with one cottage being used as a cow shed ! Block [C] has been partly re-built (nos. 9 and 11) and block [D] not much altered (nos. 1 and 3).

Until the early 1950s, lighting for Hougomont was by paraffin lamp. And mains water was not supplied until the early 1960s. It is claimed that pipes for gas lighting were found during renovation work in one of the cottages. If so, it would indicate that Speak's gas supplies reached here in the late 1800s, but were later cut off, probably when Halifax took over the supply.

Law Hill, as it is known today, is the area on the left down Pit Lane [E] comprising Low Well Cottage [L] and the much altered Law Hill Farm [K], which is said to have had such notable residents as David Essex and, more recently, TV presenter Christa Ackroyd. It was substantially altered in the early 1970s and for a while became 'Mountain Lodge'. After renovation in the 1990s, Law Hill farmhouse and attached barn became a 4-bedroom luxury house. The outbuildings were rebuilt as 8 stables. A paddock was created on the filled quarry area [H] behind Low Well Cottage. The footpaths to Nettle Hole [J], and to Clough [G], have been blocked off, though the track to Clough can be clearly seen from above.

The coal pit at Nettle Hole was still in use up to the mid 1800s. Those towards Clough closed earlier [M].

From around 1840, Clough became the long-time home of farmer Daniel Briggs. Together with adjacent cottages, it became derelict in the late 1800s, and is not to be confused with Clough House of 1902 down Laneside. Adjacent to Clough is their tip, which contains large quantities of oyster shells. Pre-railway days, oysters, together with cold punch, were enjoyed in gentlemen's clubs in towns where topical matters or business were discussed. The oysters were brought by mail– (stage) coach. In the railway era, oysters were brought by train and became the 'food of the poor', as is evident at Clough.

Seen from Hillside Place, across the main road are the 3 blocks forming Hougomont. The colliers cottages are obscured by bushes. Beyond (L to R): Low Well Cottage; Law Hill farm with integral barn; a barn (erected without planning consent – ordered for demolition but then forgotten about !); the light-coloured building far right is the new pumping station for Soil Hill reservoir; Thornton Viaduct stands behind it.

Poppy (or whatever) the pony grazes where the track lay to Clough and two pits. Hougomont is in the middle distance. The actual Treacle Tree was where the small trees are seen to the right. On the skyline (L to R): Two detached houses on the site of the Institute bowling green; Pickering (Hall) Kennels (trees behind); The Institute; bungalows on the tennis court site; the Co-op block; Grand View, modern house; West Royd; Harmony Place.

The old brick stable block at Law Hill farm (Photo: D Shepherd)

The fish pond, which had existed for more than one hundred years, behind Low Well Cottage   (Photo: D Shepherd)

WEST SCHOLES AND YEWS GREEN

On the plan, West Scholes is marked A to J, plus P. Yews Green is marked K to N.

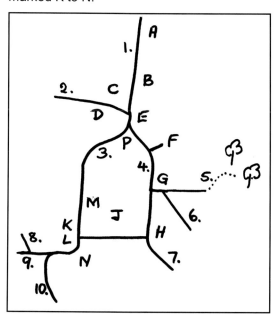

1. Laneside (to Pit Lane)
2. Carter Lane (to Queensbury)
3. Cockin Lane
4. Brewery Lane
5. Footpath to Birks Wood
6. Track (stone runners) to Old Shaft
7. Cow Lane leading to Mortons Fireclay Works
8. Bridle Stile Lane (to Lanes)
9. Brow Lane (to railway station)
10. Cockin Lane (to Thornton)
A. 'Bleak House'
B. Laneside, assorted houses
C. Wellfield House
D. Vicarage
E. 'The Junction' pub
F. Brewery, later Fearnley's Mill
G. West Scholes House/Briggs Villa
H. Ashgrove
J. Marley House
K. Yews Green Farm
L. YG & WS Mission and terrace of houses
M. Terrace of houses
N. Green Head Farm
P. 'The Bungalow'

WEST SCHOLES MILL AND THE FEARNLEYS

The former West Scholes Brewery of Briggs Brothers had been out of use from about 1903 to 1920. The property was purchased in 1920/21, by delver Walter Fearnley, together with this brother William (a former overlooker at Lister's Mill, Bradford) and a Mr Ramsden who had the necessary administration skills. It became known as 'Fearnley, Ramsden'. From the initial single loom, business expanded with the production of cut moquette. The original tower and chimney of the brewery were lowered one storey, and a new weaving shed was built on the right hand side of the building, using 'good quality stone from Haincliffe House', a demolished mansion in Hainworth Wood at Ingrow. Production of wire loom (uncut) moquette was introduced.

Walter's son Arnold was a butcher by training. He'd gone to London (age 17) with a train ticket and 7 shillings in his pocket. He took the first butchering job he was offered, in Walthamstow, where he became a curiosity ("from Yorkshire!") and well liked. His father suggested he might do some representing of the family business while in London, and he was so successful at this that he soon returned (with a London lady as his wife) to West Scholes. After a course in book-keeping he became the Mill Manager.

Virtually from the start until 1941, the mill worked round-the-clock, producing bright coloured materials for the Australian and New Zealand markets in particular. Products were carted (on barrows) from the mill to Queensbury station for transport direct to the docks. Eventually a small motor wagon was purchased.

Walter Fearnley loved machines and was usually to be found in his overalls tending the boiler (originally gas, then oil) and looms. Visitors often mistook him for 'one of the workers' and would slip him a few pence to be introduced to the Director – a situation which amused him greatly !

A local recalls: "When I wor a lad, I'd work in Fearnley's Mill for an hour or so after school, minding bobbins and so on, and get 2/6d a week. I saved up and we went to Lewis's in Leeds to get me a proper pair of leather shoes."

With the outbreak of war, the mill was requisitioned for storage by the Ministry of Supply in 1941. The place had to be stripped of machinery. Some machines were put into storage ('oiled up') at Field's Mill in Thornton. Others, like the big Jacquard looms were transferred to Feather's Mill, opposite the post office in Oxenhope. Fearnley's bought this mill, and went to considerable trouble lowering floors in order to fit in the big looms. But shortly after production began, the Admiralty requisitioned this mill for the storage of ropes.

West Scholes Mill seen from the track to Birks Wood. The size of Fearnley's extensions can be clearly seen.

Raw materials were rationed. In order to maintain their allocation, and to bring in money, an arrangement was made with Heckmondwike company Schleuper's to produce Fearnley materials. Thus after the war, Fearnley's ration was available and production resumed at Oxenhope and West

Scholes (gradually transferring back to West Scholes) as manpower became available. Eventually the mill at Oxenhope was sold to a Mr Taylor.

With the changing demands, the production of moquette ceased in the 1950s. The running of the mill had been taken over by Arnold's youngest brother Ernest in 1951. He brought in flat cloth looms to produce various materials including curtaining, using synthetics.

The company ceased in 1975. Bought by a Mr Spooner, the mill continued for a few years and was then let to a recycling company.

Above:

With the original buildings in the middle, Fearnley's added weaving sheds on the right and behind, and rebuilt on the left.

On the ground floor of the central 'tower' is the original coal-fired double oven, used when the building was a brewery. This photograph was taken in 1990.

YEWS GREEN & WEST SCHOLES MISSION

Since at least 1852, a cottage behind Yews Green Farm, being the old number 4, was used by Kipping Lane Independent Chapel as a Sunday School. In 1865 it is stated there were 75 scholars enrolled, and that new premises were being sought. However, the school closed soon afterwards.

In 1858 Rev. John C Hyatt became curate at Queensbury Parish Church. In 1865 he moved to the newly-built vicarage at Carter Lane. It is likely that he supported the idea of a Chapel/Sunday School at Yews Green. In 1871 one Samuel Robinson, age 60, of Yews Green, is listed as Chapel Keeper. This is most likely the new one organised by Hyatt. From 1881 onwards the property at 23 Yews Green remained 'empty' and from around 1900 it certainly became 'The Mission'. The ruins are to be found adjacent to Yews Green Farm yard. It consisted of two conjoined two-storey buildings forming an L-shape. The main door was fitted with a 'chapel-style porch'. It may be this porch, and other alterations, which are referred to in 1899 in the Queensbury Parish News: 'The Sunday School at West Scholes re-opened after extensions were complete'.

The final shape of the Mission building after the 1898 extension

In 1905 Rev Hyatt left Queensbury, and responsibility for the Church of England Mission transferred to Thornton Church. Its purpose was for 'Services, Christenings and the Teaching of the Children' and also served as a meeting place for Church groups such as the Mothers Union. The last christening held there was in 1925, being that of Peggy Daniels. Now staffed by Thornton Church (even the Reverend Tollit, incumbent 1909-1939, worked there), we know that Sunday School teachers from Queensbury Church would 'help out'. The Sunday School is noted, in the 1920s, as being 'worked by young ladies'. The Thornton Parish Magazine records that, on occasions, the offertories from the Mission were greater than from the main church !

In the 1920s and 1930s cricket matches were arranged with Yews Green Cricket Club at their ground nearby.

Educational entertainment was organised, for example in 1934 a Miss Whitecross presented a lantern slide show on 'Oberammergau', the lantern being borrowed from Thornton Grammar School. One wonders if the slides were being used on a circuit – the Institute at Mountain hosted the same event but presented by a different person.

Around 1933/34, Foster's (who owned the land and property around here) decided to sell. Thornton Church was not in a position to purchase. YGCC offered the use of their 'pavillion' for the Sunday School. A new hut, costing £200, was considered, but nothing further occurred. Around 1935 the Mission closed. Locals remember it was abandoned, still furnished and with books left behind 'just rotting away'.

The road made a tight turn round the corner of the Mission. Some years later a fatal road accident occurred there. Eventually the Council had part of the Mission building demolished, the road widened and the corner eased. The high wall was erected, using stone from the partly demolished Mission.

The Mission ruins, as seen from Yews Green Farm yard. The road is beyond the high wall on the left. The first house in the terrace was Daniels' shop.

Above (A) is the Sunday School run by Kipping Chapel. Above (B) is Yews Green Farm. YG & WS Mission is seen as a ruin above (C). Yew House is extreme right, foreground. A 2008 view from Scarlet Heights.

GRIMSTON GARAGES

The Grimston family came from Hull. After conscription in WW II, son John became an apprentice in Foster's Black Dyke joinery shop for about a year where his overlooker remembers "he couldn't even knock a nail in straight". Nonplussed, John began preparing and selling firewood at a yard opposite The Junction at West Scholes, the wood being scrap timber obtained from nearby Ernest Crabtree, who was busy demolishing wartime temporary barracks and Nissan huts. John was asked to make a garage for someone, and soon offered three designs. Leonard Harrison, a joiner at Foster's, worked with him and persuaded John to have only one design and to use jig construction. Two men made ends and two made sides, in wood and asbestos. Soon there were two wagons and around 8 employees, and John's sister Nora 'did the books'. Two skilled men could erect a garage in an hour – a wagon might have five or six garages aboard, for a day's deliveries around northern England.

Business was brisk, and in order to expand John bought the old Co-op Bakery at Hill Top in 1951. Concentrating on garages, he changed to using pre-cast concrete units (rather like the Wartime 'pre-fabs'). Trevor Bradley, a former Queensbury milkman, had joined Grimston's a couple of weeks before the move to the bakery. He tells that: "A single storey add-on was built on the Queensbury side of the bakery. This was done by the workforce who were employed one day a week on this, on a rota system. An office block was built by contractors at the other side. Grimston's had 6 wagons in the 1960s, and supplied nationwide. It was not unknown for drivers like myself to work 90 hours a week. My wage went up ten-fold, to £46 per week! John owned a boat - a big one - which he sometimes brought to the yard to work on."

In the 1960s John, together with two friends, was 'lost at sea' when sailing from England to Spain – the investigation into the incident was never fully resolved, but locals felt it wasn't an accident – more of a disappearing act for financial reasons. The business was sold and transferred to premises near Tong, Bradford. The old bakery and yard became a car wreckers. The 'office block' was completely clad in stone (an extra wall on the outside) and renamed Foxhill Lodge.

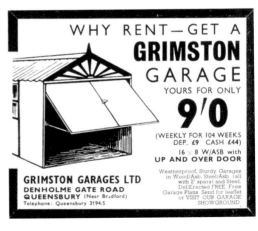

COCKEM / COCKHAM / COCKAN / COCKIN

Take your pick on the spelling! A village, documented up to the 18th century, featured in legend, but which then vanished. The name possibly means the homestead by the glen ('coc' = ravine, glen, valley, and 'ham' = homestead or village). Its location has not been noted on any map but a study of old records (by W Robertshaw, Bradford Antiquary Vol 6 1940) suggests the following: 'A family of the name Cockam (various spellings) lived in the vicinity from at least the 1300s. However, it is noted in the Clayton Fee of 1246 that Robert, son of Henry de Langley, was granted newly-cleared land at Cockam in the hamlet of Clayton. In the 1500s a Mansion House is mentioned there, and by the end of the 16th century there was a settlement of about 250 persons. In the 1600s the Mansion House was either rebuilt or replaced nearby'. West Scholes House could be a contender for the mansion: On the site of a previous (c. 1500 AD) house, the present building was erected for William Hird and his wife Isabel in the late 1600s – the date stone on the porch is WH IH 1694.

It is suggested [Bradford Archaeological Society] that the area is Medieval, with West Scholes/Yews Green occupying a tongue of land between High Birks Beck (where there are said to be ancient furrows detectable) and Hole Bottom Beck. West Scholes is thought to be West Scoles – the shed or barn to the west. [Scandinavian root skáli.] West of what? Of Cockan, perhaps?

In 1538 water rights were granted to the owner of the Corn Mill at Pinch Beck to divert water from Cockan (Hole Bottom Beck) via a mill race to his mill. The mill race can still be seen SW of Cresswell House.

By the late 1500s, there were many clothiers active in the village, producing light woollen cloths such as Shaloon and Callimancoe. Even in 1766 a Shalloon maker is mentioned at Cockan. However, by 1786 in the same area, Jeremiah Briggs is listed as a Callimancoe maker at Yews.

Land stretching from Mountain (Pineberry area) to the present Clayton Heights was known as Cockam Edge (but shown on maps as Clayton Edge). There were 3 districts of Clayton – Town, Heights, and Cockan. In the 1600s, Cockan was the most populous, and included Carter Lane (the main Bingley-Halifax road), and Fall Top. A Cockin Lane exists running towards lower Thornton from Yews Green, and another Cockam Lane was mentioned years ago running in the direction from Clayton towards Yews Green. Low Lane/Laneside at Mountain was referred to as Cockin Lane in the 1700s.

Considering Robertshaw's study of deeds, the Cockan estates seem to be mostly bounded by Carter Lane – Laneside – Birks - Hole Bottom Beck, which places the village around West Scholes/Yews Green. This seems a more suitable location than the boggy Hole Bottom valley itself. Ancient wells or springs are mentioned including Dakwell (probably a mis-reading of Oak); Hurst or Hirst (possibly Hird's) Well since we are told of a spring adjacent to the Manor House, and there is such across the road from West Scholes House; and Merwell, which refers to a boggy area; hence possibly Hole Bottom Beck.

The village is specifically mentioned in the legend of the Mixenden Treasure in 1510. Why the village should lose status and ultimately disappear in the late 1700s is not known, though one explanation could be simply a change of name.

HOLE BOTTOM

At Hole Bottom, across the road from Briggs pit and right by the beck (on the east side) was a building (early 1800s to about 1890). This is said (by historian Cudworth), to have been the second mill in the area, with Amblers at Mountain being the first.

In 1841, Joseph Firth (age 45) is shown as a 'manufacturer' here. His wife, and 12 other persons at Hole Bottom are 'Stuff Weavers', that is hand loom weavers. Many more lived in the West Scholes area. It is suggested that the property by the beck was a small water-powered spinning mill – even the pitiful flow of the beck would have been sufficient for this. Joseph probably lived at Hole Bottom Farm, adjoining his father's house.

The 'mill' seems to have been in use for 20 years or more, but in the 1840s Joseph took over the farm when his father died and by 1851 there were only four hand loom weavers remaining in the Hole Bottom area and the mill closed. On plans of the 1880s the 'mill' is shown as 'cottages'.

YEWS GREEN CRICKET CLUB

Yews Green Cricket Club was founded in 1921, using a field just beyond Ashgrove in Cow Lane at West Scholes. The Club moved to Mountain in 1957 and almost two seasons were needed to prepare the pitch which Speaks had abandoned years earlier. A new pavilion was opened in 1974, by the west end wall. On match days, high nets were hung from tall uprights along the wall by Mill Lane, to protect the windows of Luddenden Place, opposite. In the late 1990s, the landowner wished to sell the land for £22,000, and the club obviously didn't have the money. The club folded in 1999 and the pavilion was demolished that winter. Some members moved to the 'rival' club in Old Guy Road.

One former club member relates: "I'd help at t'Cricket Club I' Cow Lane, rolling t'pitch, and helping wi' t'scoring when there wor a match on. Then we'd get tea an' boiled 'am sandwiches – boiled 'am, mind you! That wor summat i' them days!"

More recent cricketers from other areas have sharp memories of playing YGCC at Mountain – mostly concerning the ever-present wind, and chasing the ball down the banking towards the main road!

TALES FROM WEST SCHOLES

Memories of Peggy Daniels

Peggy Daniels was born in 1924 at the first farm cottage at West Scholes House ('Briggs Villa'). She was christened at the Mission, and recalls attending Christmas parties there around 1930, when Santa came. The family moved to the second house from the top of the row opposite Yews Green Farm, then to the shop, which her father ran for many years next to the Mission. He had a pension of £1 per week as a result of gas poisoning in World War I, and was unable to work. Their stock came "from a firm in Halifax. Many folk baked their own bread. The yest (yeast) man called each Tuesday, and my father would get a lift in his motor van to go shopping in Queensbury. There was also Willy Ingle, a travelling grocer with a motor wagon." (George Daniels actually ran the shop in the late 1930s. Then it became Jessie Lovell's until it closed about 1951.)

When she was first married, Peggy moved to rented accommodation at Hole Bottom, owned by the Clayton Fireclay Company. "The Towers was occupied by the Whiteheads, a quarrelsome family, whose house had leaks all over, and lots of good furniture was ruined because they wouldn't do repairs."

West Scholes/Yews Green folk were more likely to go to Queensbury or Clayton for shopping and entertainment than to Mountain, although several attended Mountain Chapel, and the kids went to Foxhill. The teenagers went to Victoria Hall for dancing, and the Promenade in Queensbury High Street which was known as the 'Bunny Run'.

Memories of the Hainsworth's

Geoffrey Hainsworth and his brother Alan who owned and farmed Yews Green Farm confirm Peggy's stories, and tell us that the local kids went to Mountain Chapel "regularly and in all weathers after the Mission closed. There was a Whit Treat from Mountain – two coach loads were taken to Golden Acre Park, near Leeds", they remember.

"Morton's fireclay works had a cart, pulled by two horses, to take their products to customers. It was a slow journey, even on paved ways (which were called 'stone runners'), and it might be possible to do only one or two trips per day. The driver was Fred Lee who lived on Harmony Place, Mountain. There was also another haulier (Parson Ingle) at West Scholes, who had stables opposite the Junction."

When Hainsworth's moved to Yews Green Farm in 1936, the water supply was through seamed lead pipes from the adjacent farm. Mains water followed. Then electricity in 1948 and telephones.

"In the early 1950s a train from Bradford would arrive on a Sunday just before 10.00. Groups of men would walk from the station through West

Scholes to Birks Wood, to a gambling school". This would have been the 0915 Bradford Exchange to Halifax train, due at Queensbury at 0938.

Corinne Fearnley b. 1920

Corinne Fearnley, daughter of Arnold and granddaughter of Walter who owned West Scholes Mill, was born at No. 29 Laneside, at the time a back-to-back dwelling. She was frequently ill and seemed so on every occasion when her parents had arranged to take her to Queensbury Parish Church for christening – she was 23 before receiving this blessing ! As a child, she remembers playing out in Laneside, and how the local kids kept in close-knit groups according to where they lived: Laneside; West Scholes; Yews Green. She attended Foxhill School (Mr Kirkby was the Head, with teachers Miss Bartle, Mr Sharp and Ida Rushworth). There were two routes which the children could take – either up Laneside, Blind Lane and to school; or up Carter Lane, and Harp Lane (which they called Old Road) direct to School. In either case they were told to "stay on the pavement" – if there was one !

Corinne took piano lessons from Harry Patchett, a grocer from Chapel Street, Queensbury. He'd deliver the weekly groceries then give a one-hour lesson. Up Laneside was a small shop run by Mrs Dustan (bottom house of top block of 3, now all one and called Bleak House). At No. 27 lived the Ingle family. Mr Ingle had a motor wagon, used for grocery, coal and general haulage, which he kept in a shed and yard opposite 'The Junction'. It was known as Parson Ingle's yard, not because of any preaching aspirations but because his wife was of the Parson family (as in Taylor and Parson, Ironmongers of Bradford) and his proper name was John Parson-Ingle.

Corinne recalls her concern one Christmas Eve when Santa came to the door, and she wasn't in bed ! But she still got a present. The Santa was unknown – maybe from the Mission or the Cricket Club – but every child received a present.

Nellie Shackleton b. 1919

In 1932 Nellie and her parents Thomas and Annie moved from Horton to Mavis Farm, Cockin Lane. The farm was owned by her father and his three brothers. They kept pigs and poultry and sold to individuals and retailers, for example to Clayton Co-op.

Nellie had another year to do at school, so rather than change she continued going to Horton by train from Queensbury. Indeed, such was the frequency of the trains that she was able to come home for lunch ! She and her family rarely visited Queensbury, preferring to take the train to Horton or Clayton for shopping.

WW II was followed by the bad winter of 1947. By 1948 both of Nellie's parents had died. Her uncles wished to sell the farm straight away but she persuaded them to let her run it, at least for a few years – until 1950 in fact. She continued her twice weekly train rides to Horton to sell eggs or chickens.

Down at Yews Green, the first shop remembered was that of Mrs Wood, who was the sister of Charlie Ingle, the manager at Morton's at that time. The shop, like the other two, was a house-shop, selling bits of everything. It was situated at the bottom cottage of the Yews Green block, now number 15. Later, when this closed, George Daniels opened at the top of the block, number 21.

Charlie Ingle was an annual customer for Nellie – he'd buy goslings to fatten up (at Ashgrove) to use at Christmas gifts.

In the early 1900s the Schunimann family lived at Carr House, then moved to Mitchell Hall during the inter-war years. Karl Schunimann was German, and an engraver by profession. His wife ran a confectioners shop in Legrams Lane, Bradford, in the 1930s.

At the top house of Hollinwell Hill lived coalman Billy Vickers, of the Metcalfe and Vickers coal merchants company, well-known throughout Bradford area.

Nellie remembers visiting the Thornton Corn Mill down in the valley, where animal feed was prepared in the 1930's. Pigs were to be seen at most farms before, during and after the War. Pre-war they could also be found roaming free in Birks Wood.

Opposite The Junction was Grimston's yard, formerly Parson Ingle's. After the business moved to the old Co-op Bakery, Grimston kept pigs in the yard for some time. Fortunately the prevailing wind blew from the pub to the piggery! And also at the new premises for a while until locals below complained of the liquid run-off coming down on to their land. Grimstons offered pig sheds, with a 'working' demonstration shed on the Co-op site.

In 1955 Nellie bought Wells Head Farm in Queensbury. This has about 5 acres where for many years she continued to keep almost 100 pigs and about 250 head of poultry, supplying the Co-ops in Denholme and Skipton, and other retailers.

A medley of memories

A local born at Yews Green in the 1920s recalls:

"Yews Green Farm was rented from Foster's by Eddie Chadwick and his family but they were essentially evicted when John Hainsworth bought it. John left it all to his sons Geoffrey and Alan who never married, but they still maintained a nearby farmhouse in habitable condition just in case either might take a bride!" The 'nearby farmhouse' is Carter House Farm, which was the family's original dwelling. It was uninhabited and verging on derelict until the death of Alan in 2000. The next year Geoffrey had it 'modernised' in order to let it. Geoffrey and Alan were the last dairy farmers in this area, having a herd of about 3 dozen Ayrshires which they tended themselves, with help from Allan Atkins who was a milker for them for about 20 years (he moved to Carter House in 2003). Mr Atkins remembers Hainsworths as being meticulous farmers – everything had to be 'just so'.

West Scholes was the territory of the Briggs family from the late 1700s and through the 1800s. Apart from farm, quarries and the brewery, they had coal mining rights. One unfortunate family member, coal merchant Edward (son of William Briggs), was killed on 15 January 1871, not down a pit but by a runaway train at the Lancashire and Yorkshire (Exchange) station in Bradford. The train smashed through the buffers and into the station building, pushing Edward ahead. Subsequently his widow received £650 in compensation from the railway.

Pre-WW II, West Scholes was a typical hamlet. Down Laneside the road was of broken stone and earth, the pavements and kerbs (if any) were of cut stone, with a row of cobbles along the lowest side of the road to prevent erosion when it rained. Gas street lighting was present with the posts mounted on the road rather than on the pavement. Most of the houses in the terrace nearest The Junction were ivy-covered.

Near West Scholes House, the pavement was stepped down to a smart cobbled open yard. The garden, which was enclosed, had only one substantial tree and boasted a neat lawn. It all looked quite idyllic!

West Scholes House had been three dwellings. The end nearest Thornton was occupied by John Briggs who began brewing ale in the adjacent sheds. The Briggs family owned most of the land from Laneside down towards the brickworks, and Birks Wood.

The haulier mentioned by Hainsworths was Mr William Parson-Ingle. Although horse transport has been mentioned, he aspired to a motor wagon, and dealt in coal and green grocery as well as general haulage. His yard was opposite The Junction pub.

The row of cottages behind Yews Green Farm had no water supply until after WW II, and used the trough in Green Head Farm. This was also used by cattle – the humans were advised: "Wait till it settles after t'cows 'av drunk", before collecting water! In the 1960s Green Head Farm was occupied by Benthams, who kept hundreds of free range hens.

In the early 1960s several cottages in Laneside were semi-derelict, and eventually sold at real bargain prices. Further up, the property now known as 'Bleak House' was still cottages numbers 1, 3 and 5 Laneside.

West Scholes House, showing the carriage steps. Briggs' original brewhouse was in the buildings to the right. Note the stepped pavement. (Corinne Fearnley Collection)

West Scholes House in modern times, with rampant foliage

Laneside, West Scholes. Note the ivy-covered terrace houses and the gas lamp positioned on the dirt road. Arnold Feanley lived at No. 29, which is just left of centre. (Photo: Corinne Fearnley collection)

On the other side of Laneside was the coach house belonging to Wellfield, the well being by, or just inside, the coach house. Main access to Wellfield House was from Carter Lane. The property was erected in 1866 for William Briggs and his wife Agnes. It was built rather like a distorted L-shape, and had cavernous cellars. The date stone on the east wall has two Masonic symbols – the compass and square, and the level which may indicate that William was a Senior Warden. It is known that he was a Mason (1861 to 1874) in the Harmony Lodge in Bradford.

The modern house on the site between Brewery Lane and Cockin Lane used to be another business – Crabtree, Engineers. Around 1950, Ernest Crabtree erected a second-hand Nissan hut in the grounds of the bungalow [P] where his uncle lived. There was also a lean-to on the house, in which Ernest's son Lionel built an 'oxygen-fuelled jet engine'. On test, it propelled itself and the bench to which it was bolted through the brick wall of the lean-to. Ernest re-built ex-military equipment after WW II, when there was a big surplus. There is a local tale that Mr Crabtree was responsible for 'helping himself' to the abandoned Queensbury Vicarage, leaving only the front façade standing to mask his deed! Locals remarked that the remains "looked like a film set".

The site became a nursery (garden) run by Mr Zeltin, of Polish origin, in the 1960s. The shed was later demolished and the bungalow extended.

A few yards down Cockin Lane from Yews Green was Mitchell Hall, reached by a sweeping trackway on the left. It was originally a farm, occupied by James Mitchell in the early 1800s. It was demolished in the

1960s but the track exists and Cranmore House was built nearby. Opposite is Ashby House where Whitehead's had lived prior to building The Towers. Around WW II, Thomas Shackleton was at Mavis Farm on the left, and opposite was Green Dragon Farm (the former alehouse), and Cockin Farm. Next was Whitehead's New Works, behind which was Sun Wood Farm with Willy Yewdall, brother of Sam of the well-known animal feed merchants at Leaventhorpe Hall. Back at the Brow Lane/Cockin Lane junction, was Yew House, occupied in the 1930s by Mr Sigley, who made leather belts and straps.

West Scholes. The main road through the hamlet, today ! Ashgrove, built in 1874 by Haley Briggs, is featured. The road ahead (Cow Lane) leads to Morton's Fireclay Works. There is also a right turn just past the tree on the right back to Yews Green.

WARTIME WORLD WAR II

A Miscellany of Memories

As in many villages in England, life was not seriously disrupted. True, men left to go to war; there was rationing; women were transferred to work on munitions, on the land or in engineering; and troops were seen all around.

An ARP (Air Raid Protection) group at 'an undisclosed location'. Their job was to alert residents to possible air attack if they'd not heard the sirens; to guide those on the streets to the nearest air raid shelter; and to ensure no lights were showing at night.
(R Hunter Collection)

Messrs Shackleton and Greenwood (later owners of the Institute) were employed to clear the 'plantation' at Speak's Mill and to build an air-raid shelter, a structure some 70 feet long with concrete slab sides and roof, covered over with earth. (Mr Shackleton was also foreman of the Rescue and Demolition Squad in Queensbury area.) The ARP moved in to the Institute food preparation room – a room which is virtually underground.

Mr Stead, the curator at the Institute, would be seen in his woolly cap - his uniform - maintaining the building, the tennis court, the bowling green and the path thereto. On the left where this path to the green crossed the drive to Pickering Farm was a pagoda, locals recall. He also made peppermints and humbugs for the local kids. The 'Tute was open Monday to Saturday 0800-2200. The Library opened on Friday evenings. The two billiard tables were well used, as were the slipper baths. The ARP had taken over the Dining Room cooking area, but food was now required for the mill workers – the Institute Dining Room became the Canteen, and food was cooked in the caretaker's own cellar kitchen (next to the baths). A large Aga-style range was installed in the cellar kitchen, protruding into the room in front of the fireplace. Mr and Mrs Stead, helped by another lady, made wonderful meals – "you wouldn't have thought there was a war on", says Mr Stead's daughter. However, after about 18 months the rations were cut – someone had made a mistake – but the mill workers still ate well there! An opportunist (no name mentioned) also ate well on one occasion. A cow which had fallen in a nearby cowshed and had to be shot, was dragged by the farmer and others to the bottom of the field below the 'Tute, for collection by the knackers men. There it was, four legs stuck in the air – but by morning one had been sawn off !

Both Fearnley's Mill at West Scholes and part of White Castle Brewery near Raggalds were taken over by 'The Ministry' for food storage. There was a thriving 'black market' – eggs could fetch 4/6d a dozen, for example!

Pig farming was common, sometimes on a scale of 300 or more animals. The pigs were slaughtered at the farms – usually with a few extra for local bartering, these carcases being preserved in saltpetre and stored in empty chicken sheds. There were very few sheep, some cattle, geese "which took ages to pluck", and chickens "which could be killed, cleaned and plucked in three minutes", and which were sometimes boned and pressed into pint pots.

Raggalds Inn was such, providing accommodation as well as victuals. Several well-known performers of the time stayed there when in shows in Bradford. They are said to have included Jack Buchanan, a well-known song and dance performer of the 1920s/30s and who also appeared in many films; and Vic Oliver, who later became a radio broadcaster. Maisie Greenwood was the licensee there. The wife of a visiting officer allegedly stole money from Maisie's bedroom – it was big news at the time!

Troops (Seaforth Highlanders and others) were billeted at Queensbury New School (but not at Foxhill), with others at Wellfield and at the Vicarage at West Scholes. Off-duty, the officers frequented Raggalds; the other ranks went to the Mountain Eagle, the Fleece, or the Queensbury pubs.

At Pickering Farm lived Mr Robinson. He was a night watchman at the Mill. During the War he had 'Fire Watchers' to assist. These were employees, often women, who slept at the Mill in a room over the offices. They were provided with camp beds and blankets, and paid 3/6d a night (part of which usually went on a fish and chip supper) to be ready to provide first line action in the event of a fire caused by bombing or other eventuality.

In Mountain, Kirkbright's fish shop, like many others, produced 'steak' cakes to combat the shortage of fish. (A proper fishcake is a thin layer of seasoned fish trim between two slices of potato, dipped in batter and fried in beef dripping. 'Steak' cakes had sausage meat substituted for the fish. I mention this because many people, not familiar with Northern England, think of fishcakes as those revolting rounds of mushy mashed potato and minced fish, coated in breadcrumbs. Ugh!)

With the formation of the Home Guard, a rifle range was created at Oats Royd, Shugden. The local Home Guard group the engaged in exercises of defence and capture. One well-remembered incident concerned the 'capture' of the former Raggalds School. The attack group lost sight of the observers, and indeed, of everyone else, in thick mist, but persisted in their attempt to 'take' the school which was achieved late in the evening. However, all the 'defenders' had gone home long ago! But the attackers claimed victory because no-one had spotted their approach.

A few buildings in Mountain had electricity before the War. Nearby areas (like West Scholes) stayed on paraffin and gas until the late '40s/early '50s. At Yews Green, householders were offered electricity if they paid for installation, which a few did in 1949. Soon after, everyone was offered it for free, to the annoyance of those who'd paid !

Many locals remember the night of 31 August 1940, when the Luftwaffe bombed Bradford. Residents lined up by the Tennis Court and Bowling Green as the bombers made their run, seeming to circle round Mountain. The attack lasted about 5 hours. On another occasion after an air attack, (probably 14 March 1941), the kids down at Yews Green scoured the fields for remains of incendiaries. Further down at Morton's and at Whitehead's, some claim the kilns at the fireclay works were left open at night when an air raid was thought imminent, being a 'sacrificial target' intended to draw the bombers away from Bradford. Mr Wood, a fire-watch officer at Morton's at the time, says this was not so. The kilns just ran continuously as normal.

A stick of bombs was dropped near Morton's on one occasion but it is thought they were being dumped, not aimed. One just missed the shaft, the remainder landing parallel to the railway, towards Thornton.

On the railway during the war was a gang of Italian POWs, led by an Irish foreman, and based at Shelf Hall. They are remembered working at Queensbury station, and 'drank tea by the bucketful', which might well have been the way it was mashed ! They are recalled as helping with snow clearing, as were German POW's who were housed in Brow Lane, Shelf. One of the Germans stayed on and married an English woman. They set up an antiques business after the War.

The log book at Foxhill School tells of their wartime activities. On 1 April 1940, a Staff Meeting was held to discuss, among other things, Air Raid Protection Shelters. One was built in the school yard, being Anderson-type, partly sunk into the ground, in the northern corner of the school yard, and on the 23rd children were taken to the shelter, to get used to it. On 2nd May, the first timed evacuation took place (time taken to get everyone into the shelter was 4 minutes). On the 16th, the alarm sounded – evacuation time 5 minutes. Thereafter regular practices were held, and the time was eventually reduced to a more satisfactory 2 minutes.

Respirators had been issued, and had to be in working order and with the children at all times. Usually about 20% were faulty – the ARP people at the Institute dealt with faults in the evenings. More seriously, many children lost or forgot theirs. Often we read of a child being sent home from school for a forgotten respirator, and failing to reappear that day!

On 14 May 1940, the head teacher writes: "In view of the International situation and by order of the Government, the Whitsuntide Holiday (which had begun 3 days before) was cancelled and school re-opened at 9 am". Likewise the Summer Holidays were reduced to only 2 weeks.

The Ministry of Information Cinema Van toured the area now and then, giving useful advice on wartime 'survival'. On one occasion the children were paraded to the Hall of Freedom in Queensbury for a Ministry film show. "On arrival the premises were found to be locked and no preparations had been made. The children were dismissed." Sounds like modern times?!

Further 'information' was available in school. On 28 January 1941 the Head reports: "......... I allowed the Enquiry Office (at the school) who had an incendiary bomb to show it, and to give a few hints as to how to deal with one, to classes 1 and 2." One wonders what the 'hints' were!!

Potentially more dangerous was a break-in to an adjacent shed where the 'Military Authorities' kept materials. 14 December 1941, the Head Teacher writes: "I engaged with police from 1.40 to 3.40 pm searching for live ammunition stolen from the hut of the Military Authorities near the school building. Live rounds were recovered from various children". And the next day: "Twelve more rounds were recovered from two boys".

At Foxhill School, the Head Teacher had to teach, attend to admin and finances (eg collecting dinner money and savings money) and also DIY. "After 11.00 am the Head Teacher divided his class among the staff and for the remainder of the day was involved in fixing anti-splinter netting to windows". Continued the next day.

From 1 September 1941 evacuee children from London began to arrive, but, being few, this caused little disruption at the school.

Mismanagement was rampant in the provision of school meals, introduced in 1940. Although Foxhill School had been provided with a 'dining room' for children to eat their own food, and obviously cooked meals had been provided 'for those most needy' in the past, the Authorities decreed that the children who wanted school dinners should be walked to the Queensbury Modern School. On the first day, 21 April: "The food available was insufficient", we are told, and perhaps the dining space also. This idea was immediately abandoned. In future (from 28 April) the basement at Foxhill would be used. Food would be sent up from Queensbury Modern School at 12 noon, in containers. The Foxhill caretaker and his wife were to be paid 15/- a week to serve the food, and teaching staff were to supervise. As there were "insufficient food containers for the 91 children expected", the school was informed to restrict the number to 59. Who but an administrator would give a figure of 59? So Monday the 28th arrives – so does the cutlery and crockery but not the forms or folding tables, and classrooms had to be used for the next few days. Subsequently dinners often arrived 30 minutes to one hour late, which disrupted the school timetable, and there were shortages from the kitchens. Perhaps the catering standards were none too high. 24 March 1944: "Of 119 children who stayed for dinner, 65 refused the cabbage. A week ago, 60 refused." But then, kids will never eat their greens! And again: "A few grubs were found in the pudding – the second time this week." And other problems – 2 July 1943: "the dinner van broke down". The containers were eventually brought on a milk float "but most of the gravy spilled". The kitchen supplying Foxhill was moved to Denholme from 3 September 1943, which resulted in even more problems, especially in winter. 22 January 1945: "The Cooking Depot at Denholme is frozen up". So no dinners, although "Emergency rations at the school were sufficient for only 24". Other children were encouraged to go home for lunch, though staff and helpers managed to make some "other arrangements" – possibly courtesy of the Pineberry. On the 23rd: "all children sent home for dinner". On the 24th: "Dinners today but many children missing".

Although not the end of the School Meals saga, or indeed of other problems, the Head Teacher on 7 May 1945 writes, and perhaps with some relief: "The announcement was made this evening that hostilities in Europe had ceased and that tomorrow would be declared V Day. The school will not meet tomorrow and the following day."

HOLES IN THE MOUNTAIN

There existed many pits and quarries in the area, with coal, sandstone and fireclay being extracted.

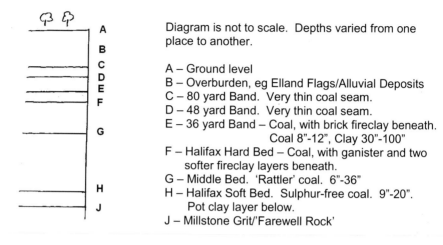

Diagram is not to scale. Depths varied from one place to another.

A – Ground level
B – Overburden, eg Elland Flags/Alluvial Deposits
C – 80 yard Band. Very thin coal seam.
D – 48 yard Band. Very thin coal seam.
E – 36 yard Band – Coal, with brick fireclay beneath. Coal 8"-12", Clay 30"-100"
F – Halifax Hard Bed – Coal, with ganister and two softer fireclay layers beneath.
G – Middle Bed. 'Rattler' coal. 6"-36"
H – Halifax Soft Bed. Sulphur-free coal. 9"-20". Pot clay layer below.
J – Millstone Grit/'Farewell Rock'

COAL

In the area of Wilsden, Thornton, Queensbury and towards Halifax, the coal strata are nominally as shown in the diagram. The bands called 80/48/36 yards are termed thus because of their distance above the Hard Bed. In some areas these bands are not present, and in many cases the distance above the Hard Bed is far less. In many places, faulting has occurred and any of the seams may outcrop.

The 36 yard coal rests on a clay bed used for brick making. The coal, being inferior, was sometimes left in place to provide a roof for the clay mine.

Next down is the Halifax Hard Bed. This coal gives out a great heat (used to fire boilers), but has a high sulphur content. Being associated also with iron deposits, it contains pyrites (locally termed Brass Lumps or Baum Pots). These were extracted at the pit head, or returned by consumers since they were of equal value by weight as was the coal. They were used in the production of Sulphuric Acid and of black or dark brown dyes. The bed rests on ganister and clay layers.

Next is the Middle Bed, a coal seam some 6 inches to 36 inches thick and known as Rattler Coal.

Finally there is the Halifax Soft Bed (not _really_ soft!) This is sulphur free, and was in demand for iron smelting. It is 9 inches to 20 inches thick on clay. Below is Millstone Grit, known to miners as Farewell Rock – "there ain't no more coal to dig for"!

From early 1600 to the early-1800s small coal pits were all over. Most of these in our area were known as bell pits or 'dayholes'. A bell pit is a narrow vertical shaft dug to a coal seam, often not more than 20 feet down. The miner then dug along the seam for a few yards in all directions. When it was felt that collapse was imminent, work would stop and a new pit would be dug. The distance between two chambers, preventing collapse, might be as little as two feet. Coal was hauled up in wicker baskets. Bell pits were operated by farmers who saw coal mining as an option to farming when labour was not needed for the latter. Thus these pits opened and closed (by boarding over the top) according to demand and labour availability. Some lasted for years – others were forgotten. Small scale mining was done by a short adit or level, also called a day hole, if a seam outcropped.

On the north west side of Soil Hill, beds down to and including the Middle Bed (Rattler Coal) outcropped. The area of Soil Hill and of Raggalds was littered with over 30 small workings listed pre-1850.

Our area is at the edge of the Yorkshire coalfield. Seams which can be up to nine feet thick in, say, Barnsley, are only a few inches thick here, hence not worthy of big investment. Neither are they suited to mechanisation. Our deepest pits were all opened with shafts less than 500 feet deep.

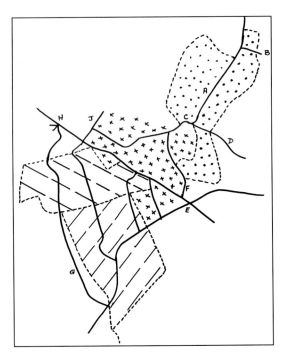

Approximate extent of mined coal 1854 - 1941

A. Cockin Lane
B. Low Lane, Clayton
C. Yew Green
D. Brow Lane
E. Queensbury crossroads
F. Thornton Rd/ Carter Lane
G. Roper Lane
H. Raggalds
J. Pit Lane, Mountain

\ Stocks Shugden
/ Stocks Ford

X X - Fosters Mountain End, etc
• • - Briggs Hole Bottom, etc

The extent of mining towards Thornton, Clayton and Halifax has not been determined.

Major operators of pits were: Foster, Stocks and Briggs.

The Foster family operated pits from c. 1810 to 1894, and were major landowners, not only in Queensbury.

Foster's acquired Harp Bottom on Carter Lane, Mountain End at Foxhill, and Ben Pit which is thought to have been the pit three fields below Harp on a line towards Hollingwell Hill. This latter pit, for which a drain was bored out to the steep valley to the north, was a particularly wet pit. A shaft to the north of Albert Road, opposite Hill Top House, is thought to be linked to Mountain End pit. Foster's pits were all linked underground.

The Stocks pit within our area is Shugden. The colliery shaft was at the end of the pit lane, mid-way between Bradshaw Lane and Roper Lane, close to Near Shugden Farm. There had been workings here pre-1800, gradually progressing east until under much of Mountain, across to Mountain End pit, and south almost to the Ford workings. The northern and southern boundaries were clearly defined by seven-yards faults, (the strata had moved up or down by seven yards), and additionally with 'water fast' areas (major water seepage) under Kitchen Lane and near Mountain Mill. Shugden and Ford (together with Shibden and Hanniker) were Stocks pits. Several other pits operated in the Shugden valley.

Stocks pit Shugden, about 20 years after closure. The winding house is on the right. Typical of the pits in the area, with the simple timber headstock.
(Harry Brooks Collection)

Joseph Briggs (born c. 1766) owned much of the land around West Scholes. He lived at West Scholes House and, although listed as a farmer, he was probably responsible for the development of coal mining on his land. In 1841 his son Joseph was innkeeper at West Scholes Gate Inn, but then inherited his father's coal business. He moved to Yew House and by 1851 he is shown as coal dealer, presumably of West Scholes Colliery.

By the early 1800s there was a pit along the border of Birks Wood: and a shaft (later called Old Shaft), to the Soft Bed in the middle of the field, half way between West Scholes and (the site of) Morton's. In 1831 we hear of 8-year old Richard Harper being "grabbed by the hair and shaken" by the gin horse he was driving at 'Ee (High) Birks pit.

The area was known as West Scholes Colliery. All that remains is a levelled area being visible near the West Scholes – Birks Wood footpath. Here was the final shaft to the Soft Bed. By around 1870 the colliery was abandoned. The stone chimney of the 'Old Shaft' winding house survived until about 1920.

In the early to mid 1800s, there was an active pit (probably Briggs) at Mavis Farm. A fault runs parallel to Cockin Lane, on the farm side, preventing expansion to the east. The pit is still visible.

An interesting view up Bradford-dale. Foreground right is Clayton Gas Works with their pit just across the road. Left is Albion Brewery (short chimney) with Briggs Fall Bottom pit (tall chimney). Beyond the brewery is The Thorntree pub with Thornton corn mill in the trees just to the right, together with the pond for supplying the waterwheel. (Frank Leonard collection)

After 1850, a new shaft was opened at the far side of the beck about 200 yards south of Sun Wood Farm, and a further shaft was sunk at Hole Bottom (Brow Lane). Other shafts at Holegate (Cockin Lane) and at Fall Bottom (Low Lane) completed this network. The Sun Wood and Holegate shafts were later used as vent shafts.

Briggs operated Holegate Pit (168 feet to the Soft Bed), which closed about 1880, and Fall Bottom (shaft 135 feet to Soft Bed) which closed in 1913. Fall Bottom, Holegate and Hole Bottom pits were all connected underground, and the whole area from Cockin Lane, Low Lane and to Brow Lane has been intensively mined, especially the Soft Bed seam.

At Holegate part of the headstock and winding house survived to around 1970, though most other structures were removed in the 1890s. The stone chimney which had a square base, octagonal stack and collar, survived intact until 1976/7, almost a century after closure.

At Fall Bottom, everything was abandoned and was still in existence some 20 years later.

When Joseph retired, his son William (who built Wellfield House in 1866) took over. By 1890, he had retired and his son John William had taken over. Soon afterwards (1893) John William opened New Pit (above Queensbury Station) with up to 50 employees. By 1913 all Briggs pits had closed.

Hole Bottom (Brow Lane) pit was situated just across the beck from Whitehead's Fireclay, and consisted of a shaft (about 160 feet deep to the Soft Bed), winding house, office at the road side, and the loading platform for the cable tramway. Across Brow Lane was another (exploratory) shaft to the Soft Bed, latterly used to drain and ventilate New Pit. The GN railway embankment was built around this.

On 7 October 1893 a fatal accident occurred at Hole Bottom pit. The use of pit props was 'at the discretion of the miners'. On this occasion, they had not been used and a roof fall killed William Jones and George W Stephenson who lie buried there. The pit closed a few days later, having been worked for over 30 years. Except for the office (still extant in 2008) the site was cleared almost immediately, and the field reinstated.

New Pit was hard by the Sharket Head/Hole Bottom tramway, on the right when ascending. A second shaft of unknown purpose existed on the Bell Wood side at this time. It has been claimed that spoil from the shaft at New Pit was taken down the tramway and dumped within the station triangle on the right of the tramway. Considering maps of 1893 and 1908, this could well be true. British Railways would have then added to this to create their siding for ash. New Pit is also referred to as Hole Bottom or Queensbury Colliery. Between this pit and Hole Bottom (Brow Lane) were two 'mares'. No mining was carried out between them except for a drainage/ventilation gate. New Pit worked Hard Bed (150 feet deep, seam 2'6" thick), and Soft

Bed (225 feet deep, seam 1'1" thick). Mining was done at either side of Queensbury tunnel but not under it except for several gates. Two further throw-ups occurred to the west, one of 5 yards and one of 10 yards, and running NW/SE, but these were mined across. The Hard Bed workings closed in 1902, the Soft Bed in 1911. The Soft workings extended from Harp Bottom pit across to Sharket Head and passed under Station Road, (near Greenland Farm) and towards the A647 at Scarlet Heights. A vent shaft is still visible in woodland on the left near the top of Station Road.

After being abandoned, many shafts were left crudely and dangerously covered over – usually a few timbers or railway sleepers. In the 1990s, local contractor David Shepherd was employed to fill the shafts, making them safe. Many were not dealt with – the land-owners would not permit access. Most sites were obvious, but in preparing to fill one shaft, others were often uncovered.

When filling in, the contractor had find the shaft, usually by moving some of the spoil (called 'Bluebind') and exploring the likely area. Although many were timbered over, some had been capped with two stone slabs. Having opened the shaft, a methane probe was lowered down. If this proved negative (ie safe to work), clean fill was tipped in to permit water flow (most pits were flooded by then); next bluebind to the shaft top, with a final topping of clean fill, and soil to landscape. Properly filled pits blend in with the terrain so as to be barely noticeable from the ground.

In our area, the final extraction of coal was from the clay mine of Morton's. In Birks Wood near the railway embankment and immediately below Morton's works is the entrance to an adit, being stone built, about 36 inches high and 30 inches wide. The adit slopes upwards very slightly, by about two feet over a tunnel length of about 330 feet, where it links to the bottom of Morton's winding shaft, then to the 'Old Shaft'. Two enterprising men from Thornton, John Brown and Roy Atkinson, took a lease after clay extraction ceased in 1965. Using the adit for access, they dug around the winding-shaft which Morton's had filled, and into the earlier part of the clay workings. A compressor provided power for pneumatic drills, etc, via a hose down the Old Shaft. In this part of the workings there was no problem with water, though other parts were now flooded. The tramway was still in place and was extended through the adit. From the entrance, a rough tramway was laid straight up the embankment to the works, the pit trucks being hauled up by means of an old motorcar engine attached to a winch. Simple screening was carried out.

The coal had been extracted from the Hard Bed. Consequently, as purchasers commented, "It spit a lot" as the iron pyrites in it tended to produce mini explosions when burnt. John and Roy sold locally '"for a few bob a bag". actually 5/- for smalls, 7/6d for lumps. The enterprise lasted about three years then the new owner of the site, Albert Danes, increased the rent significantly, so they removed their equipment and sealed the adit.

Later John and Roy turned to demolition work, one of their first jobs being the two chimneys at Morton's. Working to a quotation of £25 per chimney, they first marked the side exactly in the line they wanted the stack to fall. Working from this mark at an equal pace to either side, six or seven courses of bricks were removed and replaced with 3 x 2 timber (or whatever was handy). When they were just over half way round, the chimney collapsed where intended. Each stack was down in about 30 minutes. "A lot safer than Fred Dibnah's method", commented John.

According to the report in the local paper, "a single stack, 100 feet tall was demolished in 4½ hours". Take your pick!

A TYPICAL COAL MINE PIT HEAD

Thornton Top Pit (near Carlton House) was a Wood's shaft and was somewhat larger than our local pit heads. (Harry Brooks Collection)

SANDSTONE

Over our whole area were sandstone quarries, some mere outcrops, others huge holes in the landscape. Almost every farm had its own small quarry for farm use, being situated in the Delf Field. In the early to mid-1800s the most notable quarries around Mountain were at Hill Top (Harp Lane); by Fleet Lane; and at Shugden Head. The former was operated by David Knowles who had purchased the land in 1823. He had a high wall of excellent quality built around the area – and the project bankrupted him, it is claimed ! His quarry was purchased by a Mr Esau Gregson who used it as a private rubbish dump. In 1890 the Council ordered him to desist 'tipping fish, animal and vegetable waste' into his quarry – the pong was monumental !

The Mountain Quarry (between Glazier Road and Pineberry Moor) closed before 1900. The quarries opened from the 1870s at Pineberry Moor and at Hill Top (between Chapel Lane, New Park Road and the main road, in fact, at both sides of the main road) were developed and still operating into the 1930s. Hill Top was also known as Pickering Park Quarry, and from 1949 was used as a council rubbish tip being finally filled in the 1960s. It is now a sports field.

Left in splendid isolation, with quarrying on two sides, were numbers 2 and 4 Hill Top, at the end of Hill Top Lane which formerly cut straight across what was to become the quarry, to the top of Chapel Lane. Two rows of cottages (probably one-room low deckers) had been opposite each other at the Albert Road end of the Lane, extant since the late 1700s/early 1800s. 2 and 4 Hill Top were added about 1857. The two cottage blocks were demolished in1886/7 when George Farrar, stone merchant, acquired the land and quarrying began on a large scale.

A quarry was called a delf, and a quarryman was a delver. The stone was extracted with a plug and feathers, the latter being two metal bars shaped rather like metal tent pegs, driven into a fissure. Between them a plug, like a big mason's chisel, was driven in, causing the stone to split. Then along came pneumatic drills.

John Morton's had a quarry in the next field up Carter Lane from their farm at Lower Springhead from the late 1800s until the 1930s. Essentially it was just a big hole, with a steam crane there to lift out the blocks. Queensbury Council frequently complained about the mess from wagons on the road. The quarry eventually became waterlogged and was closed. Soon after, a child fell in and drowned. Upper Springhead Farm also belonged to Morton's. A fire which started in the kitchen burned down the whole place. A modern barn stands near the site.

Some quarrying continued at Soil Hill until the late 1900s, but stone extraction has now been completely abandoned in our area of study.

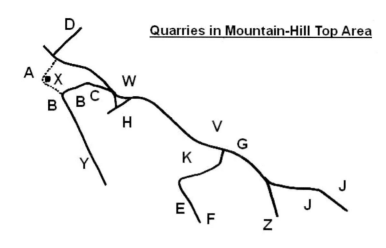

A	Behind the Cali	G	Fox Hill (Knowles'). Medium
B	Micklemoss Estate		1823-c.1850
C	Behind South View	H	Mountain Quarry. Small c.1870s
D	Behind Low Well, Pit Lane	J	Hill Top. Extensive c.1870- WWII
E	Upper Fleet	K	Pineberry. Extensive c.1830- WWII
F	Lower Fleet		

A to F All were small and closed by 1860

Localities
V	Fox Hill	Y	Old Guy Road
W	Mountain	Z	Chapel Lane
X	Guy House		

Rock & Heifer

Although there are none in our area, the nearest being Thornton, close to a large delf or quarry you might find a pub called 'Rock and Heifer'. This seems a nonsense name but, putting aside thoughts of bovines, it is suggested that heifer is a miss-spelling of a quarrying tool. An implement used by miners/quarrymen in the 1700s in Germany was a 'häckel' ('haeckel'). This, with a shaft about 75cm long, was used to test for cleave-planes in rock to assess the best way to cut or split. Could 'haeckel' have become 'heifer'?

CLAY

The existence of clay pits and fireclay products in this area can be traced back to at least 1650.

There have been many brickworks around the area, especially Thornton Fireclay; Whitehead's of Hole Bottom; and Drake's/Morton's. Whitehead's specialised in pipes, chimney pots, glazed bricks and ornamental glazed products for gardens, and Morton's made retorts for gasworks, and firebricks for hearths. Thornton Fireclay opened in the mid 1920s and was the largest and most modern in the area. Firebricks, pipes and glazed ware for the construction industry were produced. The last firing before closure was in March 1975.

On most sides of Soil Hill the 36-yard, the Halifax Hard, and the Rattler beds outcrop, and extraction of clay and coal was from open pits. The main workings were on the north side, with clay being the main resource. Clay was supplied to brickmakers around the area. These extensive workings have been in the Greenwood family since the 1880s. The family resided at Upper Shay Farm until the 1970s. After WW II Greenwood's purchased an adjacent farm in the hope of extending their workings but almost immediately found a fault (which runs between Upper and Far Shay farms) which prevented this. Extraction ceased in the 1960s, and the whole area has been filled and landscaped.

Pre- WW I to the end of WW II, a two-stage horse tramway ran from the pits, about 600 yards up the hill. A short upper stage led to a shute where the clay was tipped into a truck on the lower horse-powered line which ran almost straight to the A644, for transfer to road vehicles. This occurred at the side of house No. 102, which during WW I had been a blacksmiths, run by relative Fred Greenwood, where the horses were shod and tools repaired. All work at Greenwood's pits was done with a pick and shovel, it is claimed.

The reason for the unusual shape of No. 102 is not known, though it is thought to have been a collection point for 'pieces' (of hand-loom cloth) in the early 1800s, with a hoist on the front face.

Clay Workings Adjacent To Our Area

At Holmfield, fireclay products are still supplied by PSR (Parkinson Spencer Refractories). Now only specialist products for the glassmaking industry are produced, using the local clay (Halifax Hard Bed), which hereabouts is said to be of the best quality in Britain – indeed, the only other place where this type of fireclay is found is at Stourbridge. The bed extends from the Shibden valley (where the company still mines from an adit); under Queensbury, Thornton (Morton's tapped into the same bed) and beyond Denholme where PSR operated an open pit above Leeming until 2007. This clay which is soft and grey, will withstand higher temperatures than conventional (brick) clay.

The Hard Bed Seam

COAL 24" – 30"
GANISTER 12" – 18"
FIRECLAY. FOR SPECIAL APPLICATIONS 9" – 20"
FIRECLAY. BRICKMAKING AND GENERAL 40" – 50"

Above Holmfield, in the Ambler Thorn area, many adit entrances are still open though mostly abandoned in 1959. Some entrances are stone-lined, being about 30 inches square. Others are wood-lined and slightly smaller. The tunnels slope slightly upwards as you go in, to facilitate drainage. All are in a dangerous condition and should not be entered. The last adits closed in 1962.

When excavating at Denholme and near Cullingworth, old clay workings (dating from the 1700s or before) were uncovered, some only about 15 inches high. Other larger ones had wooden rails in them. The miners, and hurriers, crawled along these tunnels dragging a sledge to transport the clay.

In the Shibden valley are extensive old workings of both coal and clay, accessible by horizontal adits. Ancient flagged wagonways lead down the valley. Current extraction is only on the south side of the valley, however.

Shibden Valley Clay Workings, South Side 2003

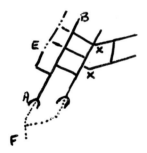

AB about 200 yards – still in use
E   working face in 2003
F   loading dock
X   closed adit/no longer used for access
••• railway track outside the mine
—   gate or level
—••— intended extension

Originally employing 7 or 8 men full-time, the operation now requires one miner and one trammer (hurrier), perhaps one or two days a fortnight, and it is intended to cease mining by 2010. Access to this mine is about 300 yards up the road from Shibden Mill Inn towards the Ski Slope. A stile on the left leads to a track which eventually curves right, up to a loading bay. On the corner, just above the track, are two old adits, with a third about 200 yards to the left. These gave access to PSR's earlier, now abandoned, mine on this side of the valley. From the loading bay, a length of L-girder track leads up to an adit, which is about 3 feet square and is now used to facilitate ventilation. The adit currently in use is adjacent to the loading bay, the entrance being about 3½ feet wide by 4 feet high. Both entrances are stone lined – originally all main tunnels were stone lined but now cost precludes that. The entrance roof is supported by wood, girders and metal sheet. The L-girder tracks are held on wide-spaced wooden sleepers, with loose stone and clay between. The clay bed is horizontal here, and the tunnels extend about 600 feet into the hillside. The seam is Halifax Hard Bed.

PSR require only the two clay layers immediately below the ganister. When a heading (tunnel) is made, these layers are extracted and trammed out. Any other material which is dug out is used to pack the sides of the tunnel, being held in with horizontal planks of wood behind the pit props. This enables a better working height to be maintained. The coal and hard ganister layer is the roof, and the working height at the face is about 3½ feet to 4 feet – comparable to the 'yard-and-six' in the coal mines.

When the heading has gone as far as the miners deem to be 'advisable', a parallel tunnel is begun, perhaps 30 or 40 feet away. As this progresses, linking tunnels are made between the two to provide air flow. These mines are all 'naked light mines', which means there are no flammable gasses so illumination can be (and was) by candles – though battery lights on helmets are now used. Water seepage is minimal. At the work face, the miner (who wears leather knee pads) kneels, or sits on a low buffet, and uses a long-handle pick to extract the clay. This is shovelled into the wagon right behind him. The trammer removes it. Where tunnels join, the wagons run on to a metal plate where they are man-handled on to the next set of tracks. The loading bay is covered with metal plates for manoeuvring. A miner can produce about 10 to 12 wagon loads (about a ton) of clay per shift.

The mining method here is known as 'pillar and stall'. When the headings have progressed far enough, the miners work backwards, extracting the clay from between the tunnels, leaving pillars of clay in place to provide support. Formerly the (expensive) pit props were then removed, being dragged out with a ratchet device known as a sylvester.

Paul trams a tub from the Shibden Pit. Trucks in our local pits held about 100kg of coal or clay.

On the north side of the valley PSR operated an open pit. The coal and clay layers can be seen, and an earlier level. On the left are two one-wheel low-sided barrows, seen upside down. The man near them uses a pneumatic drill. The tramway wagons have the usual flangeless wheels, running on L-section track. Effluent seeping from a pig farm above could make conditions rather smelly, I'm told!

The present PSR mine on the south side. The working face in the mine. The last clay miner in the area, Paul Scrimshaw, sits on his stool holding his pick. The tramway track is in the foreground.

Thanks to Paul Scrimshaw and PSR, Holmfield, for information concerning clay mining and photos.

POTTERIES AROUND SOIL HILL

Soil Hill was covered with a rash of coal pits and sandstone quarries in the early/mid 1800s, but from the 1700s, clay deposits were being worked and several potteries were established in the area.

The earliest documented venture was by Jonathan Catherall from Anglesey. He opened a pottery 'opposite Raggalds Inn' (Raggalds Farm or perhaps the pit by the Colliers pub) in the 1760s. The Catherall family lived at Keelham Hall Farm. Finished products were stored there, and years later stocks were 'rediscovered'. In 1784 his son Samuel opened a pottery at Denholme Park. This was run by the family for about 80 years. Below Roper Lane was Small Clues Pottery, opened in 1800 by James Robinson, later becoming Robinson and Wade, and closing in 1879. Also in the early 1800s until around 1870 was Hill Top Pottery at Rosemary Hall on the south-west side of Soil Hill.

Jonathan Catherall moved his operations almost immediately to the west side of Soil Hill, opening Swilling End Pottery. Jonathan's grandson Samuel opened a small pottery at Bradshaw Row, which closed after a couple years.

By the late 1870s, Catherall's had sold out and Swilling End had become a chicken farm. In 1883 it was re-opened by John Kitson, then sold to Isaac Button in 1897, who opened a new pottery further down the hill at Coal Lane nearer the A629. Run by Isaac, his sons and grandsons, it remained in production until 1964. The works was built in an L-plan, with a kiln inside one arm and the chimney outside the corner, all of brick. They produced earthenware products and slipware, and what is technically called 'black pottery'. The clay used was a fifty-fifty mix of common brick clay and fireclay from beneath the Hard Bed.

Inside Isaac Button's Kiln

Most kilns have upward draught, that is the heat only flows upwards. This kiln at Soil Hill was designed for downdraught and this gives a more even heating of the kiln.   (R Hunter Collection)

In order to prepare clay for processing it is heaped up and allowed to weather for one to two years, being turned occasionally. This improves its plasticity for moulding. It is crushed and mixed with water in a 'blunger' (a machine with paddles for blending). It is sieved and dried (usually by the sun but Soil Hill employed heat from the kiln flue). The clay is re-wetted when required; homogenised in a mixer; extruded as a continuous bar from a 'pugmill', sliced into blocks and allowed to rest ('sour') for six months then pugged again before being cut for the final working mix. For some time prior to Button's pottery closing, Isaac Button (grandson) was the only worker, doing everything from digging clay to delivering the pots!

The pottery was bought by Don Greenwood of Upper Shay Farm, who for a while, produced domestic ware and tried making 'Glass Pots'. These are made of fireclay, with a high silica content, and are vessels for containing molten glass from which the glass blower extracts his material. The venture was not successful.

Soil Hill Pottery was partly re-opened in 1973 but closed again in the 1980s and is now derelict, although with listed building status.

Interviewees who lived at Raggalds and Perseverance Road in the early 1900s remember how, as children, they'd walk over Soil Hill to Button's pottery where they might be allowed to make a pot, then go on to play at Rock Hollow. They'd collect their pots a few days later.

Soil Hill c. 1964. The last Isaac Button is pugging clay, which snakes out in the foreground. (R Hunter collection)

MORTON'S FIRECLAY WORKS

The early history of the fireclay works is uncertain. We know that John Morton (born 1847) was works manager at the family brickworks (Joseph Morton's) in Siddal, Halifax, living at 2 Mortons House. He moved to Ashgrove, West Scholes in the early 1880s. The brickworks was operating as John Morton's in 1884. John died in 1927. His son Lewis John Morton is shown as co-employer with John in 1901, and soon took over from him.

Until 1895 extraction of clay was probably from the area just west of the shaft at the Works. It then moved further west-south-west reaching the final West Scholes Colliery shaft by 1901. By 1924 the Old Shaft was reached. Mining continued south-south-east almost to Marley House and Green Head Farm by 1960. Beyond was the Great Mare fault – actually several faults. Exploration was done due east, with a shaft to the 36 yard bed and a bore to the Hard Bed, near the footpath over the railway; and a shaft close to the railway east of Mitchell Hall, to the 36-yard bed. These served as ventilation shafts for extraction in the 36-yard band, but excavation in the area was abandoned in 1957.

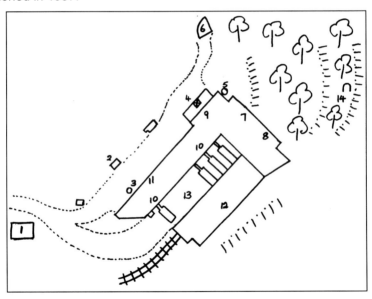

<u>Plan of Mortons Fireclay Works 1960</u> *(Not to scale)*

1. Office
2. Toilets
3. Kilns Chimney
4. Winding shaft/pit head
5. Boilerhouse chimney
6. Reservoir
7. Boilerhouse
8. Cable winding engine
9. Crusher and clay feed hopper
10. Kilns. There were nine in total
11. Moulding floor & joiner's shop
12. Siding & loading bay shed
13. Open bay
14. Adit, opened about 1904.

A view from the footbridge around 1980. The nearest building was the office, with the boilerhouse chimney and pit head gear to the left, kiln chimney to the right; the end of the moulding shed, and the dark loading dock shed is straight ahead. (D Shepherd)

Chimneys! In this view from Law Hill Farm, probably dating from the 1920s, we note the two chimneys of Birks (Morton's) Fireclay Works, with the pit head gear between them. The clay, seen white, is piled high (A). Lister's Mill chimney can be seen above, across the valley. (B) is the West Scholes Colliery (Old Shaft) winding house chimney. (C) is Whitehead's Cockin Lane works ornate chimney. Low Lane (D) leads to Clayton. The dense woodland is Birks Wood, before it was thinned out. Right foreground is the site of Clough. (R Hunter collection)

Morton's worked in close co-operation with, or was actually part of, Drake's Constructional Gas Engineers of Shay Lane, Ovenden, a company founded by Jonas Drake in 1847. Morton's trading name changed over the years, for example John Morton & Co Fireclay (Thornton) Ltd in 1941 (Birks being in Thornton district); John Morton Fireclays Ltd in 1952; and their products were marked latterly as John Morton & Co, Halifax. All the administrative work for Morton's was done at Drake's. It is even recalled that lunches were made in Halifax and brought to Morton's. Morton's abandoned mining in mid-1965, with an underground workforce down to half a dozen men. Drake's ceased trading in 1966/67 due to the collapse of the coal gas market.

Access to the works was via Cow Lane, running from The Junction pub (Brewery Lane) straight through West Scholes until near the railway (a footpath continues ahead to a second-hand footbridge over the former railway), where the lane turns left and is paved with firebricks. Entering the works area, one roadway turned left, another descended, the manufacturing buildings being in between. The upper roadway passed the moulding shed, the crushing plant and the shaft. The lower roadway led to the kilns, boiler house, storage shed and loading dock.

From about 1900, extensions were made: At the south side near the shaft; the corner of the moulding shop was extended towards the gate; a west side extension, together with a new boiler house chimney (c. 1920). A gantry and structure were erected close to (7), with a railway track beneath it. It is likely that the coal that was mined was pushed in the corves along the gantry and tipped into a hopper, or into rail wagons below for use elsewhere. It is shown on OS maps from 1908 to 1930 and on an aerial photo of 1947, but had disappeared by 1960.

After 1920, a new larger office was erected, to the east of the gate, in the area now called Birks Farm.

The winding shaft at the Works was about 180 feet deep to the Hard Bed, which was roughly horizontal through most of the mine. The 36-yard bed was between 40 feet and 70 feet above this. Both beds were sources of clay, and some Hard Bed coal was taken also. The extent of the mining was about 1000 feet south and 1200 feet east of the Works.

Many firebricks are scattered around the area, usually marked 'John Morton & Co. Halifax'.

The remains of Morton's, 1996. This part accommodated the clay storage, crushing and mixing (above) and the boiler house (below). The windows (upper left) belong to the moulding floor.

The faulting which prevented further development had occurred with earth movements in primordial times when the Pennines were being formed.

The fissure created filled with a low grade sandstone, unsuitable for building and often associated with the presence of water. Fissures of this type are called mares, and despite its name, The Great Mare, this fault is quite a localised one, and there are several others in the area. 'Mares' are rarely crossed because of the unstable nature of the area. However, if a fault is a 'Throw up' or a 'Throw down' (depending on which direction you are mining), this is when the earth has not split open but simply moved vertically, putting the seams out of alignment. By means of a steep gate (or lift), these were often crossed, and mining continued on the same seam.

For some years a manager, Mr Charles Ingle, lived at Ashgrove (also known as Morton's House) and he'd go into his cellar to count the number of charges being used to blast the ganister, as a check on efficiency. The explosives were stored in a small building about 50 yards south of the works' reservoir.

Towards High Birks was the adit, considered by some only an 'escape route'. It is not shown on pre-1900 plans, and might have been created to assist drainage. Two shafts to the east were used for ventilation and were surrounded with brick walls, as was the 'Old Shaft'.

The soft clay and ganister were hoisted to the surface in corves. The soft clay was piled outside to 'weather'. The ganister was tipped into the crusher – a pair of rollers, belt-driven from the boiler house below. First some larger lumps might have to be broken by hand. The crushed product fell into hoppers for storage until required, when it was mixed with water to form a stiff slurry and run to the brick makers. Some was made into 'standard' firebricks of 1", 2", 3" thicknesses. Other was mixed and moulded for gas works refractories, with joiners on Morton's staff making the moulds 'to specification'.

These retort mouldings might be up to 10 feet long. The moulded products were moved to the 'Hot Floor' above the kilns – clogs had to be worn here because of the heat – then after 24 hours lowered into an empty kiln. The kiln, beneath which was a system of air tunnels to provide draught, was sealed then fired from below. The chimney flue for the kilns was at the eastern end of the moulding shed.

Workers in the Moulding Shed at Morton's in the 1930s. (Jacob Ellis Collection)

After several days, the fire was allowed to die, the kiln was broken open at the front, and the still hot bricks or mouldings barrowed out to the huge storage shed erected in the late 1920s, which covered much of the yard and railway siding. The workers wore thick gloves and clogs as protection from the heat. A gantry crane in the shed facilitated moving the larger items, though the railway wagons were easily loaded by a variant of the sack cart, the wagons having drop sides and being on a level with the loading bay. The railway wagons could be hauled into the shed by cable (powered from the boiler house), and run out again by gravity. There were two sidings provided adjacent to the railway (see also 'Railways'). Some products were taken out by road, originally by horse power, later with a Bedford 'O' articulated wagon.

The site of Morton's works, and the railway trackbed from Cockin Lane to Headley Lane, is now owned by a land-fill company. All of the works has been demolished. The pit head gear was cut off at ground level and the shaft sealed. The reservoir was breached and drained. The air shafts have been filled and the brickwork removed. The 'escape adit' can still be located in Birks Wood, though now impassable.

Miners at Morton's. The man without a cap is Charlie Ingle, the Works Manager. The flat caps had extra padding, for protecting the head! The photo dates from the 1930s. (Jacob Ellis Collection)

Charles Ingle's father James William had been a yard labourer at Morton's around 1900, and Charles learned brick-moulding there, eventually becoming Works Manager.

At Morton's, in 1920, a miner was paid 27/6d for a six-day week. Of this 7/6d went to his 'trammer'.

Some employees recall a 'canteen' on stilts, located in the large store shed. Personal washing facilities on site were said to be missing, except by using the canteen sink !

Mr Jacob Ellis recalls working at Morton's for several years in the 1930s. His father worked there as Blacksmith/Engineer. Four Shire horses were kept in stables opposite the trough at West Scholes. They were harnessed one in front of the other to haul Morton's wagons up from the works to Queensbury.

WHITEHEAD'S FIRECLAY WORKS

Julius Whitehead was born at Farnley, Leeds in 1838. He trained in brickmaking, being noted in 1861 as lodging at a house on the corner of Wakefield Road and Foundry Street, Bradford, close to Bowling Brick Works. Soon afterwards, he married Caroline Townend and moved to Dewsbury then, about 1868, moved to Darwen, Lancashire, where he advanced to become manager of a sanitary pipe makers.

Having amassed some capital, he moved to Southowram Bank, Halifax, probably around 1880/81. He bought the brickworks at Hole Bottom which seems to have been in existence since at least 1840 but which in 1879 is shown as owned by Asa Fawthrop. Asa's father James had been a 'Gentleman Landowner' in the Clayton area. He died before 1871 and presumably left the brickworks to Asa, who seems to have been pleased to dispose of it. Fawthrop's brickworks was across the beck almost opposite Briggs' pit and consisted of a small workshop, single kiln and chimney, about 20 feet above the beck, with a shaft and winding house at the roadside. The workshop site can still be seen.

Mr. Julius Whitehead.

Julius came to live at Ashby House, Cockin Lane. Later he constructed 'The Elders' for his eldest son Ernest, and 'The Towers' for himself, moving there about 1891. Julius remained at The Towers until his death in 1908. He was a Freemason, being twice elected as Master of Warren Lodge, Halifax. He was an inventor, and had several patents including the 'Acme' Solid-socket Pipe Making Machine.

Claude, the younger son of Julius, took over the running of the business, living at The Towers with this wife Annie May. They had three sons – Alec, who moved to Pasture Lane when he married Annie Hough from Bradford in 1947, and Harold and Vernon who lived at home and never married. All three sons were motorbike mad, Vernie and Harold riding rough, and Alec touring Europe. If burglars were discovered at Cockin Lane, the lads would roar off, with the intenion of literally running them down. All three were inventors: Vernon had a radar background with the RAF and experimented with electrics and early TV (working with Baird); Harold was into engineering and gardening; Alec was a prolific movie maker, and the only one really interested in the family business. Claude died in 1952. May died in 1963, and soon after the house and gardens were in serious decline. Maintenance was lacking; the pool constantly sprung leaks and was drained; the conservatory where Harold kept his exotic plants, butterflies and young trout, was demolished.

A charming study from the family album thought to be Claude Whitehead and his wife Annie May (née Lowe) on tour in their thoroughly modern motorcar. (A & M Whitehead collection)

The Towers, showing the conservatory and the roof greenhouse in the pre-dome era. In the foreground is part of the frozen pond. (A & M Whitehead collection)

Alec died in 1977, Vernie in 1983. Alone in The Towers, Harold lived in the kitchen, with his perpetual soup-pot, a stock of Carrs Water Biscuits, and bits of motorbike scattered around. The rest of the house was closed. Harold, died in 1987. The Towers was sold immediately to a Mr Clarke, then a couple of years later to a Mr Sharples. It was completely renovated, and has since changed owners again.

*The three inventors – (L to R) Vernon, Harold, Alec.
(Both photos: A & M Whitehead collection)*

Around 1970, Vernon poses behind The Towers with the Dome which was to house the reflecting astronomical telescope which he and Harold made from scratch, including grinding the mirror. Note relief tiles on the wall. On the right is the indoor swimming pool, formerly housing the domestic electricity generator.

Using a temporary tramway, with 'L' rails, Whitehead's workers excavate for the ornamental pond. On the left, the low 'kiln-like' structure is in fact a pile of tiles, some of which have already been laid (behind the spade on the left). The pond was completed by 1907. (Clayton History Group collection)

The launch of the 'Rin Tin Tin'. At the ornamental pond, with tiles in place (see above), family and friends gather. Back row left is Vernon, Claude wears a hat, with Harold in front of him. Sheila Murgatroyd, the young lady on the left, was second cousin to the three brothers, and inherited much of the Whitehead 'fortune'.

Vernie made a radio-controlled boat also, which he could command from the roof of 'The Towers'.

(A & M Whtiehead collection)

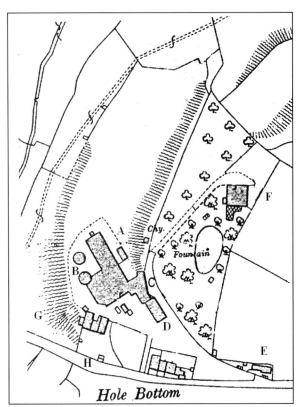

Whitehead's Hole Bottom Works and Houses 1908

Chy – Ornate Chimney

A – Downdraught Kiln (rectangle)

B – 2 updraught Kilns (circles)

C – No. 2 Shaft/ Winding House

D – Stables

E – The Elders

F – The Towers

G – Site of No. 1 Shaft

H – Brow Lane

A view from the railway bridge in 1990. Brow Lane is below. The cottages in the foreground were owned by Whitehead's. The chimney stands in splendid isolation, with The Towers on the left. The empty flat area was the Works.

'The Elders' stands at the roadside at the entrance to the track running behind the Works up to 'The Towers'. It is faced with glazed brown bricks and heavily embellished with glazed relief products. It was first occupied by Ernest Whitehead

The Towers is a listed building – including the observatory and telescope. This view is from 1990.

Turning again to the business, fireclay and coal were mined from the 36-yard seam, via Fawthrop's shaft [G] 54 feet deep. Julius immediately began to build a much larger works higher up the valley side on land also purchased from Fawthrop. This opened around 1883. Clay and coal had to be hauled up a tramway into the works. A tramway across the beck from Briggs' pit brought 'better' coal to the works incline.

When Briggs' pit closed in 1893, better coal was brought in by horse and cart from Green Clough pit, Alderscholes Lane, which Julius purchased at that time for £312. Although it had been worked for over 40 years, it provided access to 3 coal and clay beds. The pit engine house remains, and was latterly used as a brass foundry in the 1940s.

Also about 1893, a new shaft, 127 feet deep to the 36-yard seam, was sunk behind Hole Bottom works. The tramway into the works was closed and Fawthrop's shaft became a vent shaft.

Coal from the 8-inch thick seam in the 36-yard band was used for the initial heating of the kilns [B]. The 'better' coal was needed for the main firing. Beneath the 36-yard coal was 4 to 5 feet of clay. The whole of the workings extended east of, and parallel with, the beck, for about 1100 feet northwards, with a breadth of 500 feet.

On the side of the Works facing Hole Bottom Pit were two circular updraught kilns. By 1894 a downdraught kiln [A] at the back of the Works was added and the new covered headstock and winding house [C] had been joined to the main building (together with the boilerhouse) next to the stables [D]. Some of the Works was embellished with Whitehead's relief and glazed bricks. Also by 1894/5, an imposing ornate chimney was erected behind the Works, replacing the plain brick one which was on the Brow Lane side. The chimney [Chy] was, legend tells us, built by son Claude in one day! Another common misconception is that the 'cup' decoration on the chimney was in honour of Bradford FC winning the FA cup in 1911 – an amazing premonition by Claude ! The chimney had a 'fluted' top but this 'disappeared' at some time after the works closed.

Claude was a strong man and proud of it. He liked to show his workers that he could work faster than they could. During a brief spell at digging he reproached one worker for not digging as fast as he did. "It's all reet fer thee', responded the worker. "Tha's nobbut 'ere fer 'alf an hour – I've another eight hours ta do".

From 1901, the company, Julius Whitehead and Sons, Clayton, had a showroom at Century Buildings, Sunbridge Road, Bradford, opposite the bottom of Barry Street. Another premises supplied building materials and ironmongery.

This photo, taken in the winter of 1889/90, shows 'The Towers' under construction. The original Whitehead's works chimney is just to the left. The shorter chimney (far left) is for Fawthrop's shaft, which was still in use by Whitehead's. Also see 'Railways'.
(R. Hunter collection)

Below:
Whitehead's circa 1905. Note the decorative products on The Towers, the chimney and the stables block on the right. The building in the centre carries the date 1894. Far left are 2 kilns.
(Graham Hall collection)

Chimney at Hole Bottom Works

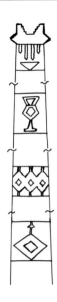

Top Removed

GLAZED DESIGNS:
White Background, Blue Pattern

White Background, Brown Cup
Green Cup Centre

Brown Background, White shape
Green Diamond Centre

Brown Background, White Shape
Green Centre

All other parts brown unglazed bricks

/\/ Plain parts omitted on diagram

In late 1908 Whitehead's pit at Hole Bottom was abandoned. New Works had been established at Cockin Lane close to, but not utilising, Holegate Pit which, having been worked out, had closed around 1880. There was no decoration at New Works except for motifs on the square-section chimney, similar to the one at Hole Bottom, and which was to the south of the main building. It was about twice the height of the nearby Holegate Pit chimney. The two down-draught kilns were within rectangular structures on the north side of the building. Initially the clay was dug from open pits a few yards to the south, and transported on a man-powered temporary tramway. The 36-yard band was used, the pits being around 60 feet deep. Further pits were opened to the north east, and some drift mining was carried out, with tramway wagons being hauled up the gradient from the adit by steam winch.

Chimney at New Works
Brown brick. The motifs are brown glazed brick on glazed white bands. White collar. Brown top. Also there was a plain white band at about a quarter of the chimney height.

From the late 1920s the Hole Bottom works was slowly demolished, everything being cleared except the ornate chimney. The round kiln bases were still discernible into the 1970s. The New Works closed in 1969. Notwithstanding this, in 1974 Whitehead's applied to extend the clay pits, but West Yorkshire County Council refjected this. The site was sold cheaply to a Mr Granville Crossley, on condition that he cleared the buildings and filled the pits. He had a bungalow and outbuildings erected, now in the occupation of his son. Many stone walls in the area are incongruously topped with Whitehead's square- or triangular-section glazed hollow copings.

Many of Whitehead's products were salt-glazed. In the 1950s the procedure would run thus:

Wednesday early morning, the fires were lit to begin heating a loaded, sealed kiln, and using the inferior 36-yard coal. Throughout the day and Thursday the kiln temperature would be raised slowly to 430°C, then allowed to rise faster so that by Friday, in the very early hours, the fires could be cleaned out, refired with better coal, and the temperature now raised at about 1°C per minute until, by around 0900, 1170°C would have been reached. The fires (there were sixteen per kiln) each received one shovelful of salt, thrown well in. This was repeated three times at half-hour intervals to allow the temperature to recover. After another half hour, the fires were left to die down slowly to maintain 900°C for several hours. On Saturday morning the fires were drawn and the kiln left to cool until broken open on the Monday morning, to be emptied, then refilled on Tuesday and the process repeated. Over 30 tons of stoneware were fired in a kiln, with coal consumption of around 8 tons.

In 1900 chimney pots cost from 6/-. Regarding decorative features, Julius reckoned that "if it can be made in wood, then it can be made in fireclay".

Cockin Lane Area

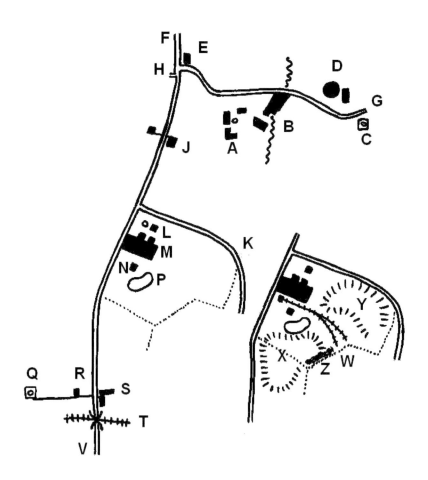

A Fall Bottom Pit. Closed 1913.
B Albion Brewery c. 1869-1930.
   Fat Refinery from 1932.
C Gas Works Pit.
D Gas Works.
E Thorntree pub.
F Chat Hill to School Green.
G Low Lane to Clayton.
H Track to Thornton Corn Mill.
J Cresswell House.
K Track to Sun Wood.
L Holegate Pit chimney/shaft.
M Brickworks.

N Ornate Brickworks chimney.
P Brickworks Pond.
Q Mavis Pit, pre-1850.
R Mavis Farm.
S Green Dragon/Cockin Lane Farms.
T Thornton-Queensbury Railway.
V Cockin Lane to Yews Green.
W Tramway to drift with winding
   engine by the works.
X Clay pit from 1904.
Y Later clay pit to c. 1960.
Z Crag.
···· = Wall

Whitehead's second (and last) wagon was this maroon Commer, seen at New Works. Thornton church is across the valley. The timbers on the right are the Holegate pit headstock. The site roadways were old railway sleepers.

A view from New Works chimney. Cresswell House is at the top of the picture, with the mill race to the Corn Mill running in diagonally from the right. Cockin Lane is on the left, with the entrance gate to the works. The Holegate pit chimney is central, with the headstock to the left and the fenced-off shaft. The winding house has disappeared. The works is below, with two rectangular kilns (dark roof left, light roof right). (Both A & M Whitehead collection)

TALES FROM THE PITS

Many early small local pits were simply shafts, with access by rope or ladder. Coal was usually hauled up in wicker baskets or 'skeps'. Hauling power was by person, or by horse winding a gin. A few collieries were moderately deep, with proper winding gear and, to some extent, safety procedures.

The name Ellis Barrett occurs in several pit tales. Born in 1848 (that is, 6 years after the Act was passed forbidding children from working underground) he was employed in 1856 as a hurrier in Shugden Head Pit. His father ('Ill Dick'), mother and sisters also worked in the pits. Ellis was one who told later generations of how gas blow-outs in the pits were regularly burned off. The scorch marks on the tunnels could be seen in many pits. The miners would hope to get rid of pockets of gas quickly, otherwise they might be told to use safety lamps instead of candles – candles gave more light! Sometimes a lad (referred to as a 'penitent') was employed to crawl through the tunnels at night with a candle on the end of a stick, to burn off any gas accumulating in roof hollows. Surprisingly, no explosions occurred !

Prior to Ellis Barrett's 'retirement' from mining around 1889, there was an accident at Hole Bottom Pit where he worked. In a roof fall, he suffered a broken collarbone when he and Greenard (Greenwood) Drake were briefly buried.

Down a mine, the colliers might work naked on account of the heat and lack of ventilation, though women often retained a garment around the waist. So far as underground work was concerned, there was no distinction made between the sexes, though women rarely worked at the coal face. Males could be of any age but females were mostly 6 to 21 years old. [1840 Mine Commissioners Report.] Miners had to buy their own candles, explosive powder and fuses, and sometimes to pay their hurrier. A miner would have to prepare his own props and walls.

In the older pits, the sledges used to move coal in the tunnels did not run on rails, so one can imagine the effort required to manoeuvre them when full. Wicker baskets were used also. Children from about age 7, and young women, wore a harness which was attached to the sledge or basket. In some pits they had to crawl on hands and knees.

On the 1851 census, Joseph Briggs (West Scholes Colliery) is shown as employing 20 boys and 13 girls. This has then been amended to 20 men and 13 boys, but one suspects the original entry might well have been the honest one!

Women of poor families would return to work straight after giving birth, and if no-one was able to look after the baby they'd take it down the pit with them, leaving it in some dry area to be tended as often as possible.

At the shaft bottom (t' Pit'ee) in larger pits, the Hanger-on (t'Inger-on) attached the corve, skep or basket to the cage or rope, then the Banksman (t'Pooller-off) took them out or off at the shaft top.

By around 1880 mineworkers not actually engaged at the coalface had 'protective clothing' in the form of a leather cap and a leather waistcoat or jerkin, leggings and clogs. By 1900 it was back to normal outdoor attire, until the 1930s.

It had been the norm for children as young as 4 to be used as 'trappers' (opening and closing the ventilation doors). Such young children sat in total darkness. There would be a string tied to their arm and the door so they didn't have to grope around in the dark. They'd have water and food (if the rats didn't get it !) for the 10 or 12 hour shift, 6 days a week.

The Mining Act of 1842 prohibited underground working by women and children under 10 years of age. It was frequently ignored. On the rare occasions when Mine Inspectors visited our 'back-of-beyond' area, and if they could gain access at all, they might be made most welcome with a tot or two of whiskey, so that the underage workers could be spirited away before the inspection. In this area, children were working at the coal face up to 1878, since they were able to fit in to the thin seams better than men.

Young lads were sent by their families in other parts of the country to areas where there was work. In 1871 the census records Abraham Smith, coal miner, with his wife, son and daughter, taking as boarders from Liverpool two lads aged 12 and 14, working as coal pit boys. And in Luddenden Place, Greenwood Drake, coal miner, and his family had boarders from London, being two 13-year-old lads listed as coal miners.

A certain 'Willie Nigger', a collier, took time out from boozing at the Fleece to let his young son down the pit (presumably for night duties). On stepping from the skep, the lad encountered a live but badly injured horse which had recently fallen down the shaft. (Horses were not used underground at any local pits or mines.)

A Mountain collier called John Willie Drake was killed while working down Ford pit. Born in 1876, he lived on Luddenden Place, then moved to 12/14 on the Cali in the 1920s. He'd been a collier all his life and was known as a very methodical worker with an eye for safety. While working on his side, a large block of shale fell from the roof, crushing him. His hurrier raised the alarm and others came to his aid but, in the cramped conditions, the block could not be shifted. The foreman arrived, and morphine was administered to John Willie, so that a fellow miner could split the fallen block enabling it, and John Willie, to be moved. He died soon afterwards, and his body was taken to Mountain. On the day of his funeral, 6 miners carried his coffin to Queensbury church, and the mine manager and colleagues attended the service. He was buried in the Council cemetery. He died in June 1937 at 61 years of age.

It was not only the miners who were susceptible to pit accidents. In early 1871 an inquest was held at the Fleece Inn, Mountain, into the death of John 'Dobbin' Greenwood, 63, of no fixed abode. John was 'regular' in Mountain area, sleeping rough. One Thursday night in January he'd slept in the pit top hut at Foster's pit, Mountain End, Foxhill. On the Friday morning, he helped the workers to clean the hut and to sweep the snow from around the pit head. During this cleaning, a pair of old trousers caught fire in the hut. John said he'd take them to the waterbutt by the boiler, to dowse them. It is thought that smoke from the trousers obscured his vision and he fell down the shaft onto the cage which was about halfway (73 yards) down. It took some 3 hours to retrieve his body. He was 'laid out' by Ann Kirkbright, 34, of Mountain, who stated that "his brains had been knocked out, and there were other injuries".

In many pits conditions were really cramped. Tunnels were of minimum dimensions, since to enlarge them would be to produce more spoil (waste material) which was uneconomic. Everything was done in a crouching position, though at the coal face the collier would work laid on his side, using a pick, then pass or scrape the coal back to his hurrier, who would load a corve or baskets for transporting outside, or to the bottom of the shaft. In order to progress at all, more than just the coal had to be excavated – although the coal seam might be only about 18" thick, the tunnels might be opened out to "a yard and six" which was 42" high. The top would reduce down to about 36" over a period, as the ground settled.

The miners' illumination was candlelight until the early 1800s, when the Davy lamp was invented. Miners claimed that candles gave more light!

Apart from the obvious spoil heaps and flakes of coal, little remains of the coal industry on the Mountain. However immediately before Foxhill School (travelling from Mountain), a higher boundary wall indicates the site of Mountain End pit. The access for colliers, called t'bob'oil (bob hole) because you had to bend or 'bob' under it, is still obvious. "There's many weary bones passed through that hole", intoned older residents. Also in the wall running down the field is an integral but blocked up archway some 54 inches wide. Were this excavated down, the level of the pit yard would be found, but the area has been 'landscaped'. The pit site extended from the bridleway Blind Lane to about the Mountain side of Foxhill School yard and was known as Mountain End Pit – nowhere near Mountain End Farm! It closed in 1891. The underground workings extended down to Harp Bottom and Ben pits, and towards Hougomont.

The "bob 'oil" at Mountain End pit. Donald Haigh who is 5' 9" tall, stands by to demonstrate the size of the aperture. The builder of the wall was paid 1½d per yard.

Little remains visible of Mountain End pit. This filled-in archway gave access between the pit head and the yard. It can be seen from Foxhill School looking towards Mountain.

The coal pit which closed last was Ford. There was a shaft around 480 feet deep to the Soft Bed. The main tunnels, or roads, were wide enough for a double track tramway. The Soft seam was about 16 inches thick on a 4-feet thick bed of clay. The workings extended about 400 yards east and west of the shaft, and about 1300 yards from Ambler Thorn towards Mountain. Two faults were crossed – an upthrust of 20 feet, and a downthrust of 10 feet, under Old Guy Road. The Hard Bed seam which was about 70 feet above the Soft Bed, connected to the Shibden workings It was worked less extensively.

Stocks Pit at Ford

The shaft took two years to sink. Production began in 1900 and was expected to provide 500 tons per day. After closure it became the site of the Council depot. (Harry Brooks Collection)

A former miner who worked at Ford in the 1920s relates the following:

"The work space at the shaft bottom (the 'Pit'ee' or 'Piteye') was about 9 feet wide by 7½ feet high. After about 12 yards this dropped to 4 feet high, and the passageway about 7 feet wide. There was a double-track tramway one for full corves (wagons), one for empties, on a slight uphill grade. The wooden sleepers (ties) were about 3 feet apart, and the trackway on the empties side was covered in wax droppings from lads' candles. After about 500 yards, the tunnels split. There were turn plates to manoeuvre the corves, and the track became single, the tunnels narrower and undulating. There were 'turn offs', side passages with a height of a "yard and six" which settled to only 3 feet high. Here was the 'stall' – the workplace at the coal face – where the miner would remove his clothes. The seam is about 17 inches thick. A working face of about 8 yards wide would be exposed, with the collier working on his side. In the centre of the area, an additional 18 inches height was blasted out for the corves to be run in. As he works, the miner uses props for about 4 feet, then uses the waste that has been blasted out to back-fill where the coal has been extracted. The props, and rails, were moved forward to the next face. A miner might fill 12 to 17 corves per shift. "

The hurriers usually worked without trousers – they had to stride from sleeper to sleeper in a semi-crouched position and trousers would soon split! They had many scratches on the back from contact with the low roof. In the 1920s, a miner might produce 2 tons per shift, for which he'd be paid 8 shillings per ton.

Mr John Brown of Thornton was the last coal miner to work in our area. Having been a member of Mine Rescue teams which became a legal requirement from 1911, he has provided the following comments:

Apart from the possibility of collapse, the following hazards may be present in coal and clay mines:

Blackdamp: This is a lack of oxygen in the atmosphere due to poor ventilation. If a naked flame will not burn, blackdamp is likely the problem.

Firedamp: A build-up of methane. Small accumulations, initially at roof level, could be carefully burned off. Any spark or flame can cause an explosion if sufficient methane is present.

Stinkdamp: Gases produced by rotting timbers which reduce the oxygen content of the atmosphere.

Dust: Fine dust particles in the air produce a flash fire or explosion if ignited.

Flood: Water may pour in from the surrounding ground if a part of the mine gives way.

In our area, slow flooding occurred in some pits. If the slope of the seam was appropriate, this could seep out.   Otherwise pumps had to be used, which were expensive and brought about closures by making the pits uneconomical, though most pits closed because they were worked out.

In Thornton Colliery/Fireclay pit, water drained towards Green Lane, where there was an access shaft by the viaduct. Periodically a miner would proceed from the main shaft, clearing blockages on the drainage channel as he went – because of the high iron content in the water, mini dams frequently impeded the flow. It was claimed that a bottle of Whiskey was let down to the bottom of the access shaft as an incentive for him ! Variations of this tale include: that the miner was given a £2 bonus; or a new suit. Having reached the level of Pinch Beck the mine water drained out, producing an ochre colour (from the iron) and providing the local name of Red Beck.

John Brown in 2007. Age 71 and happily retired !

At Ford, and at Mountain End, small accumulations of methane occurred. At Morton's, there was blackdamp.

Incidentally, the 'damp' term does not refer to wet but to 'dampf' (the German word for vapour).

When a pit was opened, the shafts were brick lined, using a technique of building downwards. Except in small and shallow mines, at least two shafts are needed for ventilation, and from the early 1900s on safety grounds. If the mine is an adit, then two adits are required.   Doors within any mine control the air flow. The tunnels were referred to as 'gates'. The main tunnel, used for transporting materials, was the 'roadway'.

Coal and clay were extracted in the local pits by the 'pillar-and-stall' (also known as 'post-and-pillar') working – pillars of coal or clay are left to support the roof. In the more modern pits elsewhere 'longwall' mining is used whereby the whole seam is extracted, the roof being supported with props.

If only clay was taken, the coal was often left to provide a roof. If coal was taken later (as Brown and Ackroyd did at Morton's), great care had to be exercised – if too much was taken the roof could have breached and the wet material above, rather like ready-mix concrete, could have quickly flooded the gate.

One of the many sayings of miners was: "Big 'uns follow little 'uns". If small pieces fall from the roof, get out because a collapse may be imminent!

In some local coal mines you'd find them 'swept clean'. No coal left. But at others, coal was loaded into corves with a fork, so that the smaller pieces (slack or smalls) were left behind because they fetched a lower price. In fact, if you dress your home fire with smalls, even coal-dust, you'll find it fuses together to form blocks which then burn like lump coal.

When mining coal. a lot of dust may be created. It could block your nose and make breathing difficult. Many miners took snuff down with them.

Some pits had a main shaft serving two seams or levels, the separation at Mountain End being about 180 feet, at Fall Bottom about 50 feet, while at Morton's it was only about 20 feet. The winding cable, which was checked and marked every day to correct any stretching (so that the cage would stop at exactly the right place), was controlled by the banksman. By a system of bells, buzzers and indicators, the miners could contact him for raising or lowering the cage. On occasion, the method failed – Mr Brown recalls a miner who fell from one level to the shaft bottom when the cage moved upwards unexpectedly. He crashed right through the timberwork which covered the sump at the bottom and was killed.

LOCAL PERSONAGES

John Bates b. 9/4/1815, d. 1903

Born of a poor family, he received a rudimentary education in a 'private school' at Small Tail run by one John Briggs.

Then he went to Ambler Thorn school until age 12 when his father, a banksman, was killed in an accident at one of Foster's pits (probably Black Mires, Queensbury). John had to go to work to help to support his mother and sisters – fortunately mum and a sister soon got work since John received only 3/- a week as a gin horse driver for Foster's! He trained as a weaver, at Ambler's then at Foster's. By the time he married at 30, he was earning 12/- a week, having retrained as a power loom weaver at Foster's, then at Speak's.

He lived in one of the two small cottages opposite Mountain Mill with his wife, Fanny, and 4 children. He seems to have been a man of community spirit in that he wanted to help the under- privileged, and became politically active with the Chartists who 'fought for workers rights and better working conditions'. However, they became militant – they would drill on Soil Hill and practice guerrilla tactics in Birks Wood – resulting in confrontations with mill owners and the law, and the death of a local Mountain man during a skirmish in Halifax. John would have nothing to do with physical violence: He joined the Temperance Society instead!

He is listed in the census as a Tea Dealer. He was a School Attendance Officer for Clayton Board, and active in the early years with the Queensbury Co-operative Society.

John Bates, his wife and two of four children

Albert Edward Briggs b. 1869

Albert was of the 'Briggs of West Scholes' family, being the son of brewer Haley Briggs, when they lived at West Scholes Gate Farm. He lost an arm in an accident at work when a young man. In 1920 he bought and moved to Travis Farm Cottages. He was a skilled joiner and cartwright, and repaired drays for Fielding's Brewery. Fielding's always used horse transport – they tried a motor wagon once but reverted to horses. Albert kept cows, pigs and chickens, and he was able to milk a cow faster and more effectively than many folk with two arms, it was claimed. Compatriots referred to him as the 'One Arm Wonder'.

A Mr Law had a Dennis motor wagon for general haulage. Together they became Briggs and Law. On summer evenings and on Sundays the wagon was converted into a charabanc, and excursions were run to, say, Knaresborough for 2/6d.

In 1935 Albert bought the Foresters, and converted it into a private house, which he sold in 1936. In 1939 Albert sold Travis Farm Cottages to Bethel Cockroft who was resident at 25 Raggalds, the former Foresters property.

Mrs Turnpenny b. 1907

Her mother was a Bastile child, sent from the workhouse in Liverpool and adopted by the family at the Gray Horse. Mrs Turnpenny went to the Church School (Russell Hall). She became a Sunday School Teacher at the Parish Church, and sometimes taught at Yews Green Mission. Her 'cousin', Jimmy Cooper, was a postman who died on his rounds at Scarlet Heights, in the snows of 1947 – presumably of a heart attack.

Mrs Turnpenny worked at the Queensbury Co-op during the War, and occasionally deputised at the Mountain Branch: "The shop was quite small, with a display counter, shelves and a side office. The manager, Edgar Ambler, had one assistant. At the back, and on the floor above, was storage and 'weighing out' space (goods arrived in bulk and were re-packed). A hoist at the side of the building brought in the bulk produce to the top floor."

Mrs Turnpenny recalls that very few Mountain residents were _really_ poor – indeed some seemed relatively well off. Some families in Luddenden Place "weren't short of a bob or two", and one resident, a Mr Edward Rake, even displayed a monocle (considered very aristocratic). One woman of a 'better off' family was a known kleptomaniac and all staff were warned to keep an eye on her. Those not so well off (often with large young families) could get vouchers from the Council for use at the Co-op for food. Often cigarettes were supplied instead – it was all money to the Co-op !

Mrs Turnpenny and her husband were licensees at the Fleece, then at the Pineberry until the 1960s. She retired to Cullingworth.

Ratcliffe Feather 1882 - 1948

Ratcliffe Feather is a personage remembered by many from their youth on the Mountain. Born the son of a farmer in Oxenhope, when adult he occupied Shugden Farm near Raggalds, and also Warmlee Farm lands. He had a butcher's shop at Range Bank in Halifax (now demolished). He allowed his animals to graze on Roper Lane, and if anyone dared to complain he went ballistic ! During World War I he supplied horses to the military, getting good prices. When demand fell, and until 1937, he supplied horses for meat, to France it was assumed. He was known as the 'Dead Horse and Donkey Dealer'. The carcasses of horses which died were said to be thrown into the old pit shafts at Shugden. One wonders what archaeologists of the future will make of that? A society based on equine sacrifice? The graveyard of dozens of pit ponies?

He drove a horse and trap, and is well remembered for his weekly visits to the Mountain Eagle – "a frightening personage, with a black moustache, dressed in bowler and cape, driving his trap like the Devil himself". He also visited other hostelries, and is remembered at the Royal Oak in Queensbury where, having arrived in his trap, he'd become so intoxicated that at closing time he'd be loaded back into it, the horse would be sent on its way and would take him back home where he'd sleep in the trap until he sobered up.

Sam Gledhill
12/8/1857-17/9/1918

When Sam married Harriet Crowther, they moved into the Mountain area (Mount Pleasant) and had a daughter Minnie in October 1880. It seems likely that Harriet died at or soon after the birth. Sam then married Dinah, daughter of Alfred and Mary Pilling of Mountain. They moved into Harmony Place, then by 1901 to 5 Fascination Place, with additional daughters Maud (1891) and Phyllis (1896). When Speak's sold this property in 1954, Maud and Phyllis bought it for £235.

In the early 1900s, before the Institute was built, Sam seems to have been the organiser or treasurer of a 'gentleman's social club'. A club is remembered at one or more of the first three

Sam Gledhill with daughter Phyllis at Birks Wood (Phyllis Gledhill Collection)

houses of Hillside Place. This seems the most likely venue, although there was a Working Men's Club at this time situated between Hill Top Farm and the former Hill Top Lane, at the side of the main road. However, this is thought to have continued through WW I. Perhaps Hillside Place was the 'Mountain Club' wrongly ascribed to the Institute? Nothing is known of its activities other than brief extracts from accounts from the winters of 1904 and 1905, as in the following examples:

1904				1905 (In Total)	
7lb	Monkey Nuts	@	2½d/lb	16lb	Nuts
2lb	Chester Cut	@	4/- /lb	22lb	Monkey Nuts
2lb	Black Bird	@	3/8d/lb	28lb	Barcelonas
½lb	Thick Twist	@	3/7d/lb		

Chester Cut, Black Bird and Thick Twist were tobaccos. Barcelonas are Hazelnuts (filberts). Possibly the nuts were for some winter treat for local kids, or else the Club members were nut addicts !

However, in September 1909 the club was wound up and its assets sold. Most items, such as draughts, chess, dominoes, cards, pictures, black lead brush, corkscrew, and 2 broken chairs were bought by individuals, probably club members. A selection of chairs, spitoons and checks were sold to Boothtown Conservative Club.

A selection of the local ladies take the sun on Mill Lane, outside the Sunday School.
Phyllis Gledhill is standing on the right.
(Phyllis Gledhill Collection)

Phyllis Gledhill with sister Maude

Sam was a prominent member of the local community. He was an overlooker at Mountain Mill, on the committee at the Institute, and long-serving (45 years) bell ringer at Queensbury Parish Church for which he was presented with an engraved silver teapot. His daughter Phyllis was the last surviving family member. In her late 90's, she could still be seen on fine days walking slowly from her house to the corner of Mill Lane and back again. Her lifestyle, she said, was: "Get up when it's daylight and go to bed when it gets dark" and "Take one day at a time". Her memory of events from her childhood was crystal clear, as proven when compared to official records. She died peacefully aged 105.

Mufton Pullit (William Barker) 1857-c 1930

Mufton Pullit hated his nickname, the origin of which is not recorded. One suggestion is that it related to noises he made when struggling to get bales of hay into the loft at Foxhill Farm where he worked. The kids at the school would make fun of him, and on occasions he complained to the headmaster.

He was a man of violent temper, but also of artistic accomplishment, though most of his drawings were on scraps of paper and cigarette packets and none seem to have survived. When going about, he wore a long black coat, bowler, and carried a large brolly in any weather.

He seems to have been one of those people of whom others make fun. On one occasion a local, Ezra Bateman, dressed in false beard and hair and approached Mufton in his local (The Fleece). Ezra claimed to be an American whose flying machine had come down on Soil Hill, and he needed accommodation for the night. To the amusement of the regulars, Mufton was taken in, and scuttled away to his house in Northern Street to make arrangements while Ezra got rid of the disguise.

Ellis Barrett 1848-1932

He was the son of Richard ("Ill-Dick") Harper, miner, and Martha Barrett, who both lived at Mountain Delves. Being illegitimate he was named Barrett. Richard and Martha married later. When Ellis came to marry, his father was shown as Richard Barrett, not Harper.

In his late teens he became enamoured of Sarah (Sally) Rushworth, daughter of Jonas Rushworth, one of the founders of Mountain Chapel, and head of a family of some substance. He married her on 26.4.1869 and left the area in the 1870s. They had a daughter Lucy. In 1881 he is known to have been working at the Duke William pit at Liversedge. On the death of her father in 1889, Sarah gained an inheritance and Ellis was able to leave the pits. They returned to live at 1 Derwent Place and began a greengrocery business. In 1908 he is listed as being a 'shopkeeper' in Mountain Place, in the centre property that had been the original Co-op.

He was a good musician, and acquired a harmonium (probably from the Rushworth's). This was used for the chapel 'walk-abouts', and still exists.

Benjamin Bartle 1823-1907

Born 8.4.1823 at Upper Spring Head farm cottage near Foxhill, the son of John Bartle and Mary Ridley. He was christened at 'Queenshead General Baptist Chapel, Clayton-by-Bradford'. John died of Cholera in 1846. Benjamin trained as a woolcomber and handloom weaver, then, like many others, retrained for powerlooms. He was a Chartist, and a part-time horse dealer and trainer. In April 1847 he married his first wife, widow Mary Downsbrough. Mary died in 1866, and her older sister Ann moved in with Benjamin. However, he took a fancy to Sarah Brooks, a widow some 14 years his junior. In August 1872 they had a son. Benjamin married Sarah some 8 years later. The son was christened Tom Bartle Brooks. Benjamin died of bronchial pneumonia at Upper Spring Head in April 1907, having lived in the same house all his life.

Tom Bartle Brooks 1872-1953

Tom was a specialist at breaking-in horses but never used whip or cruelty. Horses would be brought from afar. A gypsy horse dealer came to spend several winters in Travis Laithe (Travis House), and Tom trained his horses. The gypsy had a secret horse liniment formula, which he gave to Tom, with the warning to buy the ingredients from several pharmacists rather than all from one, lest they discovered the formula. This embrocation, which was also used by rugby-laikers and knur-laikers up to World War II, consisted of: ½ oz each Oil of Vitrio (dilute sulphuric acid), Spirits of Turpentine ("Turps"), Saltpetre (Potassium Nitrate) and "extracts of lead", in a quart of vinegar. Powerful stuff !

Latterly, Tom lived in the Navvy Houses (15 Great Street), and had a smallholding next to the Delf – the adjacent quarry. Known as "the Pen", he kept rabbits and chickens and grew vegetables, for selling. He was a dealer in firewood and firelighters, and had a donkey and cart for transport.

Tom was a bit of a joker. Around the late 1800s the Minister at Mountain was Owd Jacop (Old Jacob), a real fire-and-brimstone type. One evening Tom was in the process of getting his friend Owd Eli home – Eli, they said, got drunk at the smell of a barmaid's apron, and on this occasion he'd been drinking for 5 hours. Eli was piled into a wheelbarrow and Tom was pushing it to Eli's home down Laneside. As they passed Treacle Tree at gone midnight, one house lamp was still on – Gurt Grace, a local gossip. As she peered out, Tom shouted: "It's all right. It's nobbut Owd Jacop". The story got around and Jacob threatened legal action until Tom made a public apology.

The first Penny Farthing cycle in Mountain was owned by Tom. Unfortunately a segment of the front solid tyre was missing. Tom managed fine, but others who tried his cycle failed to heed his warning "Don't use the brake!" and usually fell over the front wheel when the brake jammed in the tyre gap. He also had the first cycle with pneumatic tyres – he acquired this from a cyclist visiting the area whose tyre punctured and couldn't be repaired there and then. Tom swapped the disabled cycle (known as a 'Safety') for a solid-tyre version and one crown (5/-).

At 'The Pen'. Tom Bartle Brooks sits next to his donkey.
(Harry Brooks Collection)

WEATHER

Nowadays, with modern snow clearing methods, winter is rarely a disruptive problem on the Mountain. But many tales of snows are recalled. 1800 must have been a bad winter – it was referred to as "the dead year" – with snow up to 14 feet deep. Said to be "coldest since the dead year" was 1861 when tree branches broke under the weight of ice. Over a one month period, temperatures from as low as 15°F (-10°C) only rose to 32°F (0°C) on four days. Despite this winter, we are told later that harvesting began especially early (in June) and a good crop was achieved. In January 1891 storms reduced the attendance at Raggalds School from a registered 140 to actually only 8 pupils. In early 1895, 13 weeks of frost caused many outdoor workers to be laid off. Soup kitchens doling out soup and bread, groceries and coal were set up to relieve hardship. In March 1900 it took 90 men 2 days to clear snow from the road to Queensbury station.

1933 and 1937 were bad winters. And 1947 is well-remembered. Snow clearance, locals insist, was partly carried out by German and Italian PoW's. A 'trench' was cleared – wide enough to walk in – from Mountain to the Co-op Bakery, and supplies brought to Mountain and Raggalds in baskets carried on the head, the snow being head-high. In the houses, frozen water pumps in the cellars could be a problem, but since it was only the <u>pump</u> which froze, water was always available from the many wells.

Rennie Briggs worked for Shackleton & Moore, a haulage firm (with motor lorries) in Queensbury. They were based at the bottom of Fleet Lane at premises which became Carter's Forge, demolished 1999 for road widening. He recalls walking on wall tops from his home on the Cali to the garage when snow was deep. There were no motor ploughs – at best a 6-horse plough might clear the less deep snow. Anything else needed digging.

Much dateable evidence, and sober comments, are found in the school logbooks, for which I make no apology for frequent references. Comments have been made of deep snow and blizzards affecting Raggalds School. More recently, as recorded at Foxhill School, the weather has been sufficiently severe to afford mention.

<u>8 January 1937</u>: "Attendance greatly affected through the week by (1) Influenza, (2) Gales and heavy rain."

<u>29 January 1937</u>: "Owing to the prevailing arctic conditions …………" and all through February, until 11 March ….. "Blizzard raged from 10 am ……..." 12 March: "Yesterday's gale subsided but much further snow has fallen". On 14 March, defeat was conceded – the school closed that afternoon, and the next day !

Gales were common. At the Mountain end of the school the Girls entrance door often had to be kept locked because of the number of children getting caught and injured as it blew shut. Also the glass roof over the assembly hall was a regular cause for nail-biting tension. Sometimes panes broke and it is several times described as 'lifting'.

Snow on the Mountain is not confined to winter. The school records 10 May 1943: "Snowfall overnight". And light falls are fairly common even now well into April or even May.

But the snow in living memory was 1947. It had been a bad winter anyway. Gales even in September 1946 had blown down walls. By the first days of February 1947 there were heavy snowfalls and considerable drifting. Drifts of 8 feet to 12 feet were not uncommon. By the 5th, the school tells us: "Conditions worse. The road is blocked in both directions. 13 children are present" – they were sent home. There were about 140 kids on the register.

On the 7th: "Seven children present. Sent home. School closed."

On the 11th: "15 children present. The road blocked both ways. The snow plough is useless due to the wind." The school was closed until 17 February (which also coincided with the half-term holidays). Although it re-opened then, the 'arctic weather' continued.

28th February: "Gales all day. No dinners or milk". (Roads still blocked.)

3rd March: "No dinners. 38 children brought their own foods."

4th March – the dinner van gets through ! "Some children preferred to eat their own food in preference to the school dinner" for which they had paid.

However, it's more snow, blizzards, freezing rain, and no more dinners get through until 19th March ! The school remained open, but, as happened over many winters (usually January and February but often extended to March) there was a later (0930) starting time.

Even the railway line was blocked by snow, and a locomotive, derailed between Queensbury and Thornton viaduct, remained thus for several days. Many locals remember having to walk 'on wall tops and trucks' (vehicles stuck on the road) from Perseverance Road to Mountain, and also down Old Guy Road to Ambler Thorn. Eventually traffic traversed the main road, but with Perseverance Road still closed, coal and supplies were dragged on sledges from Raggalds.

In April that year the weather was still cold and wet, with a gale blowing – not uncommon nowadays ! The school heating failed on the 21st but despite classroom temperatures of 42 to 48°F, Foxhill remained open until things got back to normal on 6th May.

It is difficult to know if poor workmanship, foundations, or the weather has been to blame for things collapsing on the Mountain: Certainly demolition by lightning strikes is recalled; The Eagle pub has been shored up with buttresses for over 100 years; The Chapel school room fell down during construction. Stone and mortar walls some six feet high have been blown down.

Possibly connected with the severe winter, we have this report by the Foxhill School Headmaster: 14 April 1947. "During the holidays part of the boiler house has given way. The caretaker drew my attention to a screen wall in the girls lavatories which was leaning ominously. A touch of the hand made it rock. We estimated [the weight] at about 3 tons, and decided it was unsafe for children to play [there]. I gave it a push with one hand whereupon the whole wall collapsed to ground level."

Even in January 1949, Foxhill children were still expected to attend when the boiler (well past its prime) burst. This was patched up (literally!) after a few days and the caretaker told not to let it go out until the next holidays when a replacement could be fitted – if the 'patch' cooled down it would split again. But until the patch was fitted we are told: "There was no heat. The walls were damp, the temperature 36°F". It was deemed warmer outside "due to the slight thaw", so the kids came to school, had games in the yard or in the park opposite, had their milk, their lunch, and then had the afternoons off.

Also at Foxhill the young children are often recorded as having been blown over. For example 24 November 1943: "Gales. R. W. age 8, was blown down the yard, off his feet, struck his head against the boundary wall." First Aid was given at the school and R's mother was sent for to collect him. He'd only gone out to go to the lavatory!

1979:
The main Queensbury road to Ambler Thorn. Although the odd vehicle has passed, the roads to/from Queensbury were closed, and it was fortunate that snowploughs were based at Ford ! Pavements are impassable so the road becomes 'pedestrianised'.

From Christmas 1962 there was a Big Freeze for about 4 months. In places the temperature dropped to -22°C. Many households were without water when the main supply froze under the road. This lasted around 9 weeks.

In 1979 severe weather lasted for several weeks. Many problems were caused by fallen overhead wires: With a slight thaw followed by freezing, or by freezing rain, "ice of considerable thickness" built up on power and telephone wires, some of the latter becoming "so heavy that they stretched and touched the field wall tops" in places.

Through the 1980s winters were often harsh but not too prolonged. Into the 1990s, conditions became milder, the main problem being black ice on the slight dip of the road from Mountain to Pit Lane, which could bring traffic to a standstill for several hours.

Another aspect of weather and elevation is the spectacular mist conditions. Until the 1960s, industrial haze or fog was prevalent, with the whole of the Halifax and Bradford basins totally obscured for days on end. With the reduction of visible pollutants, such as from coal burning, natural mists often form. It is fascinating seeing a sea of morning mist filling the valleys, while Mountain is bathed in sunlight. However, low cloud or hill mist can give the reverse effect – Mountain may have visibility down to 10 yards, but descending to The Junction, all is clear. One noticeable phenomenon of the 1990s was the thin layer of yellow polluted air hanging over Bradford on calm days, like a mustard-coloured and clearly defined stripe immediately above the city, but not reaching Thornton or Clayton.

1953:
Kenneth Holmes and Dolly (the horse) deliver milk in Queensbury. The heat from Dolly helped to prevent the milk from freezing. (Dorothy Kitchin Collection)

"WHEN I WOR A LAD – AN' AFORE THAT!"

A selection of memories passed down in local families, to whom I am most grateful but who are too numerous to list. Memories being what they are, some 'embroidering' of stories may have occurred, though where possible facts have been checked.

In the late 1800s/early 1900s workhouses for the poor were sometimes known as Bastiles. Young children of these poor folk often roamed the city streets. In Liverpool before World War I there were many very poor Irish immigrants. Some of their children, boys and girls, usually of near working age, were adopted by families in other parts of the country – some came to Mountain. Although the children were better off, they were often exploited by their adopted family and put to work as soon as possible, in mills and mines. With the advent of World War I many joined the Army, often encouraged by their bosses who doubled as (paid) recruiting officers. Many lads failed to return, being killed in action. Some of their names – obviously not of local origin – can be seen on the memorial in Queensbury.

In the early 1900s, the Sun on Soil Hill is said to have been the local base for a troupe of Cowboys and Indians who staged Wild West shows around these parts. The kids in the area used to run along shouting and playing as the troupe passed in their gigs. This was likely to have been one of the groups 'impersonating' Buffalo Bill Cody's Wild West Show, which visited Yorkshire in 1903, last appearing at Keighley on 7th October and Savile Park Halifax on 8th October. It was billed as the 'Final European Tour' and 'The Real Thing' implying that imitators were around.

A newspaper report of 1861 tells of J (actually it was Isaac) Tempest, 75, farmer, of Mountain (actually Mountain End Farm) who suffered from gout and had to have his lower arm amputated. He refused chloroform (the anaesthetic in use then) and watched the whole procedure "with interest".

Infant mortality was higher in the late 1800s than now. Babies are said to have been placed in a box or bag and put in the grave with any adult who was being buried at Ambler Thorn – the parents couldn't afford a burial. Newborns could be insured for 1d a week by "the man from the Pru" or at least his equivalent. Of course the infant had to have a name. "What's 'ee called?" asked the insurance man. "We've not thowt on it yet" said the parents. "'Ee's gotta be called summat, fer t'forms – 'ow abaht Thomas Henry?" (the name of the insurance man). So that was the child's official name, but the family would eventually call him by his decided name!

If a woman's breasts became inflamed after childbearing, the local remedy was Cow Clap Poultice (poultice made with cow dung – but it had to be still warm and fresh!).

There was no doctor or pharmacist on the Mountain. Pharmacist Arthur Hanson is noted in 1888 at numbers 1 & 3 Gothic Street, Queensbury – he was also skilled in extracting teeth ! A doctor mentioned in early tales is 'Owd Fawthrop'. There were three Fawthrops who were doctors in Queensbury, 'Owd Fawthrop' being in practice from 1844 to 1864. He was remembered on the Mountain because sometimes he'd be called upon to 'sew up injured fighting dogs'. There were several doctors surgeries in Queensbury.

Several rows of terraces were owned by Speaks: Luddenden Place and Jester Place for example. In Jester Place the rent was 4/6d per week (pre-World War II), while the identical house in Luddenden Place was only 3/6d. This, it is maintained, was because Jester Place, being south facing, got the sun: Luddenden didn't. In one of the houses lived a Mrs Gledhill, who used to sit huddled up to a very small fire at any time of year. She always expressed her poor opinion of the Mill sending a 'young lass' (of only 14 or 15) to collect the rents – but she always paid.

The last original property in the area known as Mountain Delves was, (by the 1920s) two derelict low-deckers used to house chickens. Pigs were kept by a Mr Hill in the next field where the brick bungalow now stands.

There are three 'farm houses' close together on Roper Lane – Warmlee Hall which has several cottages and outbuildings; Warm Lee Farm; and Warmleigh House which is nearest to Ambler Thorn. Here at Warmleigh House (right), in the early 1900s a wind pump drew water into a 500 gallon tank. When the tank was filled it overflowed into a bath and the wind pump vanes would be turned out of the wind to stop the pump. If there was no wind for a long time there was also a hand pump. The farm below (Sutton's) was also supplied from here. The water was considered 'very pure'. Normal extraction from the tank was with a bucket. A local doctor would call to collect water in jars, for his patients.

The gable end of Pickering Farm barn was struck by lightning and demolished, without consequences too serious. Not so around 1935 when lightning struck Sun Farm. Actually it was one of the two attached labourer's cottages that was hit. The occupants at the time were a very poor 'family' and many of their possessions were destroyed. People in the area collected clothes, furniture and toys to help replace their losses. Some mystery (or romance) is associated with this 'family'. With no parents, it was a teenage girl (herself partly crippled) who was looking after her brothers and sisters.

The building, a low-decker of drystone construction, had a 'shut-up' bed, no running water but a set pot to provide hot water. It was not rebuilt for many years. The 'family' moved to Hillside Place, or Halifax, it is thought.

Jack Hodgson, regularly seen in the Mountain area but of no fixed abode, was a painter and decorator, and also a regular guest of Armley Jail where he passed his time doing paintings. On one occasion, he was released before finishing his artwork, so immediately went and smashed a tram window so he'd be put back inside to complete his picture. He associated with Mufton Pullit, at times lodging with him, and the pair decided the house would be improved with a stair carpet. Lacking funds, they painted a patterned one on the stone stairs.

Several odd characters lived in the central area of Mountain where the shops were. In the smaller block of five properties once considered to be 'fairly decent', lived Mrs Greenwood and her daughter, both said to be quite mad and not bothered about personal hygiene. On going out Mrs Greenwood used to cast a spell by saying "No intrudence in my house while I'm away". The local kids considered them 'witches' and remember them shouting and screaming at each other behind closed doors. Nearby, over Mr Farnell's property, lived another lady with antisocial ideas on hygiene – she'd empty her chamber pot out of the window, like the old fashioned 'Gardez l'eau!' custom, but without any warning.

At the back of the Mountain Eagle were two attached cottages known at the time as 'Sam Dawson' houses (the name of the owner). In the yard was a pump and the village mangle, complete with heavy stone rollers, for use by anyone. This is possibly 'Langdrake's Mangle' mentioned as being "the best in Mountain", and Langdrake could be a corruption of Long Drake (Drake-who-was-tall) since no-one called Langdrake is known to have lived here, but there were plenty of Drake's. The cottages were demolished in the early 1990s, and the pump site a few years later.

The Mill was the place to go in an emergency such as an accident or fire, as when the inhabitants (Hannah and her retarded son 'Happy Frank') of Lee's cottage went looking for a gas leak with a lighted taper !

Telephones did not become common until the 1950s, though poles and wires can be seen on photos from forty years before then, Speak's Mill and Mill House being the first to have phones in Mountain. In 1914, Speak's phone number was 'Thornton 21', and later their telegraphic address 'Speak, Queensbury'. The unfamiliar 'buzz' of wind over the wires is remembered. Before telephones, to summon a doctor for a home visit when he came to Mountain on his rounds (usually by horse and trap), an open envelope would be placed in the window of a house in Mountain Place, telling the doctor where to call. Or someone had to run to Queensbury ! The doctor most remembered was George Shields (in practice in Queensbury 1900-1924). Another alternative ("but only if you were desperate", I'm told) was

Ambulance Annie (Mrs Dean) who was trained in First Aid. She lived in Mountain Place, and it was probably her window which displayed the envelopes.

When Raggalds school was in use, pupils wrote on slates. A domestic variation of this was the slate notebook – a small piece of slate, say 9 x 12 cm, fixed to a leather back with a leather covering flap (to prevent accidental erasure), and carried in pocket, purse or bag. These are known to have been in use locally well into the 20th century, for shopping lists.

The local Council Office (foundation stone laid by Paul Speak on 19 May 1895), was between Thornton Road and the Stag's Head, Queensbury Behind the offices was a mortuary. The undertaker was said to bring a "shovel-full of bits" round from time to time to dispose of in the coke-fired boiler.

To catch a tram to Halifax or Bradford necessitated walking to Queensbury where the two lines met. A Mountain local recalls taking the tram from Queensbury to Halifax. A big-breasted woman with a baby got on. The conductor, who was a youngish pleasant lad, took her fare. She then opened her blouse for the baby to feed, but it wouldn't have it, and began yelling. Mum says to it: "If tha's noan bahn t'ev it aw'sel gi'e it t'conductor", (if you won't have it, I'll give it to the conductor), much to the embarrassment of the young lad !

Locals knew their neighbours in adjacent villages as Clayton Claht'eads (Cloth-heads), Haworth Flar'eads (Flourheads), but we're left guessing for the names for Thornton and Denholme folk.

Queensbury folk considered Mountain to be the 'back of beyond', and the inhabitants thereof to be quite thick. In fact, Mountain folk were quite observant, and sometimes knew more about Queensbury than did the locals, as in this example: On Queensbury High Street was a shop owned by Joseph Knapton, known locally as Owd Dooad. He was a dealer in ironmongery, and had supplied such to the new Council Offices when first erected. His shop was number 80. At the side of his shop is a very narrow alleyway or snicket, referred to as Mawksome Nick, which leads to Chapel Street. Part way up the snicket are some old cottages bearing the not-very-obvious name plate 'Cambridge Place', situated behind Knapton's shop.

"Does ta knaw where t'Cambridge Place ligs?" asks the Mountain resident. Most Queensbury-ites wouldn't. "Up Mawksome Nick", a few might respond. "Ay, an' what wor t'name o' t'ginnel afore then?" This would usually stump them completely. Triumphantly, with a mischievous glint in his eye, the Mountain person would say: "Nay, tha should knaw – it's t'Dooad Knapton's Backside !"

In cricket, for important matches the Mountain team used Job Taylor's bat (he was the publican at the Fleece and later at the Eagle) – the only decent bat available in early days. The players also paraded in top hats – known locally as 'Rahn Squaruns' (Round Square Ones).

Unlike Queensbury, Mountain had no brass band. The Denholme Band was called "t'pit shaft band" because they played by a new pit when the shaft reached the coal seam. Clayton's band was referred to as "t'ale an' bacca band" (ale and tobacco), presumably for social reasons.

Sometimes you had to go to Queensbury for your entertainment. For film shows, for example, there was the Victoria Hall (films from 1912 to 1960) and also the Hall of Freedom in Nelson Street. Some remember films Monday, Wednesday and Friday, a different film each night, from 1913.

For indoor swimming, from the late 1800s there was the Victoria Hall baths. There were dances held on Saturdays. And dances at the 'Tute, of course, from 1913.

On a Sunday evening there was the Queensbury 'Prom' – between the Parish Church and the bottom of High Street was the place to be and be seen, to meet up with potential partners. Some locals called the Prom the 'Bunny Run', others knew it as the 'Monkey Run'. Those who were successful might "hole-up in shop doorways, only to be cleared out by the local bobby". The technique was for the officer to remove his cape (which was weighted) and swing it – quite heavy enough to knock down a person. Others might head for Foxhill Park, and the 'Chinese Temple' – a circular shelter with radial partitions but otherwise open (like a sea-side shelter): If you were first there you could get a more intimate place in a back corner. The main activities there were 'kissing and fumbling'.

Foxhill Park, owned by the Council from 1897, was originally un-named, but called Queensbury Park from 1905. It is the triangular area with apexes at Upper Fleet House, Pineberry pub and the top of Chapel Lane. About half of the area had laid-out paths, a pond and shrubbery from 1899/1900, existing into the 1970s.

The Fair Ground (behind the Old Queens Head off High Street, Queensbury) was the annual venue for Marshall's travelling amusements for a few days around 14 August. As well as the sideshows, Gallopers, 'Shamrock & Columbia' steam swingboats, etc, there were other events like boxing challenges and biscuit eating ! In this latter event, contestants coats were removed and tied together in a pile. Each contestant was to eat 3 dry biscuits (cream crackers: no drinks !) then had to extricate their coat and put it on. The winner received a prize ---hopefully a pint of ale ! The Queens Head fair was originally a cattle fair, in October in the early 1800s. In 1853 it was revived in September to coincide with Fair Week, with travellers, shows and a Gala at Foxhill Park. In 1871 we are told the fair was held on the last Monday in August. "There were cattle and a good show of geese, all of which sold. There were extremely high prices on horses. The pleasure fair had roundabouts, swingboats, velocipedes, waxworks". It became a fair only, held at the Fair Ground, and known as 'The Thump', surviving into the 1980s.

All work and no play led to certain members of the community periodically 'going on the rant' – a booze-up lasting several days. Miners especially, who sometimes worked a seven-day week, and never saw daylight in winter. In the 1930s, George Glew, joiner and coffin-maker, based at the old Raggalds School, would take to drink after a funeral. And Jack Hodgson, a painter and decorator specialising in marble-effect painted fireplaces, who lived on Glazier Row, and always wore a long tail coat when not at work. When he went on the rant, he'd stand in the street with one arm in his coat, bellowing "Napoleon !" and throwing half-pennies for the kids to pick up.

Many people remember picking bilbers (bilberries) at Soil Hill when they were young. In Spring the kids would also visit Birks Wood to collect young dockings – dock leaves, for which neighbours might pay ½d a bag, to make Dock Pudding. The young leaves – the large older leaves are very bitter – were known locally as Passion Docks. To make the savoury 'pudding' (Calderdale recipe), wash the leaves and boil for 20 minutes with chopped onion. Add oatmeal and boil another 20 minutes. Strain, form into patties and fry in bacon fat.

In the 1920s there were fields of rhubarb down 'Sam Loine' (Old Guy Road) the business of one Jack Howarth.

There was plenty of livestock around the Mountain – pigs, sheep, cattle, horses, geese, and hens. The sunrise racket of the cockerels was referred to as the 'Lark Song'. And there were lots of wild birds, rabbits and foxes. Even into the 1960s, the fields between Micklemoss and Fleet Lane were known as the Hare Fields

In the early 1900s, Rat Dan was a part-time rat catcher. Sometimes he took a couple of live ones with him. In the local pubs he'd bet a pint of ale to bite off the head from a live rat. He laboured for Dan Briggs at Law Hill Farm, and slept in his laithe. Briggs was described as a 'nit-scrat' of a farmer.

John Willy Sutcliffe (Pig Willy) kept pigs at Pickering Farm in the 1930s. He'd trade Yorkshire Mixture (sweets) with the local kids in return for pig swill. Although of a local family he lived in the Navvy Houses in Queensbury.

Around the late 1940s, John (or Jack) o'Goth lived in the cottage at the Mountain end of the low-deckers at Travis. He sang a lot, to the annoyance of the neighbours, and often became so drunk he'd be found at the roadside, totally incapable, but with his faithful dog waiting at his side until he could make the journey home. He is remembered as looking big and tough but with a squeaky voice, and sometimes wearing a Davy Crockett hat.

Previously another character who lived in this vicinity, probably at number 31, was Sam o'Tom (o') Ikes. He shared the one room with his donkey, which helped to keep the place warm in winter, he said.

Another animal companion was a house-trained pig belonging to Tom Bartle Brooks in the Navvy Houses. He'd take it on a lead for a visit to the Granby in Queensbury or to the Fleece on the Mountain.

To bring in a little extra money, women and girls who were at home knitted pullovers (ganzies) for fishermen – three or four times a year a dealer from Filey would call to buy them.

In 1933 the novelty of manned gliders was seen in the area – a one-off visit. Flying from 'The Rough' on Roper Lane, they were hauled manually into the air to fly over Bradshaw and to return. One part of the plane was secured with a Fokker pin, a name which amused the local lads.

Ronnie Cook lived with his parents in Denholme during WW II. His father worked at Speak's as an overlooker. By 1947 they moved to 4 Jester Place. Ronnie got work in the railway goods yard at Thornton. Major freight from there was maggots from Jerusalem Farm. They were packed in tin boxes, like the old wholesale biscuit boxes, with small air holes in the top.

On one occasion in 1947 Ronnie and a couple of friends had been playing snooker in the Institute. They were thrown out by Mrs Stead, the curator's wife, for being too noisy. Soon after, the Institute's heavy roller was found to have run down the field at the back and demolished a chicken shed. Naturally Ronnie and friends were suspected and interviewed by the local bobby, which terrified Ronnie. Actually they'd not been responsible.

A subject for gossip and speculation in 1966 was the attempted murder of the Mountain Post Mistress. Memories having become a little hazy with time, the event as reported in the Halifax Courier and Guardian runs thus: "On Friday 26 August 1966 George Buckle (27), single and a labourer, of 1 Mountain Villas, went to Mountain Post Office for a 4 shilling postal order. He then went round the back of the counter and attacked Miss Ivy Sutcliffe (63), the Post Mistress, with a spanner, and stole about £48 from the till."

Now George was obviously not a person who thought things through very well. He did it, he admitted eventually, because he was 'flat broke' and the Post Office was a place which had money – there were no banks on the Mountain. And he didn't mean to hurt anyone. Okay so far, but on the down side, George had lived at Mountain Villas for about a year and had been an occasional customer at the Post Office. Before the robbery, he armed himself with a spanner. He hit Ivy over the head five times, fracturing her skull, grabbed the money and went back home. Within 30 minutes the police paid him a visit. They found the 4 shilling postal order hidden in overalls in a child's pram (don't ask!) and most of the cash in £5, £1 and 10/- notes stuffed up the bedroom chimney. George initially refused to believe he'd done it. As he claimed, he'd "never used violence before". He was arrested for Robbery with Violence, taken to Halifax, and eventually sent to Leeds Assizes. Ivy was stitched up but never fully recovered psychologically, and moved from the Post Office soon after.

Nicknames and Colloquialisms

There was a local rhyme presumably referring to Pauls II and III:
"Old Paul and Young Paul
Old Paul's Son
Young Paul will be (a) Paul
When Old Paul's done."

Descriptive nicknames used to be more common than now, and a whole range of nicknames of Mountain locals has been preserved by Harry Brooks. From his father's list of names in use in the late 1800s we find: Family descriptive names, such as Jack o' Liddie's (Olivia's son Jack), Ann o' mi Uncle Jack's (Ann, my niece). There were personal descriptive names such as Gurt Grace (Grace was a big girl !).

Posy Billy lived in Glazier Row. He was considered effeminate and said to "hang out his britches with his wife's".

Piss Plonk-arse may not be as derogatory as it sounds. In the West Riding wool trade in the 1800s, urine (called 'lant' in the trade), was required in cloth making. It was collected by carters who had the forename Piss added to their known name (eg Piss William) denoting their profession. The Plonk-arse may refer to this individual's tendency to readily sit down "for a natter" (gossip) with anyone.

Other local names included:

Dont = Jonathan; Dooad = Joseph; and Pilt = William.
Alt o'Bob Shack's was the eldest of Bob Shackleton's sons.
Prin Rusha was Prince Rushworth – not a Royal at all!
Jim o' t'Owd Raw was James who lived in the old row of cottages.
Gowd Aarm was Gold Arm, a local second-hand dealer who kept his large stock at the Hall of Freedom in Queensbury.
Cleean Teead was not Clean Ted at all – he had a penchant for picking up horsemuck and taking it home in his pockets !
Now ponder on these. Pistil-Rig, Jack o' Three Steels, Curn-box, Bumsticks.

For the bird-watcher, local names in the late 1800s included:

Shepster	- Starling	Pienot	- Magpie
Wall Snacker	- Wheatear	Tewit	- Lapwing
Blue Dunnock	- Tree Sparrow	Linnet	- Finch

Like most areas or towns, Mountain had its own pronunciation and phraseological variations. In particular, Lane is always 'Loin'. If you lived on California Row, you lived 'on the Cali'. Indeed if you were local, Mountain had the definite article in front – "I'm going to/live on the Mountain". (See also 'Mountain in Verse'). The pronunciation of words in Mountain area is likened to that of Halifax and of Lancashire, especially the apparent insertion of an 'i' after 'o', for example: coal is pronounced coil; hole is 'oil; noon is noo-in, school is schoo-il.

'Living Tally', also known as 'living ower t'brush tail', was co-habiting.

"Thornton puts out white flags on Monday", referred to washday at Thornton, all streets being clearly visible from Mountain.

When someone died, a euphemism was to say "t'Green Cat's called".

The Mountain locals who were non-chapel-goers were called 'John Barleycorn's Disciples' – their chapel was the Fleece, Eagle or Raggalds !

A NOTE ON ARTIFICIAL FLOWER MAKING

John Klose (See 'Banks Alarum') trained as an artificial-flower maker. Usually men performed only the first part of the process, which was to stamp out the petals or leaves from a wad of fabric, using a machine in the main workplaces, or a sharp hand-stamp which, when struck with a hammer, could cut around 15 thicknesses at a time. The material may be pre-coloured, or hand-coloured later. After cutting, veining may be added by applying pressure to each piece in a suitable pair of dies.

Young women or girls, with their more nimble fingers, would now separate the cuts of petals, perhaps apply further colouring detail, and thread a fine wire through layers of petals. If a curled effect is required a goffing iron is used – somewhat like a flat soldering iron heated in the fire which when touched on the fabric causes local contraction. Final assembly of the flowers, and binding of the wire stems in green thread or thin strips of fabric, completed the product.

Some, like John Klose, worked from home and supplied local milliners. Others supplied undertakers. Usually the whole family was involved, working wherever they could in their already cramped living conditions. Eye strain was common, working with small items and by gas light, and the brightness of the colours can affect the eyes over a period of time. Colours were often brushed-on powders, such as arsenic green (little used by 1870) and copper sulphate, both of which created a dust especially when the 'cut' of flowers or leaves was separated. This irritated the eyes and respiratory system. And even in summer a fire had to be kept alight to heat the goffing irons. The main periods of work were February to May and August to November.

MOUNTAIN IN VERSE by Harry Brooks

If your dialect is a bit rusty, there's a 'translation' of the poem as well !

1) Nine lang month' o' Winter,
   Three mooar o'cowd weather
   Mak a year at t'Maantin,
   But ta 'en all together,
   T'wind an t'rain an t'blizzards,
   T'frost an t'ice an t'snaw
   'Elped ta fashion t'Maantin
   Inta t'place we knaw.

2) T'fields – ther' all ruff pasture
   T'fowk – ther ruffer still! –
   An' ther's nooan a tree theer
   Up o' t'top o' t'ill.
   T'chimleys all leyn ovver,
   T'fowk som'times an' all
   E' ta leyn o' t'wind a bit
   (If it stopped the'd fall).

3) Ivvry 'aase at t'Maantin's
   Built o' local stooan,
   Law-raamed uns
       or cham'er'eights,
   Brick boxes? – ther's nooan !

Pig-'oiles, pubs an' nessies,
T'Institewt an' t'meln,
Coil-'oiles, t'schooil an' t'chappil,
T'varry graand itseln.

4) Seeams ta be stooan riddled,
   T'dry-stooan walls all raand –
   The' wor built o' stooan 'at cawm
   Aat o' t'Maatin graand.
   Roofs, door-jawmbs an' lintils,
   Winder frames an' stees,
   Causeys, gurt field-rollers,
   Skep-'oiles made fo' t'bees.

5) Sooa ther's little wunder
   T'fowk 'at live up theer
   Seeam 'ard faced an' rugged,
   Speyk ther minds baht fear,
   Knaw 'at <u>ther</u>' a race apaart
   Feel it i' ther' booans,
   Even thaw t'off-commed uns
   Think ther numb as stooans !

'Nine long months of Winter and three more of cold weather make a year at Mountain. But the weather has fashioned both the place and the inhabitants. The fields are rough pasture. The inhabitants are rugged. There are no trees at the Mountain. The chimneys all lean over because of the wind; likewise the inhabitants, who would fall down if ever the wind dropped.

All the houses at the Mountain, low single storey and two storey, are made of local stone – there are no 'brick boxes'. Pigsties, pubs, privies, the Institute and the Mill, coalsheds, school and chapel, even the ground itself seems full of stones. And all around the drystone walls are made of stone quarried from the Mountain. Roofs, doorframes, lintels, window frames and stairs; the paved tracks, and big rollers for levelling fields. Even beehives.

So perhaps it's not surprising that the folk who live up there seem strong willed and rugged, and fearlessly speak their minds. They know they are a race apart; they feel it in their bones. They don't care that those new to the area think the locals are as numb as their stones.'

GHOSTS 'N' BEASTIES

Ghost stories are not common in our area, and despite occasional fatal accidents, the spirits rarely lingered.

Until the early 1900s, boggards roamed the area, visited the mines, and were regarded with due respect. Some locals, like Ned o' Putts, would regularly shout, if out in the dark, to "flay t' boggards away".

Scrat Hall, noted on early maps as Boggard Houses, was along a track a few yards beyond Travis. It had a selection of spooks, and was considered by the local children to be a place for supernatural adventures. From the late 1800s the houses were empty. Local kids used to go to explore all the rooms, trying not to show fear. Then they'd go down to the cellar where there was a well, said to be the home of a green dwarf. One brave soul would drop a pebble down, then all the kids would run 'like Hummer Nick', yelling "Little Green Man's coming!" Later, Sandal Farm was incorrectly referred to as Scrat Hall on account of mysterious scratching noises being heard.

Soil Hill could be a place of concern for adults. Not only as in the Mixenden Treasure story, either. One Sunday morning, in daylight, two local men had been to a coin-tossing school (gambling group) on Soil Hill. On the way down they were accosted by a tall, impressive gentleman who asked them where they had been. On being told, he shook hands with them and gave each a sovereign, then disappeared. They looked at the coins and found only cinders. Totally terrified, they ran home to Mountain and told everyone they'd met Old Nick himself!

At West Scholes a male ghost has the habit of climbing over a roadside wall into the path of motorists. And in the same area, one evening in the 1970s, two sober, sceptical and subsequently terrified witnesses saw a ghostly horse with female rider in 'old fashioned' clothes jump walls across Cockin Lane. Witnessed by locals from time to time, the spectre is known as 'Lady Cockin'.

In the 1950s, Yews Green Farm was the venue for unexplained ghostly knockings. These emanated from under the lounge floor (which is timber over a solid base, with no pipework below). Repeated at about one second intervals, in short sequences, over a period of a few minutes, they provided a talking point (or consternation!) for visitors. After a few years the knockings ceased.

Several owners of a house in Jester Place have been disturbed by a 'presence' of unknown origin. Likewise one in Luddenden Place – perhaps the same spook, since the houses are back-to-back. There is said to be a spook at Jester House, also a ghost reportedly wandered the weaving shed at the Mill when it was latterly being used as a bakery prior to demolition.

Ghosts at The Institute are mentioned in the chapter 'Mountain Hall Hotel'.

A recent spirit has made itself felt since 1986 at Micklemoss Farm house. This is Allan Scott who committed suicide there with a shot to the head.

MAGIC AND TREASURE !

The classic story involving Magic is that of the Mixenden Treasure, here in abridged form based on that related in 'History of Queensbury' by Barratt.

At the end of the 15th Century, there were stories of a great treasure buried in the area of Soil Hill. In 1510, various interested parties met and planned to find the treasure. They included Sir John Wilkinson, a canon of Drax Abbey (he claimed knowledge of Black Magic), Richard Greenwood (a priest at Bingley Church) who claimed to know the area, and seven others. They reckoned there was probably a demon guardian, so proceeded with a mixture of Christian and Pagan ritual, invoking Belphares the treasure hunter's demon. For reasons known only to themselves, the search was to be made in winter.

They agreed to meet at sunset (probably with the intention of a midnight ritual) at the west end of Soil Hill, travelling in twos and threes to avoid arousing suspicion since all were unsure of the legality of the operation. One carried a censer and holy water sprinkler but lost them en route; another carried torch ends in his coat, and so on. Seven of them made it to the moor known as Wilsden Lee. The mist came down, and they lost their way, eventually arriving at Cockham (below Mountain) on the old Bingley to Halifax road. They then proceeded over the Mountain, to Micklemoss Cross, about a mile from their intended meeting place. After an unsuccessful search of the area, they met up again at Cockham, where some spent the night.

Two months later, the remaining interested parties met to summon the spirit of 'Oberion' to help them. However, at this point the Ecclesiastical Authorities stepped in. The group surrendered themselves, and several punishments involving parading and whipping in public were carried out. They abandoned the search for the treasure.

Oberion, an alternative spelling of Oberon, is best known as King of the Fairies, as portrayed particularly by Shakespeare. His spirit is said to be able to be conjured by magicians into a crystal stone. He seems to have a special, though rarely used, characteristic of assisting in operations involving digging.

THE MURDER OF BETHEL PARKINSON

"It has seldom indeed been the painful duty of the journalist to speak of a murder so brutal, and so entirely horrible, as this ...... within the last day or two", began the report in the Halifax Courier on Saturday 16 January 1858.

The initial report speaks of the mystery of the murder. It also pinpoints the locality quite well – about one mile from Hebden Bridge railway station, two miles from Heptonstall, half a mile from Old Town, towards Wadsworth Moor. There is 'Common Farm' occupied by one William Shackleton. The body was found on his land, half way between Common Farm and the next farm. On two sides of this field are lanes, or deep ruts, some three or four yards deep, formed mainly by the action of water, and known as The Dark Lanes. "A bleak, obscure and unfrequented spot."

The murder was thought to have occurred on the Wednesday night or Thursday morning. From a distance, the body was originally perceived as a pile of manure. However, realising it was a body, Shackleton and three others went to examine the site. A coping stone weighing 18 lbs was found near the battered head of the body, and half of a butcher's carving knife blade was found – the deceased having had his throat cut. The police were called and the body removed to the nearby 'Hare and Hounds Inn', Lane Ends, where examination revealed numerous gashes – the attack was consistent with someone kneeling on the victim's chest and stabbing with the right hand: The wounds were mainly to the left side of the body where there were at least 42 stab wounds. The right eye was black. There were broad jagged wounds to the forehead, and small cuts on the crown and back of the head. The skull was fractured just behind the right ear, and a similar wound on the left. The left ear was cut through. The throat had two deep cuts. There were two cuts between the ribs, and another just below the armpit. Another wound, thought to have been made with a skewer, was on the left breast. From the raised arm of the now rigid deceased, he seemed to have been trying to protect himself to the last.

On the Friday morning, a positive identification was made by a local – the deceased was a man named Parkinson, farmer and cattle dealer, from Raggalds Inn, near Queenshead.

At first it was thought that Parkinson had been going to or from Preston market. The most direct route was from Raggalds via Wadsworth Moor to Hebden Bridge station, though why he should walk so far rather than take a train from Halifax was not questioned. It was realised later that he had intended going to Preston Lane near Halifax, to do a deal – much more likely than to Preston, Lancs ! For some reason he changed his mind on the way. It was supposed that he had been murdered by someone known to him – opportunist robbery in such an unfrequented location was most unlikely.

Leads were established, and one Joseph Shepherd was arrested. He actually gave himself up to the police ! He professed innocence but claimed to know who had done it: Someone who lived near Raggalds. Shepherd claimed to have been party to getting Parkinson to the remote spot. He said the motive was revenge, not robbery.

By the time of the inquest, and due to the extreme diligence of the police, several witnesses had been found. On the Tuesday, Parkinson had been trying to raise money to buy cattle. He wanted £30. Shepherd was with him, on the road from Halifax to Queenshead. In the evening Parkinson asked his wife for money – she left 2½ gold sovereigns and some silver for him when she went to work just after 5 am on Wednesday. Parkinson intended borrowing the rest from his brother-in-law George Normanton who was a grocer on the Mountain.

Parkinson and Shepherd had known each other for years, as attested by Joseph Mann (alias Dooad o' Manuels), licensee of Raggalds Inn. On the Wednesday he saw Shepherd call on Parkinson. They left together. Parkinson called at Raggalds toll house to leave his door key for his wife to collect on her way home. Hannah Garth, the toll bar keeper's wife, concurred.

The two men left down Bradshaw Lane, and various witnesses confirmed their route on tracks and over fields via Lane Head (Illingworth), following the present Calderdale Way to beyond Wainstalls, crossing near Low Bridge, over Wadsworth Moor and down Keelham Lane, where the murder took place, and where they would have arrived at about 5.15 pm.

A man 'like Shepherd' was noted asking directions to Luddenden railway station 'after 7 pm' on that day, and purchased a ticket to Halifax at 7.40 pm. Arriving at 8.05 pm, he took a cab through the town, via back streets (at his request). Having been a cab driver in Halifax himself, he was known to this driver. Shepherd then walked to 22 St James Road, a brothel run by a Mrs Eastwood. Two of the girls there testified that he had blood on his hands and trousers – he claimed he'd been 'set upon' but had thrashed his assailant. He asked for sponge and water, and a bottle of sherry. He said he had plenty of money, and stayed the night with the two girls who said he was "restless, and spoke often of his mother". At 6.30 am on the Thursday, he dressed, noted that blood was still on his trousers, and left. Shepherd handed himself in at Halifax police station on Saturday evening, though professing his innocence.

On the other hand, Shepherd's 'alibis' were inconsistent or uncorroborated. It was also mentioned that Shepherd had been charged with highway robbery on the 6th of January – Shepherd and an accomplice attacked one William Parker, beerhouse keeper of Ovenden, when on his way home from Halifax. Parker was knocked to the ground, Shepherd kneeled on his chest and threatened to run a knife into his heart unless he handed over his money, which Parker did. After being kicked about the head, Parker was allowed to get up and go home.

Now Shepherd was detained at Halifax, then York. He protested innocence yet said he deserved hanging, though he would prefer to be shot. All who met him considered him hard, callous and unremorseful. He was duly sentenced to be hanged. He was 22 years old.

On the day of the execution (Saturday 3 April 1858), a crowd estimated at around 14,000 assembled in front of the scaffold in York. Many had walked considerable distances – others had come on holiday excursion trains. Halifax, Ovenden and Queenshead persons were evident. Benjamin Bartle of Mountain organised a wagonette for locals from Mountain to Bradford and then by train to York. At the execution were Parkinson's widow and his father; and Shepherd's father and mother with whom he lived at the time, and his estranged wife who lived at Queenshead. The execution was carried out by Mr Askren of Rotherham. We are told that, unusually, neither the sacrament nor burial service were provided on the way to the scaffold. The body hung for one hour, was removed and buried within the prison precincts.

At the time of his murder Bethel was 30 years old. In 1851 he is shown as living at Mountain Delves, at the family home. His father, Sam, farmed some 20 acres at Micklemoss, so was probably quite well-to-do. Later the family built or bought houses for renting in the vicinity of Mountain Delves. Bethel was listed as a waggoner at that time. By the time of his death, he lived at Law Hill with his wife Mary, a mill worker, with his occupation given as farmer.

The following description of Bethel was provided by the Halifax Courier, to help identification. It is of interest for the description of the attire of the time.

"The man is of 28 to 30 years, strong, healthy, 5'9" tall. His features are 'irregular': Large forehead, high cheekbones, small nose. Sunken light grey eyes. Long and curled sandy brown hair. Whiskers are thin and curled, being lighter than the hair. He has a florid complexion.

The clothing is of the kind usually worn by farmers or labourers. An old black cloth cap in front of which are 3 small buttons and a small bunch of ribbon, the peak of leather (which had been scorched at some time) being broken and jagged. He has a blue cloth jacket, with buttons of common grey horn, and with pockets at the back. A waistcoat of drab fustian velveteen. The trousers are of well-worn fustian corduroy, with leg buttons hard and stiff from dirt. His boots are 'Blucher' quarter boots laced to above the ankles, with the soles well-nailed. His stockings are grey worsted, with bright coloured garters cut probably from a 'poncho piece'. His neckerchief is of well-worn black silk."

The site of the murder may be visited today. Near Old Town, above Hebden Bridge at the top of Lane Ends Lane is the Hare and Hounds pub, where the body was brought from the field. A rough track (Popples Lane), runs from above the pub towards Wadsworth Moor. Follow the track to the gate of Keelham Farm. Turn left and you enter the Dark Lanes. After a few yards turn right over a stile. The body of Parkinson was discovered at the top of the bank on the left, just over the tumbled wall. Commons Farm is the nearest farm up and across this field. The Calderdale Way runs across the top. There are several adjacent habitations, but it is not now the 'bleak, obscure and unfrequented' spot that it was 150 years ago.

References

'History and Topography of Bradford'	J. James 1841
'Round and About Bradford'	Cudworth 1876
'Pleasant Walks around Bradford'	Speight 1890
'Queens Jester'	F W Wallett 1884
'Historical Sketches of Clayton, Old Dolphin, Queensbury District and Shibden Dale'	J Parker 1901
Vint, Hill and Killick files Queensbury District Council Minutes Queensbury Co-operative Society Minutes Thornton Parish Church Minutes	Bradford Archives
'History of Northowram'	Mark Pearson
'Memoirs of an Old Collier' (Northern Mine Research Society)	J Aked 1974
'Queensbury Lines'	Whitaker and Cryer 1984
Queensbury History Society Pamphlets	J H Patchett et al
'Queensbury Centenary 1863-1963'	Brochure 1963

And thanks to:
> Shibden Folk Museum, Halifax;
> The Omnibus Society;
> York City Archives;
> West Yorkshire Archives;
> The Coal Mining Authority, Mansfield
> Bradford Industrial Museum

A point to note:
O.S. maps are pretty good on details, except for place names and precise dates!